The
Bio-Sexual
Factor

The Bio-Sexual Factor

by Richard Hagen

DOUBLEDAY & COMPANY, INC.
GARDEN CITY, NEW YORK   1979

ISBN: 0-385-14591-8
Library of Congress Catalog Card Number 78-20236

Acknowledgments

In September 1977, I dropped by the office of Dr. Glayde Whitney, a colleague whose specialty is behavioral genetics. I suggested that I wanted to write a book on "sociobiology and human sexual behavior." Did he think the time had come for such a book, I asked, and would he be my consultant if I should attempt such a project? Dr. Whitney assured me that such a book should be written. He also fed me many books and articles, tutored me in genetic theory, suggested many of the ideas that appear in this book, and, perhaps more important than anything else, encouraged me to stay with it until it was done.

I also want to thank Dr. Charles Wysocki, behavioral geneticist now at the University of Pennsylvania, for his careful reading of the manuscript and his helpful comments. Glenn Cowley, my agent, was the aggressive link between me and Jim Wilcox, the energetic Doubleday editor who helped put the manuscript in its final form.

To all of these people I owe thanks. But my special appreciation goes to Carolyn Nielsen, who not only spent many hours in the preparation of the manuscript but who also supported my efforts to expand my own talents and interests.

Contents

1   *We've All Been Hurt*   1
2   *Sociobiology: A Struggle Against the Tide*   14
3   *Evolutionary Logic at Work*   22
4   *Nature and Nurture: Bringing Them Together*   51
5   *Who Wants Sex More? Who Has More Fun?*   65
6   *A Naturalistic Experiment*   112
7   *More Evidence: Hormones and Sex Drive*   120
8   *The Promiscuous Male and the Faithful Female*   137
9   *The Fast, Indiscriminate Male and the Coy,*
    Fussy Female   162
10 *Extending Sociobiology and Sexual Behavior*   178
11 *Exceptions, Emotions, and Ethics*   205
12 *Putting It Together*   222
    Postscript   250
    References   257
    Index   269

". . . human sexuality can be much more precisely defined with the aid of the new advances in evolutionary theory. To omit this mode of reasoning is to leave us blind to an important part of our history, the ultimate meaning of our behavior, and the significance of the choices that lie before us."

Edward O. Wilson
On Human Nature
1978

1

We've All Been Hurt

I'll Never Trust a Man Again

"I don't trust men anymore. I think they're all a bunch of animals. They're only interested in one thing. . . ."

I sat perplexed. Before me was a tearful nineteen-year-old college sophomore, child of the sixties, sexually "liberated," depressed, angry, and not quite sure she wanted to tough it out in a world where half the human race is sexually depraved. She was a pretty girl, but socially insecure, and consequently had a hard time saying "no." Right after her abortion, unusually severe depression had pushed her through my office door one day following class.

I was just beginning my career as a college professor. Although decidedly on the stuffy side and very straight sexually—at least in my speech and actions—I was somewhat jealous of the sexual freedom my students were experiencing. On this particular occasion, however, I was flooded with confusing emotions. I sincerely hurt for her. I felt angry at those who had abused her. But that anger could not just be directed toward the dirty few who had enticed her to bed. That anger was directed at *all* those licentious animals from time immemorial who were "only interested in one thing."

My problem, of course, as I sat there struggling to find some way to help her, was that I too was one of those animals at whom she and I were both shaking our fingers. Not in behavior, but certainly in character. Held in check by all sorts of religious and cultural norms, I knew full well that if I had been of her generation I'd have made a pass at her at the first opportunity. I was angry at myself. And ashamed of my kind. A large part of me felt vicious and indecent. Being a man at that moment was a very painful experience. I only remember mumbling something about "time heals things" and "try not to lump all men into one pile." The rest of the experience fades into a welcome repression.

Like most others who sit in a counseling or teaching position, I've since heard that record played many times. But my response today is quite different. And it is that difference that impels me to write this book. Let me recount a recent conversation that may illustrate my changed view of man's sexuality.

She was thirty-four, slightly overweight according to the standards that fashion designers and women set up, but just nicely rounded and quite sexy from the average man's standpoint. In addition, she had all those beautifully seductive, graceful, highly feminine characteristics in her movements, her voice, her eyes, and her posture. We had been friends of long standing because of a common professional interest. Perhaps for this reason I felt more free than usual to express my true feelings about her personal horror story.

"People warned me," she said, wearing her most disgusted mask, "but I really didn't know what I was in for. As soon as I was divorced, all of my best friends wanted to climb in bed with me. I was hurt, and I was angry. I was interested in friendship and companionship. All those bastards were interested in was sex. Frankly, I don't think I will ever trust . . ." And you can fill in the rest by now.

"That's too bad," I said, "because you are angry at the way the world is. And that's not very adaptive. I hear your story, but my reaction is very different from yours. I'm a member of that class of bastards you describe, and I'm not at all ashamed of my brothers. We're the product of thousands of generations of selective adaptation. We came by our preoccupation with sex very honestly, and frankly you should be glad we are as we are or you might not be here. Our sexuality is as much a part of us as are our brains, our words, and our companionship. From an evolutionary standpoint, probably more important. You can either learn to accept us for what we are, or you can spend the rest of your life moaning about reality."

Male Pride and Male Anger

Anger in my words? Yes, anger is obviously there. The same kind of anger felt by religious, ethnic, and racial groups who for generations were told that they were not quite human. The same kind of anger women feel as they look back on their history and see thousands of years of lies about the inferiority of not having a penis.

Yes, I feel anger. I'm tired of being told that men can't be trusted, that we are rip-off artists, that our sexual aggressiveness is base and inhuman. I find it disgusting that any man over forty-five who acknowledges his sexual nature is called lecherous and any man under forty-five who does the same is "trying to prove his masculinity to the world and himself." Both characterizations are equally degrading.

Degrading and psychologically damaging. Some men, lucky they be, probably don't care a wit. But there are no doubt many "closet males" who for years have been ashamed of their internal sexual world and have felt out of step with the rest of humanity. This is the essence of psychological trauma. There is nothing more crippling than feeling like a cripple. Nothing that causes sickness as much as believing one is sick. Nothing more depressing than wallowing in a slimy self-definition.

Our sexual aggressiveness is a healthy characteristic, as much our birthright as any other human quality we possess, yet we have been made out to be animals for not fitting into a mold poured by angry women, misguided moralists, and cowardly behavioral theoreticians.

The reasons for this put-down are legion. I shall not begin to explore them all, but some have earned special mention.

The Stuff That Myths Are Made of

The view of men and women being equals in sexual desire and expression has its roots in the writings of Havelock Ellis, whose landmark six volumes on sex were published between 1897 and 1910. Carrying a vendetta against the repressive attitudes of nineteenth-century Victorianism, Ellis argued eloquently for female as well as male sexual liberation. Whether his own research really convinced him that sexual desire was no less intense in women than in men, or whether this conclusion was merely adopted to strengthen his crusade, we shall never know. Nevertheless, his views were certainly instrumental in shaping what has become "modern sexual orthodoxy" (Robinson, 1977, p. 17).

THE ROLE OF PSYCHOLOGY

The pronouncements by Havelock Ellis on the sexual nature of human beings represent only one minor skirmish in the age-old philosophical struggle concerning the broad picture of human nature: Are our behaviors the reflection of inborn traits or life experiences?

This "nature-nurture controversy," as it has been called, has occupied a central role in the social sciences since their infancy. During the latter part of the nineteenth century academic psychology supported the "nature" view. But by the 1930s, psychology, especially in America, was dominated by behaviorism, a view that stressed the role of environment and thus provided an ideal soil for the nurturance of Ellis's culturally oriented views of sexual behavior.

In Chapters 4 and 6, we deal more in depth with "nature vs. nurture" and how these two views can be integrated with sociobiology, which is the main topic of this book. But at this point, the important matter for us to note is that American academic psychology has for the past fifty years been overwhelmingly behavioristic and has generally interpreted all human behavior as the product of learning.

Even the clinical wing of psychology, ignoring Freud's emphasis on instinct, sought "psychological" explanations for the whole range of human behaviors. In the sexual realm, rather than bother to look, people merely assumed biological data did not exist. Furthermore, they often compounded their lack of scholarship with fallacious logic about what this supposed absence of data should mean. As recently as 1971, a respectable scientific journal allowed a writer to argue what *must be* from what *is not:*

> Sex is supposed to mean different things for men and women, but there is no acceptable evidence for inborn biological differences between their sexual behavior. This means that the point of departure *must be* [my italics] the psychological aspects of sexual expression for males [Hessellund, 1971, p. 263].

And this view has certainly generated interesting attempts to explain the actual behavioral differences that are observed. The male who acknowledges a powerful sex drive is characterized as insecure and constantly seeking conquests in an effort to affirm his masculinity. If he likes variety in sex, he is described in one of the most current professional views as unable to form meaningful, emotional, interpersonal relationships. He flits from one "shallow" relationship to another, and because of his own psychological inadequacy is never able to experience the essence of healthy human existence. This view states that people who are truly human, those who are able to love and receive love, will not even desire sex outside of the monogamous relationship they have been able to establish. If you find yourself looking twice at a sexy pair of legs walking by, you should sign up for therapy, the sooner the better.

Even William Masters and Virginia Johnson, who at one level have done very important scientific research, contributed to the myth of sexual identity. Robinson (1977) points out that Masters and Johnson *began* their project with the commitment that there are no differences in sexual responsiveness. Therefore, it is not surprising to note that although they found differences between males and females, they carefully play down these differences and draw our attention to the similarities. In their introductory chapter of *Human Sexual Response,* they clearly tell us:

> Attempts to answer the challenge inherent in the question, "What do men and women do in response to the effective sexual stimulation?" have emphasized the similarities, not the differences, in the anatomy and physiology of human sexual response [Masters and Johnson, 1966, p. 8].

Furthermore, the data they generated coupled with the highly unrepresentative samples they used render their studies essentially useless in answering questions that relate to drive, desire, and preference, those characteristics we think of as comprising the psychology of sex. Nevertheless, they try to use their data to oppose any view implying that a woman's need for sexual expression is less compelling than that of a man. Robinson (1977, p. 188) somewhat cruelly, but correctly, calls them on their unwarranted generalizations:

> It is precisely because their research stops short of true causal knowledge that they got bogged down in amateur psychologizing: They have to invent psychological explanations because the physiology of sex is still largely a mystery to them.

During the past half century, whenever psychologists, or those posing as psychologists, have made pronouncements on male and female sexuality, either out of ignorance or out of personal conviction, they have told us that we are all the same at birth. Any behavioral differences we observe must somehow relate to differences in experience. Many psychologists are finally beginning to realize that something else may be going on. It's about time.

SOCIOLOGY AND ANTHROPOLOGY

The two other major disciplines that also emphasize human behavior, sociology and anthropology, must also accept their share of blame for the "sexual identity" myth. Mitchell (1973, p. 128) points out that sociology has been one of the most influential voices in popularizing the crude simplicity that "it is only the role assignments made to young children by a sexist society that make otherwise versatile, sexually neutral infants into girls or boys." Furthermore, in spite of rare reminders from members of their own profession that biological factors should be attended to in cross-cultural studies (for example, LeVine, 1963), anthropologists almost invariably characterize personality, including sexuality, as a function entirely of cultural factors (Bolton, 1973).

Like psychology, sociology and anthropology also claim a scientific frame of reference. If there really are the innate genetically based sexual differences I will suggest in this book, how could these disciplines accept such nonsense? Barash (1977) gives us what may be the best explanation:

> . . . sociology and anthropology have had a curious love-hate relationship with Darwinism. . . . By the later half of the nineteenth century, evolution by natural selection was becoming increasingly acknowledged. . . . This was the era of laissez-faire capitalism in the Western world, and the captains of industry eagerly embraced . . . Darwinism as a justification for the social inequities prevalent at the time. "Social Darwinism" therefore flourished, with its reassuring message that social and economic exploitation simply represented the inevitable unfolding of nature's way. Sociologists and anthropologists contributed to this travesty, much to their later chagrin, and in fact they subsequently did penance for their sins by proclaiming that human beings enjoy absolutely unlimited behavior potential, as *tabula rasa* (blank slates) upon which experience can write as it will. So, after a brief fling with evolution, sociology and anthropology embraced a conception of human behavior that attributed everything to early experience, socialization, cultural norms, etc. [Barash, 1977, p. 7].

RADICAL FEMINISTS

In this land of illusion, psychology, sociology, and anthropology sauntered down the yellow brick road hand in hand, but

radical feminism (sometimes called "neofeminism") raced
ahead to embrace the ultimate in absurdity. In their zeal to pro-
claim how much the same men and women are, some have even
suggested that differences between the sexes in physical strength
and size are totally a function of the kinds of games and activities we are exposed to during the developmental years (for example, Dworkin, 1974, p. 178). Morton Hunt (1972) points
out that this kind of "utter nonsense" comes from a minority of
feminist writers, but even a few such writers alert us to look
very carefully at the scientific integrity that may or may not be
represented in any of the neofeminist pronouncements. From
what I've seen, none of the discourses on sexual identity that
have come out of feminism are based in any science whatever.
Rather, they are simply assertions of what kind of world the
writers would like to live in.

In *The Female Woman,* Arianna Stassinopoulos (1975, p.
22) points out "the fundamental tenet of the Women's Lib ideology is that there are no innate differences between men and
women—other than reproduction." Clavan (1972, p. 301) says
that in recent feminist literature "emphasis is being focused on
the idea that sex differentiation may be biologically determined,
but attributes of gender are culturally imposed."

In 1974, an entire issue of *Women: A Journal of Liberation*
was devoted to the "androgynous role" concept. Capitalizing
on this word, which means "hermaphroditic" or "having both
male and female characteristics," Blanchard (1974, p. 16) tells
us that people are "inherently androgynous" and that the sex-
role socialization process is what "splits the whole into two
halves, 'feminine' and 'masculine.'" Shulamith Firestone, a
guru in the movement, colorfully paints for us the following ultimate culture in which all the nasty differences we now see will
totally disappear:

> What we shall have in the next cultural revolution is the
> reintegration of the Male . . . with the Female, to create
> an androgynous culture surpassing the highs of either cul-
> tural stream, or even the sum of their integrations. More
> than a marriage, rather an abolition of cultural categories
> themselves, a mutual cancellation—a matter-antimatter ex-

plosion, ending with a poof culture itself. . . . We shall
not miss it. We shall no longer need it. . . . [Firestone,
1971, pp. 214–15].

Robert Trivers, noted Harvard biologist, characterizes these
current efforts to argue biological identity between the sexes as
a "functionless swamp" (Dawkins, 1976, p. vi). A swamp?
Yes, in terms of the clouded, misty vision one must have to
hold such a view. But I'm not sure the sexual-identity myth has
been entirely functionless. There may have been a point in the
development of the women's movement when this myth did
have some redeeming value. Maybe it helped women feel more
human at the time they were beginning to struggle for social
equality. But myths, whatever their nature, are usually more
destructive than they are helpful. This myth is no exception.

Women Have Been Hurt Too

After all this chauvinistic talk, I should like to make it clear
that I can appreciate the fact that women have also been hurt. I
do not sense the hurt of women as personally as I do that of
men—I'm not a woman—but I can understand it at an intellectual level, and perhaps at some gut level.

Myths require constant nurturance or they will shrivel and
die. And in defense of the motto that men and women are
alike, some women decided they would show the world that
they could be just as aggressive sexually as men. This effort
probably caused some women needless emotional hurt, but flag
wavers are sometimes called on to act out their beliefs. In
Bitching, Marion Meade tells us just how fierce this pressure
was for women to become "sexually liberated":

> . . . the new climate . . . encourages a woman to bounce
> from Simmons to Simmons without concern for morals. In
> fact, now that virginity is generally regarded as a terminal
> disease requiring immediate surgery, the woman disin-
> clined to treat her crotch as a subway turnstile is worse
> than a prude. She's an infantile human being whose inabil-

ity to relate makes her an ideal candidate for therapy [Meade, 1973, p. 77].

During the early seventies, many women played this game, jumping frantically in and out of bed with many partners. Some lasted several years. Few, if any, found that they could continue this lifestyle beyond four or five years.

Some became bitter and turned off altogether to sex for long periods of time. A young woman patient of mine comes to mind. She played the numbers game for about three years between the ages of twenty-one and twenty-four. Now she is very much frightened and nervous about sex and doesn't want any part of it.

The women who turned off to sex altogether were the exceptions. But there were, no doubt, many others who experienced anger and disappointment at their own inability to enjoy what they thought they should have been capable of enjoying. Even that amount of trauma was unnecessary.

Some of these women who sought to prove a biological myth still suffer. But many probably buried their failure under a myth of equal incredulity—"Oh well, I guess you can't erase two decades of environmental training so easily"—and then once again adopted a typical women's sex role.

Regardless of the outcome, the trip should never have been made. Women should never have had to prove anything about their sexuality. Largely, they came by it genetically. They have a right to be what they are.

The myth of biological equality in sexual matters has also been responsible for much gnashing of teeth by several other groups of women, many of whom have probably never looked twice at the women's movement. There are those who at some point in their lives found to their great disappointment that their mates didn't feel emotionally about sex, relationships, and the like, as they did. And there are those who are chasing the dream of finding a man who does feel the way they do.

Recently, I was talking to an "over thirty" woman who wants very much to be married. Her major complaint was that she couldn't find a man who felt the same way she did about the importance of the emotional relationship. Many men seemed to at first, but as time spun itself out, it became clear that her world and that of the man were just too different. At this point, she feels desperate and figures on making a compromise—not marrying the best but grabbing what she can find, compatibility or not. What a tragedy! If she could only realize that men and women really do live in two different worlds and accept a man on that basis, she would not have to feel that she is taking second best. Rather, she would be accepting a man for what he is by birthright and adjusting to the reality of difference, perhaps even finding some excitement because of that very difference.

Then there are the hurts, doubts, and questions experienced by those women who thought that they, somehow, were responsible for the reactions of men to them, and they couldn't figure out why.

Not long ago, a young woman told me of her most recent excursion into male-female social relationships. She said that during the past two or three months, she had established friendships with a number of males, and she was beginning to believe that men and women can really be "friends" without this sexual thing rearing its ugly head. Then two of her "friends" made their move. She was disappointed in the men, because she was not interested in them sexually, and she had thought a good understanding of their "friendship" existed. But she also had serious questions about her own social sensitivity.

"What do you suppose I did to encourage their response?" she said. "I don't think I was leading them on. I was just enjoying their friendship. But maybe I was . . . maybe I don't realize what my behavior is like. It makes me feel really strange about myself. . . ."

Questioning her own viability as a social creature, wondering if she is okay. Of course, it bothered her. By now, the reader probably has a pretty good idea of my response. I said, "I'm quite sure you didn't do anything to lead them on. You were, indeed, being friendly. From what I know of you, you are sensitive socially, and you have a pretty good handle on your behaviors."

"But then why would they start getting sexual with me if I hadn't done anything to seduce them?" she questioned.

"Because they are men," I answered. "Women don't have to do anything to get men aroused. Men often just get aroused in the presence of a woman, period."

She persisted with puzzlement. "But I wasn't thinking anything sexual about them. Why should they have been thinking it about me?"

I wasn't quite sure what else to say. How do you explain a book full of theory and data in a casual conversation? The point is that this young lady was hurting unnecessarily. She was doubting her own ability to think, perceive, and react as a well-put-together human would. And she shouldn't have doubted this at all.

The nature of sexual encounter itself can produce just as many if not more hurts and disappointments. Lonnie Barbach, a sex therapist with the University of California Medical Center in San Francisco, cites recent statistics showing that "approximately half of the sexual encounters that end in orgasm for a male partner do not end in orgasm for a female partner" (Barbach, 1976, p. 2). She then goes on to describe the nagging doubts and fears that often result from this distressing state of affairs:

> Expecting [to be as orgasmic as the man] . . . can lead to all sorts of erroneous conclusions. "Maybe it's not love" is one way of dismissing the difficulty. After all, you might feel that if it were really love, you would feel so turned on that you would naturally have orgasms. Because you don't have orgasms, you may assume that your partner must not be "Mr. Right," and you must not really be "in love" with him. Besides, if he really loved you, wouldn't he know how to "give" you an orgasm? Since he doesn't give you orgasms, you may conclude that he must not love you enough [Barbach, 1976, p. 6].

For the male, of course, the same kind of troublesome questions arise. "If she loved me, she would respond." "Maybe I'm not the kind of guy who turns her on." "Maybe my technique is sloppy."

Why did we ever start the myth that women are just as orgasmic as men? There is no evidence for it. In fact, there is all kinds of evidence against it. And from an evolutionary standpoint, there is no logical justification for it.

For Pity's Sake, Let's Be Realistic

Self-recrimination, playing roles we're not fit for, disappointment, anger, distrust—indeed, we've all been hurt to one degree or another. Hurt because of myths. Hurt because we can't get inside the other person's skin and really see what's there. Hurt because we can't accept differences where differences exist.

And most of these problems between the sexes seem to center—not very surprisingly—around those differences we cherish the most, the differences that define us as male or female.

If you are a woman, possibly your behavior, quite certainly your thoughts and desires about sex, are different from mine. That is not because you are insensitive, uncaring, selfish, or the captive of a prudish socialization process. It is not because I am base, lecherous, weak, psychologically crippled, or the product of the wrong kind of crowd. It is because you are a woman and I am a man. We are biologically different. The difference lies in our genes. For too long this bio-sexual factor has been pushed aside by the myth of sexual identity. The sooner that myth is put in perspective, the sooner we can get on with the important business of accepting our own sexuality for what it is and hopefully even learning to accept these differences in each other.

2

Sociobiology: A Struggle Against the Tide

Human Instincts? Heresy!

Of course it is heresy. Fifty years ago, John B. Watson, the father figure of behaviorism, told us that innate responses in humans are limited to a few primitive "beginnings of emotional reactions" (Watson, 1924, p. 152). And even these were relegated to decidedly unimportant roles in complex behavior patterns. Just how extreme the environmentalistic position became is illustrated in Watson's famous passage from *Behaviorism:*

> Give me a dozen healthy infants, well-formed, and my own specified world to bring them up in and I'll guarantee to take any one at random and train him to become any type of specialist I might select—doctor, lawyer, artist, merchant-chief and, yes, even beggar-man and thief, regardless of his talents, penchants, tendencies, abilities, vocations, and race of his ancestors [Watson, 1924, p. 104].

In regard to sexual behavior, Watson most certainly would have seen environmental factors as being all-powerful. If we can put words in his mouth, they might well have been something like this:

> Give me a dozen healthy girls and a dozen healthy boys, and my own specified world to bring them up in, and I'll guarantee that the girls will be the sexual aggressors, talking about it all the time, begging, cajoling, and having intercourse with everyone they can, while the boys will be making up excuses about headaches and fearful of going out alone at night lest they be raped.

Sound kind of silly? Silly or not, that expression is today's sexual orthodoxy. Especially with sex, and in many other areas as well, popular and professional literature present the socialization process as one that is independent of and all-powerful over the very weak, or nonexistent, biological nature we are born with. Such a characterization may be true of some specific practices and may be a valuable tool in arguing for much-needed social changes, but it does not pass muster as a broadly applied principle.

Today, however, there is a remarkable retrenchment concerning the role of instincts in behavior. Yesterday's heretics are apparently rapidly becoming today's gurus in a movement labeled "sociobiology."

The Newest Fad

Sociobiology has been described as "the systematic study of the biological basis of all forms of social behavior in all kinds of organisms" (Wilson, 1977, p. xiii). Grandiose claims, indeed. But no less grandiose than the breadth of disciplines its principles embrace. Drawing from biology, genetics, ecology, ethology, and physiology, it has ramifications that reach into all of the social sciences. Nor are the claims of breadth paled by the style with which this movement is sweeping through the scientific world.

Without any doubt, sociobiology qualifies for the title "The Newest Fad in the Biological and Social Sciences." But unlike most fads, this one comes with a long, distinguished history, incorporating the work of dozens of the world's most respected researchers, some of whom have received Nobel Prizes for their outstanding contributions. With the publication by Darwin of *On the Origin of Species* . . . in 1859, sociobiology had its beginning. By the 1930s, Darwin's ideas were integrated with modern genetic theory into what became known as "the synthetic theory of evolution." During the following decades, which were dominated by behavioristic notions, the "minority report" researchers worked carefully and quietly, providing the dry tinder from which "sociobiology" was soon to spring. Throughout the 1940s and 1950s, conferences were held dealing with genetics and behavior, and the term "sociobiology" began appearing in titles of symposia at these conferences. Then in 1964, William Hamilton struck the match by publishing two articles outlining a general genetic theory for the evolution of social behavior, making special application of that theory to the social Hymenoptera (ants, bees, and wasps) (Hamilton, 1964). During the following decade, the notions smoldered and grew within small academic circles. But not until 1975, with Edward Wilson's book *Sociobiology: The New Synthesis,* a massive, scholarly integration of many decades of work by many researchers, did the theories generated by the sociobiologists rush through the academic world like a raging forest fire, creating controversy, heated arguments, and even public demonstrations.

Will this movement, like so many other fads, fade into oblivion when people tire of it? Clearly, I do not think so, or I would not be writing this book. And the bold predictions of leading theorists in the field show an arrogant confidence that may not be at all misplaced. Robert Trivers, the Harvard biologist whose pioneering work has given sociobiological doctrine much of its credibility says, "Sooner or later, political science, law, economics, psychology, psychiatry, and anthropology will all be branches of sociobiology" (*Time,* August 1, 1977, p. 54). Fad, or in the Kuhnian sense, true scientific revolution? Perhaps a little early to tell. But its strong historical underpinnings coupled with the apparent lack of any scientific evidence opposing it suggest that it will probably be around for a good long time.

New Wine . . . or Only New Bottles?

Time magazine describes the concepts as "startling—and disturbing." A psychologist said to me, "Sociobiology represents a whole new way of thinking. My generation was trained to live in a different world. I don't know how to adjust. . . ."

Indeed, for the majority of social scientists these ideas are startling, confusing, and difficult to accept, but only because we are not old enough to remember what the social sciences were like seventy years ago. Largely through Darwin's influence, late nineteenth-century psychology was based on concepts from biology and evolution. The importance placed on the biological basis of behavior is seen in the writings of Francis Galton, Sigmund Freud, and a most influential American psychologist, William James. American functionalism was strongly aligned with evolutionary dogma. Certainly, Edward Thorndike, John Dewey, James Angell, Harvey Carr, and George Herbert Mead would have had no trouble talking to today's sociobiologists. William McDougall, with his huge list of instincts, would have been right at home, as would the early investigators of animal behavior, Lloyd Morgan, Jacques Loeb, and Leonard Hobhouse.

This list of names may mean little to anyone other than a student in an introductory psychology course. It includes, however, those writers who, during the latter part of the nineteenth and early twentieth century largely set the pace for thinking about behavior. Psychology was, indeed, no stranger to instinctive theories sixty or seventy years ago.

Banishing the Unbanishable

But then all this is so much ancient history to us youngsters in social science. Most of us were not yet born when the rise of behaviorism during the second and third decades of this century changed the face of the social sciences and attempted to disown the idea of biological influence on behavior. Instinct was stricken from our vocabulary and everyone focused on the "learning environment."

How could scientific thinking change so quickly and dramatically? For those interested in the history of science, it may be noted that behaviorism rushed in at a time when evolutionary biologists were facing a crisis in theory. Between 1900 and 1925, much argument went on between the Darwinian evolutionists and Mendelian geneticists. In order for evolution to "work" the two theories had to be integrated. But the development of these two disciplines at the time was not yet advanced enough for a true integration to come about. Thus, struggling with problems in their own field, the champions of instinct were in no position to ward off the behavioristic onslaught led by John Watson in the late 1910s and early 1920s. As I mentioned earlier, it was not until the 1930s that the biological evolutionists achieved an integration of modern genetic theory and Darwin's views (the synthetic theory of evolution). And by that time, behaviorism had such a head start it was not soon to be contained.

During the 1930s, 1940s, and 1950s, the behaviorists appeared to sweep through the social sciences with absolute confidence, but they could not shake the dogged footsteps of "genetic influence." The efforts of psychology could not stand without support from this old-timer, so an attempt was made to sneak him back into the family by changing his name from "instinct" to "need" or "drive." Even then, he would often slip off his mask and laugh in the faces of the behaviorists. But they struggled to ignore his presence because he was a social embarrassment.

A particularly instructive example of the kinds of problems behavioristic psychology faced with the concept of instinctive behaviors comes from a report back in the early 1960s by Keller and Marian Breland, students of B. F. Skinner. The Brelands (1961, p. 681) tell us of their awareness that the "neobehavioristically oriented experimenter is apt to consider 'instinct' an ugly word . . . [classed with] other 'seditious notions' which were discarded in the behavioristic revolution." Furthermore, their own narrow background in behaviorism did not prepare them "for such gross inabilities to predict and control the behavior of animals with which [they] had been working for years" (p. 683). To illustrate the causes of their consternation, they list "misbehaviors" of pigs, chickens, raccoons, porpoises, whales, rabbits, and cows that they feel "represent a clear and utter failure of conditioning theory" (p. 683).

In spite of their rigorous behavioristic indoctrination, fourteen years of experience applying operant conditioning to more than six thousand animals representing thirty-eight different species brought the Brelands to the following conclusion:

> The notion of instinct has now become one of our basic concepts in an effort to make sense of the welter of observations which confront us. When behaviorism tossed out instinct, it is our feeling that some of its power of prediction and control were lost with it. From the foregoing examples, it appears that although it was easy to banish the Instinctivists from the science during the Behavioristic Revolution, it was not possible to banish instinct so easily [p. 684].

As a "conversion experience," the Brelands' story is particularly striking. But as an argument for the genetic influence on behavior, it is only one of hundreds that appeared during the dominance of behaviorism. McClearn and DeFries (1973, p. 31) survey the past fifty years and conclude: "This majority view [behavioristic view] was not without opposition. In fact, since Watson's pronouncement, no single year has passed without publication of some evidence showing it to be wrong."

Indeed, it was not possible to banish instinct so easily. Today we find not only the concept but also its spokesmen enjoying an unprecedented revival. Riding the crest of that revival is sociobiology.

Sociobiology: What Is It?

The term "sociobiology" derives from the application of the principles of biological evolution to the broad spectrum of social behaviors observed throughout the animal kingdom. Although Darwin articulated the basic principles, because of the nonexistence of the science of genetics at the time Darwin wrote, he had difficulty accounting for many commonly observed social phenomena. Thus it remained for more recent writers to integrate modern genetic theory with Darwinian principles and resolve some of the difficulties. (See Mayr, 1972, and Wilson, 1975, for in-depth discussions of this integration.)

The basic principle of Darwin that concerns us in this book is that referred to by Herbert Spencer as "the survival of the fittest." Through recombination of genes and possible mutations, some members of a given generation are likely to be "more fit" than are others. More fit for what? More fit for survival and, in particular, more fit for producing viable offspring. We need not totally identify this idea with the notion of animals fighting it out among themselves to see who wins. Both intra- and interspecies battles may occur, and, of course, the winners are better off in the evolutionary game than are the losers; however, animals may also vary in their abilities to cope with weather conditions, tight food supplies, and the nuances of interanimal relationships.

In Darwin's view, whenever an organism has inherent qualities that give it an advantage in producing offspring—who in turn mature and reproduce—no matter what those qualities might be, that organism is "more fit" from an evolutionary standpoint. The more recent formulation of this notion, the one that allowed a broad application to social phenomena, is this: Whenever an organism has inherent qualities that result in a greater contribution of its genes into the gene pool of successive generations, that organism is "more fit." At first glance, these two formulations may seem identical, but there is enough difference to generate some rather important implications for evolutionary theory.

The kernel of the theory has been expressed in the title of Richard Dawkins' book *The Selfish Gene*. Dawkins' notion is that genes that first take care of their own survival—or genes that give animals an advantage in putting those genes in the next generation—are the genes that eventually become dominant in the gene pool. Hence, the "selfish genes" ultimately become the most influential, and those genes that "do not take care of themselves" eventually die out.

With this basic idea, we are ready to look at some very simple examples of biological evolution having an effect on sexual behavior.

3

Evolutionary Logic at Work

Amoebas at the start
Were not complex;
They tore themselves apart
And started sex
　　　Arthur Guiterman
　　　(1871–1943)

Why Bother with Sex?

With very few exceptions, the animal world requires the participation of both male and female in order for reproduction to take place. If they tore themselves apart, why on earth do they bother to get back together in order to produce offspring? Is it to their advantage? I'm not referring to the advantage of the species. Is it to the advantage of the individual parent to reproduce sexually? In this question, we may find the best illustration of the basic point we'll be working with throughout this volume. That's exactly why it is being raised.

Why have sex at all? If we were to ask around, we might not learn much. With humans, of course, we must deal with such factors as social pressure—everyone ought to replace himself/herself on the earth—or plans for old age and the like. People have the unique power, it appears, to conceptualize the future and to act in order to bring about events they believe would be desirable. And that ability makes it difficult to pinpoint the reasons a particular couple have children.

But with other animals, things are much different. Dogs and cats don't—so far as we can tell—sit around planning to have kids for certain reasons. They just do it and have them. Why? Is it to their advantage? I'm not referring to the advantage of the species. Is it to the advantage of the individual parent to reproduce sexually?

From all appearances, it is not. The act of breeding consumes both time and energy. Although domestic animals don't have many demands on their lives, in the wilds the appropriate use of time and energy can spell the difference between life and death. Furthermore, the act of copulation itself places animals in an unusually vulnerable position toward predators. Just think of the difficult time you had as a teen-ager trying to make love in the back seat of a car and watch for the local gendarme at the same time. In the middle of a hostile jungle, you would really have had difficulty.

Not only are the acts of courtship and breeding time-consuming and sometimes dangerous, but also, once the offspring arrive, they must be provided for and protected. And if that were not enough, there is considerable evidence (for example, Taber and Dassmann, 1957) showing that parental lifespan is reduced by the toll of breeding.

Margaret Mead points out some of the advantages of not reproducing in the following passage:

> In the primate horde, females periodically show receptivity, and the males who respond mount them if they are accepted. To the male who doesn't become aroused, nothing happens at all. He doesn't get into fights with other males that day, he sits peacefully grooming himself. Or, he may even get a better share of the food because his more sexually active contemporaries are busy elsewhere [Mead, 1949, p. 204].

This monkey is no dummy. Considering all the factors we have outlined, we would have to grant that he is being pragmatic, at least. But what is it that impels his contemporaries to get in there and scrap for a piece of the action when they have such heavy fees to pay? Even leaving aside such concepts as "wisdom" and "pragmatism," one would think that over a period of time, by trial and error perhaps, animals would learn that they can be more comfortable, have fuller stomachs, get more rest, be safer from predators, and live longer if they just forget about the reproduction bit. Still they reproduce. Why?

Actually, the question is not very profound. Animals reproduce because they have been "selected" to reproduce. Animals that didn't copulate didn't have any offspring. Animals that did copulate did leave offspring. Obviously, there was a genetic selection going on there, leaving in the genes that said "do it" and weeding out the genes that didn't say anything at all about it.

Let's return for a moment to people, since this book is about people. We want to copulate because our parents did, and their parents did, and their parents did, on back through thousands and thousands of generations, even before the development of language, before a man and a woman could say, "Hey, let's have some kids so we'll have free help on the farm." Simply put, people who wanted to copulate were more likely to have children who wanted to copulate than were people who didn't want to copulate. The children of people who didn't want to copulate didn't want to do much of anything because they didn't exist.

Our monkey friend, for example, the one described by Margaret Mead three decades ago, probably lived a healthy, happy life, but he "died with his genes in," you might say. There are no little monkeys around with his genes influencing their behavior. On the other hand, some of the genes of his contemporaries, the ones who got in there and fought, live on, and are making scrappers out of their hosts.

All this boils down to the basic principle of evolution stated in Chapter 2: Inherent traits that enhance the organism's chances to successfully produce offspring, no matter how slight or strong the enhancement may be, will eventually become predominant in the species. Our example is about as basic as one can get. With sex, offspring are produced. Without it, they are not. Undeniably, there is genetic survival value in the tendency to copulate.

No arguments. No objections. No hackles raised. But this is

as far as we go with such pleasant, noncontroversial discourse. The focus of this book is on differences between males and females. And our particular interest lies in the application of evolutionary biology to sexual selection, or traits that are passed on to males and females differentially because of structural differences between the sexes. That's where the fun begins.

Sexual Arousal

A simple, very basic notion about male-female sex differences to derive from this evolutionary principle concerns sexual arousal. That's where we will start.

The vast majority of human characteristics fall under what is referred to as a normal, or bell-shaped, curve. Personality traits, intelligence, weight, height, you name it. Almost everything we can measure in humans is normally distributed. It is reasonable, therefore, to assume also that sexual arousal is, or at least was at one time, normally distributed, with extremes of "never get aroused" and "constant arousal." Diagrammatically, we can represent the frequency of such different arousal characteristics like this:

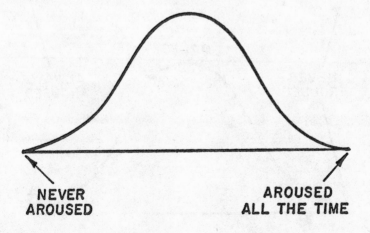

**NEVER
AROUSED**

**AROUSED
ALL THE TIME**

To read this diagram, imagine thousands of tiny little people piled up on the horizontal line. Then imagine that a line has been drawn over the top of the heap. Each person is right over that spot on the line that represents how often he or she is aroused. You can see that very few people are represented as "never aroused" and very few are represented as "aroused all the time." But many are piled up in the center.

Second, let's assume that males and females *do not differ* in this characteristic—that is, if we draw frequency distributions for males and for females, we will have something like this, with the area under the right ends of the curves representing the frequency of males and females who are aroused all or most of the time, and the areas under the left ends of the curves show-

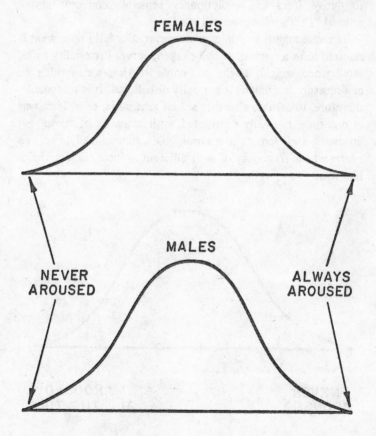

ing the frequency of males and females who seldom or never become sexually aroused.

If these representations were true, it would be the case that in a given heterosexual encounter there is no reason to predict that the male would more likely be aroused than the female, or vice versa. Now, for the sake of playing with some mathematics, let's choose two females and two males from these two distributions. For simplicity—but it still won't be simple—we'll choose one female who is aroused, or becomes aroused 100 per cent of the time when she is around a male, and one female who never becomes aroused when she is around males. In order to be perfectly fair, let's choose a male who becomes aroused 100 per cent of the time around females and a male who never becomes aroused around females.

So far, so good. We have

> One aroused male
> One aroused female
> One uninterested male
> One uninterested female

Now let's toss these four out into the wilds somewhere and let some heterosexual encounters take place. Of course, encounters between the two males and the two females are also likely to take place, but since these encounters would never end up in producing offspring, we'll ignore them.

One of our females meets one of our males. Perhaps in a large clump of bushes while hiding from a rampaging tiger. Or perhaps at a romantic stream while they are both picking berries. Maybe we happened to choose two who were already mates, so the encounter takes place at home in the cave after one or the other, or both, have been looking around most of the day for some food. Keep in mind that this encounter doesn't have to be the first meeting. It may be any one of a large number of meetings throughout their lives. For the sake of our example, that doesn't make any difference.

At any rate, an encounter takes place between the female and the male. What we want to figure out is the probability that any one of these four individuals will pass on their genes. Again, for simplicity's sake, we'll assume that both females have just ovulated and are ready to conceive.

In order to calculate the probability of any given individual having an offspring, we have to take the probability of coitus occurring in the encounter times the probability of fertilization. Given an encounter, what is the probability of coitus? Obviously, this probability will depend largely on who is aroused and who is not. If the always-aroused male meets the always-aroused female, and they have any kind of communication skills at all, the chances of coitus should be pretty high. Certainly not 100 per cent, though. The neighbors might stay late, or there is the possibility that one or the other might have a headache. Let's say that when these two meet the chances of coitus are 20 per cent.

Suppose the always-aroused male meets the never-aroused female. What are the chances of coitus then? They might be close to zero, but they are not zero. The male could talk the female into it—that is, she might say, "Oh well, it's not worth the hassle. Do it if it's so all-fired important to you." Let's say that the probability of coitus taking place under these conditions is one chance out of a hundred, or .01.

What happens when the never-aroused male meets the always-aroused female? The female might try to talk the male into having sex, and in this case, he would be the one saying, "Oh well, it's not worth the hassle. Do it if it's so all-fired important to you."

What are the chances of coitus? (Remember that the uninterested male doesn't become aroused). Zero. Even if he decided he would like to help this poor horny female out, unaroused he faces a task not unlike pushing a wagon uphill with a rope. Clearly, the probability of coitus taking place is zero.

One other possible encounter exists: The never-aroused male and the never-aroused female meet. No one begs; no one pleads. They smile at each other and go about their business. Even if they talked it over and decided they would like to have kids, the unaroused male still wouldn't be able to perform.

What information do we have at this point?

TYPE OF MEETING	CHANCES OF COITUS
Aroused male meets aroused female	.20
Aroused male meets uninterested female	.01
Uninterested male meets aroused female	.00
Uninterested male meets uninterested female	.00

I assumed that the females in this example were ready to conceive. What would be the chances of fertilization given coitus? Data from Barrett and Marshall (1969) suggest that if coitus occurs at the time the ovum is ready for fertilization, the probability of fertilization is around .70. We will use that as a value to be plugged into our analysis, but I should also point out that any value greater than .00 would lead to the same conclusion we will reach by using .70.

Now we are ready to figure the probabilities of offspring arising from each type of encounter.

TYPE OF MEETING	PROBABILITY OF COITUS	PROBABILITY OF FERTILIZATION GIVEN COITUS	PROBABILITY OF SUCCESSFULLY PASSING ON GENES
Aroused male and aroused female	.20	.70	.140
Aroused male and uninterested female	.01	.70	.007
Uninterested male and aroused female	.00	.70	.000
Uninterested male and uninterested female	.00	.70	.000

The next question is the critical one. If these are the only four individuals living within proximity of each other, what is the probability that any given individual will pass on his or her genes in any given encounter? We derive these probabilities by summing the probabilities of offspring over all possible types of encounters. The always-aroused male, for example, has a probability of .140 of having offspring if he meets the always-aroused female, and a probability of .007 of having offspring if

he meets the never-aroused female. The sum of these two probabilities divided by 2 is .0735. In like manner, the probability
of the always-aroused female having offspring if she meets the
always-aroused male is .140, and the probability of offspring if
she meets the uninterested male is .000. The sum of these probability values divided by 2 is .0700. The other probabilities are
computed in the same manner:

Probability of the aroused male passing on his genes   = .0735
Probability of the aroused female passing on her genes   = .0700
Probability of the uninterested male passing on his genes = .0000
Probability of the uninterested female passing on her genes = .0035

Now let us look carefully at what we have. In the long haul,
the always-aroused male is more likely to pass on his genes
than is the always-aroused female. Obversely, the uninterested
female is more likely to pass on her genes than is the uninterested male. In addition, the always-aroused male has a
strong reproductive advantage over the never-aroused male.
The always-aroused female also has a reproductive advantage
over the never-aroused female, but this advantage is of much
smaller magnitude than in the case of the males.

Have I played some tricks with mathematics? No tricks, I as-
sure you. The differences are the result of one basic biological
difference between the sexes that no one would dispute: Males
must be aroused if they are to pass on their genes; females *do
not have to be aroused* in order to pass on their genes. As long
as this biological reality exists, no matter what values one plugs
into these equations, the values *always* favor the aroused male
the most and *always* favor the nonaroused male the least.

If we had chosen a male and a female each of whom was
aroused 80 per cent of the time and thrown them in with a male
and female each of whom was aroused 20 per cent of the time,
we would have gotten similar results. The reason I did not do
this is simply that the mathematics would become so much
more complex to make the same point. Consider, for example,
the difficulty of just calculating the probability of coitus when
the 80 per cent-of-the-time aroused male meets the 80 per cent-
of-the-time aroused female. The probability that they are both

aroused on any given encounter is the product of the individual probabilities of arousal: .8 × .8, which equal .64. Then you have to figure what the chances are that coitus will take place and that they are both aroused. Using the .2 probability we used before, the answer would be .64 × .2, which equal .32. But we are not through with this couple. There is also the possibility that he will be aroused and she won't be (.8 × .2, which equal .16), or vice versa (.2 × .8, which equal .16). What is the probability that these conditions will occur and that coitus will take place? In the first, the male might beg the issue, and coitus might occur, perhaps 1 out of every 100 times this type of encounter occurs (.8 × .2 × .01, which equal .0016). In the latter case, the female might also beg, but of course we know the probability of coitus is .00. When both parties happen to be uninterested (which happens 20 per cent of the time for each), coitus also does not occur.

Obviously, it is too complex to do the whole analysis that way. But it is true that the same conclusions would be reached if we chose males and females from anywhere in the spectrum as long as each probability value was represented by both a male and a female. Considering all possible encounters, the more-aroused man always has the strongest advantage in passing on his genes and the least-aroused man always has the least advantage in passing on his genes. For women, frequency of sexual arousal is less important in determining reproductive advantage, and women will always fall between the two male extremes.

Let's go back now to our original density curves showing hypothesized equal distributions of arousal for both males and females. According to our figures, genes of the males on the right end of the distribution have a strong advantage over the genes of the males on the left end of the distribution. And the genes of the females on the right end of the distribution have a weak advantage over the genes of the females on the left end of the distribution. Something like this:

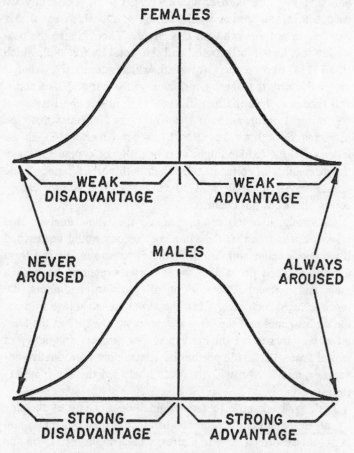

Over thousands of generations, we would expect the distributions to change, with the male distribution changing more rapidly than that of the females.

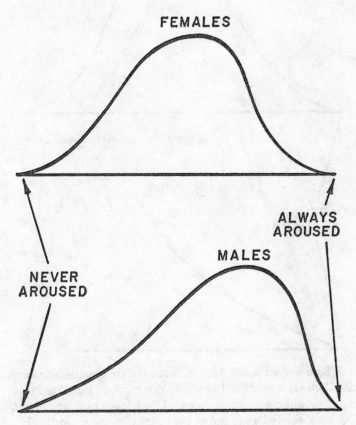

And change more, like this:

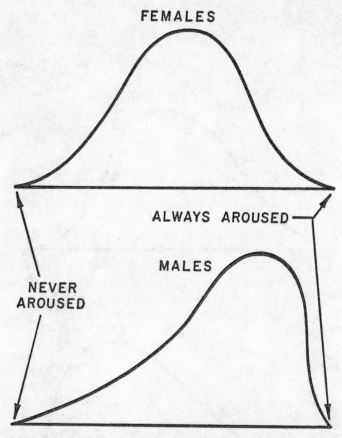

Where are we now? That is, what do the twentieth-century distributions look like? I certainly don't know. But if the synthetic evolutionary view is correct, I do know where we are *not*. We most assuredly are not at the point where the distributions are equivalent. To be there after as many generations as we have in our history would defy all the known laws of genetic selection. I suppose it could be done, but it would be very difficult to find some logic from which to argue that the average man and the average woman should experience the same frequencies of sexual arousal. Based purely on the single principle that what is advantageous in reproduction gets passed on to the offspring, we would have to predict that men would experience arousal a great many more times per day than would women.

How Does This Logic Square with What We Know About the World?

From his epic study of human sexual responses, Kinsey and his colleagues (1953, p. 682) report:

> . . . the average younger male is constantly being aroused. The average female is not so often aroused. In some instances the male's arousal may be mild, but in many instances the arousal may involve genital erection and considerable physiologic reaction. Nearly all . . . younger males are aroused to the point of erection many times per week, and many of them respond to the point of erection several times per day. Many females may go for days and weeks and months without ever being stimulated unless they have actual physical contact with a sexual partner.

As an aside, it is probably important at this point to make a few comments about Kinsey's work. Many times throughout these chapters I will refer to Kinsey and will use his ideas and his data to support points I wish to make. The reader may wonder why more recent researchers are not quoted as often. There are several reasons. First, Kinsey has covered far more topics than others have; hence, on any question raised in this book he has something of interest to say. Second, although Kinsey's work is not above criticism, it is clearly the best that has been done. Martin Daly and Margo Wilson (1978), who have synthesized more than five hundred books and articles into an impressive treatise called *Sex, Evolution and Behavior,* conclude that even though more than twenty-five years old, Kinsey's work, along with that of Ford and Beach, "are still unsurpassed" as the two major sources of information on human sexual behavior. Speaking of Kinsey's studies, Shere Hite says, "In many ways, this is still the standard that sex researchers refer

to when trying to establish the validity of their findings. . . ."
(p. 233). The reason his work is so highly respected is that
he was a meticulous researcher who went to enormous trouble
in his sampling and interview techniques. No recent study can
approach his methodological strength.

Let's return to Kinsey's statements on sexual arousal. You
can verify Kinsey's report if you wish—in a not very scientific
way—by just asking around. Not long ago, a female in her thirties said to me, "I just haven't thought about sex for about the
past four or five months." Another young woman, recently divorced and not anxious to pursue any males, said, "Sex? Oh
that's no problem. I can just turn it off and not think about
it." To find a male who would give a similar response, you are
going to have to do a lot of asking.

The evidence suggests that these differences are not as great
after men and women reach maturity, but the differences do
seem to persist throughout adulthood. For example, Wallin and
Clark (1958) found that the percentage of marriages in which
husbands reported a greater desired frequency of coitus than
their wives was twice that of marriages in which wives reported
a greater desired frequency of coitus than their husbands. More
recently, Hesselund (1971) found for a sample of married and
unmarried young adults that males desired intercourse more often than the females. No study I have ever come across suggests
that the reported frequencies of sexual arousal ever become
equal at any age.

Even more impressive are the data on overtly sexual dreams
and nocturnal emissions. Kinsey et al. (1953, p. 215) tell us
that up to age forty-five only 70 per cent of the females report
having had overt sexual dreams while "nearly 100 per cent"
of the males report such dreams. Furthermore, the frequency
of such dreams is far greater for males than for females.

The data are not voluminous, but what we have do support
the prediction (or postdiction, if you wish) made from evolutionary biology. More than that, the example serves to illustrate
the kind of logical games we will play throughout this book.
Let's consider another example.

How About Orgasmic Responsiveness?

Frequency of arousal? Yes, the data do support the predictions. But that doesn't mean, does it, that once aroused, males and females are likely to differ in the ability to have orgasm. Don't we all know that the level of sexual excitement is equally strong in both sexes? If we are to believe the popular literature, we "know" this. But then the popular literature has no basis in either data or logic.

As we did with frequency of arousal, let's show, for a large group of individuals, a density function for the percentage of orgasms given a certain number of experiences of coitus.

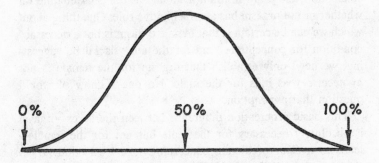

PERCENT ORGASMS

To read this diagram, as you did before, imagine that thousands of tiny little people are piled upon this line and a curve is drawn over the top of them. Each person is placed along the line at the percentage of coituses in which he or she experiences orgasms. You can see that there are very few piled up at 0 per cent, not many at 10 per cent or 20 per cent, but then the height grows with the largest bulge at 50 per cent. The curve could be skewed either way—for example, with bulges at 30 per cent or 80 per cent—but since this is all hypothetical we might as well make it look normal and have the bulge at 50 per cent.

We don't know what the curve might have looked like thousands of generations ago, but no matter—the outcome would be the same regardless of what curve we start with.

In the previous example, I argued that arousal is necessary on the part of the male in order for the genes of either the male or the female to be passed on. Hence, there is a genetic selection for the number of occasions *per unit of time* males and females experience arousal.

But that's not the whole story. Just arousal isn't enough. Biology is very clear in its message about the necessity of male orgasm in the process of procreation. On the other hand, the role of the female orgasm in pregnancy simply is not known. Although Masters and Johnson (1966, p. 172) suggest that arousal may lead to the creation of a "pool" that may facilitate conception, there are no data available at the present time on whether or not orgasm has any facilitative role. One thing about which we can be certain is that female orgasm is not a necessary condition for conception. And for the analysis I'll be suggesting, we need only establish that orgasm for the female is not *as necessary* as it is for the male. No one I know of would question that assumption.

This basic procreation difference between the sexes—orgasm is absolutely necessary for the male but not for the female—leads to a clear prediction concerning sexual selection: *Even if males and females should have somehow remained equal in frequency of sexual arousal, a selection process should have taken place for number of orgasms per arousal.* Again, I will go through what might be considered a somewhat tedious mathematical evolutionary logic. But because this topic has been the cause of much discussion in recent years, it is important for us to look at it carefully.

Once again, let's draw two density functions, showing percentage of orgasms for the two sexes.

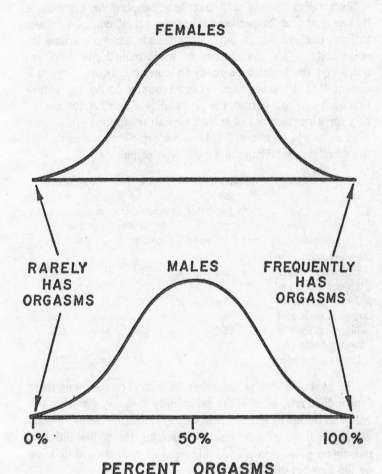

FEMALES

MALES

RARELY
HAS
ORGASMS

FREQUENTLY
HAS
ORGASMS

0%   50%   100%

PERCENT ORGASMS

From these distributions, we will again select four people:

High-orgasmic male (orgasms 80 per cent of the time)
High-orgasmic female (orgasms 80 per cent of the time)
Low-orgasmic male (orgasms only 20 per cent of the time)
Low-orgasmic female (orgasms only 20 per cent of the time)

We'll throw these people out into the wilds and let them encounter each other. Again, we'll ignore, for obvious reasons, the encounters between the two males and between the two females.

Since we've already said that these people have orgasms at 80 per cent and 20 per cent *given* the act of coitus, we have to limit our interest to those male-female encounters that involve coitus. This time, just to be more realistic, let's not require that the females be ready to conceive. Instead, we will assume that the encounters occur randomly during the ovulation cycles. If this is true, the probability of fertilization occurring for a random act of coitus, given that the male did have orgasm, would be about .04. Now we can figure the probabilities of offspring arising from each type of pairing:

PAIRING	PROBABILITY OF FERTILIZATION GIVEN MALE ORGASM		PROBABILITY OF MALE ORGASM		PROBABILITY OF SUCCESSFULLY PASSING ON GENES
High-org. male and high-org. female	.04	×	.8	=	.032
High-org. male and low-org. female	.04	×	.8	=	.032
Low-org. male and high-org. female	.04	×	.2	=	.008
Low-org. male and low-org. female	.04	×	.2	=	.008

The next question, as before, is the critical one. Among these four individuals, what is the probability that any given person will pass on his or her genes in any given act of coitus? Again, we derive these probabilities by summing the probabilities of passing on genes over all possible types of partners and dividing by the number of partners.

Probability high-org. male will pass on genes: $\dfrac{.032 + .032}{2} = .032$

Probability high-org. female will pass on genes: $\dfrac{.032 + .008}{2} = .020$

Probability low-org. female will pass on genes: $\dfrac{.032 + .008}{2} = .020$

Probability low-org. male will pass on genes: $\dfrac{.008 + .008}{2} = .008$

Who has the advantage? Clearly the high-orgasmic male has

a selection advantage over all others. And this advantage is particularly strong over the male with low orgasmic capacity, who happens to be on the bottom of the pile. On the other hand, the high-orgasmic female has *no* advantage over the low-orgasmic female.

In pictorial form, the advantages look something like this:

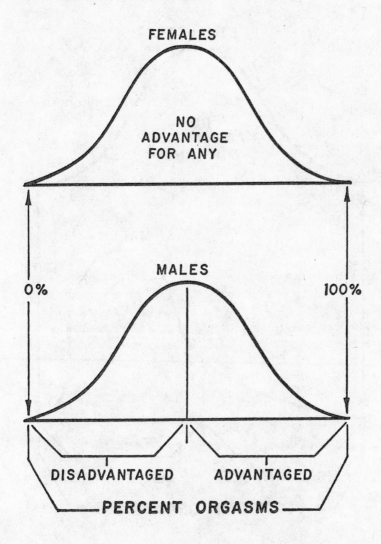

As we saw in the last example, over thousands of generations, we would expect the differential selection process to give us progressively more and more separation between the distributions. The female distribution might remain pretty much the same, while the male distribution should show a piling up at the "high orgasmic" end:

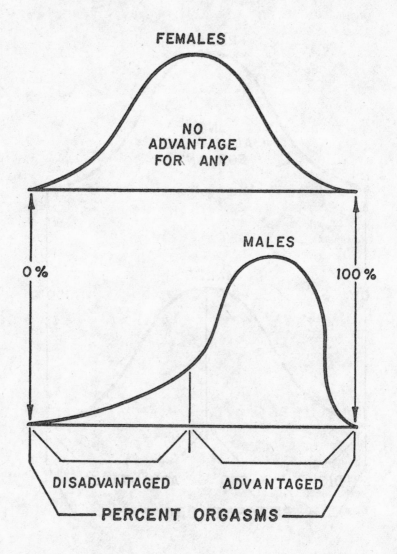

At this point, one may raise the objection that we really don't know whether or not female orgasm facilitates conception. Indeed we do not. But that matters little. As long as the importance of female orgasm to conception is *less* than that of the male—which it clearly is—the high-orgasmic male will *always* have a much greater selection advantage over the low-orgasmic male than the high-orgasmic female will have over the low-orgasmic female. And as long as these relative differences in advantage are there, males will be selected for orgasm more intensely than will females.

Is This Idea Supported by Data?

I've argued that basic biological fact (males must have orgasms to reproduce; females do not have to) combined with evolutionary theory insist that given coitus males should more frequently have orgasms than should females. Logically, the case is very tight. We should be surprised if we looked at coital orgasmic response and found no differences between the sexes. Indeed, we should be very surprised if we found women having more coital orgasms than men.

No surprise awaits us, however. The data *all* clearly support the prediction. In 1959, Shuttleworth wrote: "It is inherently easy for all males and inherently difficult for at least a few or some females to reach orgasm" (p. 167). His data show that between the ages of twenty-one and twenty-five, married men report 1.8 times as many orgasms from coitus as do married females. Almost twenty years later, Carmen Kerr, who appears to be in the forefront of the sexual revolution, writes, "From all the information about women's sexuality, many women in our society still don't have orgasms—while most men do" (Kerr, 1978, p. 11). Dr. Lonnie Barbach, a woman and a sex therapist, even makes the picture look a little more bleak. She says, "Basically, the findings show that most women *do* have trouble having orgasms with intercourse" (Barbach, 1976, p. 2). Furthermore, she cites statistics that show that about half of the sexual encounters that bring a man to orgasm do not end in orgasm for the woman. In Hite's (1977) sample, only 30 per cent of the women reported that they could orgasm regularly from intercourse.

The results of a 1972 study sponsored by the Playboy Foundation found that of women who had been married an average of fifteen years, only about half achieved orgasm 90 to 100 per cent of the time during intercourse. Of the single women interviewed, only 30 per cent were consistently orgasmic during coitus, and approximately 15 per cent never or almost never experienced orgasm (Hunt, 1974).

Barbach points out that when the data from the Playboy Foundation study are compared with the data gathered some twenty-five years earlier by Kinsey and his associates, "not much progress has been made in orgasmic responsivity among females" (Barbach, 1976, p. x). This despite the "sexual revolution" of the sixties, with all its manuals on how to do it, its emphasis on sexual freedom, and its proliferation of sex therapists.

"I always knew it," some angry critic may respond. "All those selfish men are just alike. They are so interested in their own satisfaction they pay no attention to the woman's needs. The data you are quoting prove it. Even if there are a few men who might care, they are so poor in technique it's a wonder any woman ever has an orgasm."

Poor technique? Men don't care, or they don't try to satisfy the women? Undoubtedly true in some cases. But that argument does not hold up on a broad scale.

Pietropinto and Simenauer (1978) claim that one of their major findings was "completely contrary to the widely publicized feminist complaints that men are selfishly concerned only with their own orgasms and are not interested in a woman's gratification" (p. 170). They report that more than half of the men in their sample "were willing to go to any lengths to ensure their partner's satisfaction" (p. 170).

Fisher (1973, pp. 397–98) concluded the following about male technique and female orgasm from his own studies and those that preceded his:

> The notion that a woman's orgasm difficulties reflect her husband's poor love-making techniques . . . does not

stand up well against the available research evidence. The
extensive studies by Terman, in which wives and their husbands were evaluated in detail, turned up few, if any, consistent correlations between diverse husband attributes
(including sexual behavior) and wife's orgastic ability. It
is also true that Kinsey . . . and others have generally
been unable to show that a woman's orgasm consistency
is related to several different aspects of the husband's sexual behavior (for example, how long he persists in applying sexual stimulation to his wife). In the present writer's
studies there were no consistent correlations between variables that certainly reflect the husband's sexual behavior
(number of intercourse positions, amount of foreplay, and
duration of sexual stimulation) and the wife's orgasm consistency.

A woman might counter this by saying that women just
aren't given the opportunity or encouragement to practice.
However, some sex therapists claim that even with specific
training, practice, encouragement, feedback, and a co-operative
partner, some women are still going to experience difficulty, or
perhaps never achieve orgasm either through masturbation or
in coitus (for example, Zeiss, Rosin, and Zeiss, 1977; Schneidman and McGuire, 1976). Kinsey (1953, p. 384) claims that
practice can have an appreciable effect on the ability of females
to reach orgasm in marital coitus, but he did not make a strong
case for practice. Fisher (1973, p. 406) concluded that even
his mild optimism was overstated:

> If after five years of practice only 1 per cent of the women
> studied show an increase in being really consistently
> orgasmic, or if after five years of practice only 8 per cent
> of those who are *totally* nonorgasmic begin to have an oc-
> casional orgasm, how can one attribute much influence to
> practice effects?

There is at least one other last-ditch effort to explain away
the data on orgasmic difficulty in women. We all know that a
certain proportion of men and women are neurotic. Maybe then
neurotic women don't have as many orgasms and that fact

brings the mean down. Fisher, however, maintains that in his studies he has found

> . . . no indication that women who do not attain orgasm consistently are generally more anxious or in poorer "mental health" than women who do reach orgasm consistently [Fisher, 1973, p. 398].

The simple facts are that females, once aroused, don't have orgasms as often or as easily as males do. Among the candidates for explanation, evolutionary logic seems as strong as any; in my view, stronger than any others I know of.

Number of Orgasms—Evidence That Confounds Frequency of Arousal with Level of Arousal

Sheer number of orgasms may result from either of two factors: frequency of arousal and orgasmic ability—that is, if males and females have orgasms with equal ease but males experience more frequent arousal, males should have more orgasms. In like manner, if males and females experience equal numbers of arousal but males are more orgastic each time arousal occurs, males should have more orgasms. Hence, if males do, indeed, experience more total orgasms than females, such evidence would be inconclusive about the independent role of either of these factors. However, such data would argue strongly that at least one, if not both, of these hypotheses about male-female differences would be true.

What evidence do we have? Robinson (1977, p. 109) pulled together data from several sources and concluded that the average male has over 1,500 orgasms before marriage, while the average female has fewer than 250. Shuttleworth (1959, pp. 168–69) stated: "In the age range from adolescence to age 15, single males report 20 times as many orgasms from all sources as do single females." Furthermore, throughout life, the orgasm frequency of the average man is higher than that of the average woman (Kinsey et al., 1953).

Even more impressive are the data from reports of nocturnal dreams. Kinsey (1953, p. 215) found that only 37 per cent of the females in their sample reported orgasms with sexual dreams, compared with 83 per cent for males. Furthermore, among those individuals who do have sexual dreams, which includes far fewer women than men, the incidence of orgasm given a dream is much higher for men than for women. Shuttleworth (1959, p. 169) found that in the age range from adolescence to 15, "single males report *131* times as many orgasms from nocturnal dreams as do single females." And when we stop to realize that females attain puberty almost two years before males, presumably giving them a big head start, the data should really cause us to take notice.

The apologists for orgasm infrequency in women argue that males have been taught by our culture that they should have more orgasms and that this difference in learning accounts for the kind of data we see above. But if we look closely at both principles of learning and the evidence, we gain quite another impression.

From the standpoint of a psychological concept called "stimulus generalization," we expect the effects of learning to be stronger under those conditions in which the behavior was learned than in other conditions. Presumably learning about orgasms and the like takes place when we are awake. Hence, learning theorists would predict (or postdict, as the case may be) that the effects of learning on orgasmic activity should be more pronounced during the awakened state than during sleep —that is, if male orgasms are more "learned" than female orgasms, we should find that males should have considerably more orgasms than females while awake, but that this difference should not be so great while asleep. Actually, the data show just the opposite. Consider Shuttleworth's study cited above. From adolescence to age 15, males report 20 times more orgasms than females from all sources but *131* times more orgasms from nocturnal dreams. If learning theory has anything to say about these data, it suggests that male orgasmic activity has been *dampened* by the effects of culture, certainly not that it has been enhanced.

How could cultural factors dampen the male's desire for orgasm? One does not have to go very far back in history to find professionals scaring the daylights out of the individual who might contemplate masturbation. Consider, for example, the following excerpt from G. Stanley Hall's famous two-volume work entitled *Adolescence: Its Psychology and Its Relations to Physiology, Anthropology, Sociology, Sex, Crime, Religion and Education:*

> One of the very saddest of all the aspects of human weakness and sin is onanism [masturbation], and to say that it is as important in treating adolescence as it is painful to consider is to say very much. Until recently it has been met on the one hand with either prudery and painstaking reticence or treated in terms of exaggerated horror, as in the "scare" and quack literature. . . . One thing can safely be assumed, namely, that no one ever fell into the habit of reading a serious work upon it [Hall, 1905, p. 432].

It is of particular interest to note that in this introduction to his own discourse on masturbation, Hall wishes to set his own ideas apart from the "scare" or "quack literature." He plans to tell us how things really are from a "well-modulated, scientific" viewpoint. Does he set our minds at ease? You can be the judge of that:

> The old phrase, *post coitus triste,* is illustrated in excess of all forms, and especially in self-abuse. Weakness always brings more or less depression, and in some cases the physical exhaustion of muscles and nerves, if intensified by excess, brings pain and traces of convulsion, epilepsy, palpitation, and photophobia, differing according to individual predispositions and powers of resistance. Neurasthenia, cerebrasthenia, spinal neurasthenia, and psychic impotence generally result not more in the loss of fluid than from expenditure of physical force and often by tissues connected with the sympathetic system. Subjective light sensations, optical cramps, perhaps Basedow's disease, intensification of the patellar reflex, weak sluggishness of heart action and circulation seen in cold

extremities, purple and dry skin, lassitude and flaccidity, clammy hands, anemic complexions, dry cough, and many digestive perversions can be often directly traced to this scourge of the human race. [Masturbation] . . . seems especially to predispose to convulsive disorders like epilepsy, to which it is so akin, but weakness of memory and attention, paranoia, agitation, cachexia, various neuroses of the stomach which Preyer and Fournier have studied, dwarfing or hypertrophy of the organs themselves, and many of the lighter and transitory forms of psychic alienations, are produced. . . .

The power of pity and sympathy is often almost extinguished. Self-control and will-power, purposive self-direction, resolute ability to grapple with difficulties mental or physical, to carry work that is begun through to completion, are certain to decline. . . . The masturbator's heart, so often discussed, is weak like his voice. . . .

These effects might perhaps be summed up as phenomena of arrest. Growth, especially in the moral and intellectual regions, is dwarfed and stunted. There are early physical signs of decrepitude and senescence. Gray hairs, and especially baldness, a stooping and enfeebled gait, the impulsive and narrow egoism which always goes with overindulgence, marks of early caducity which may crop out in retina, in cochlea, in the muscular or nervous system, in the stomach—all the troubles ascribed to this cause are distinctly senescent in their nature" [Hall, 1905, pp. 442–44].

If that wouldn't terrify an individual about autostimulation, I don't know what would. What must the "scare" literature have been like before Hall's work? Although these ideas were presented seventy-four years ago, many of them prevailed until relatively recently. They were no doubt still widely held among the generations from which Kinsey obtained his data.

Indeed, if one wishes to argue from a "learning" position, one can easily garner evidence to suggest that the effects of culture have been negative rather than positive with regard to frequency of male orgasm.

In this chapter, I've presented two examples of the application of biological evolution to human sexual behavior. Evolutionary logic tells us that because of basic differences in the requirements for procreation, males should be selected for greater frequencies of sexual arousal and for greater orgastic ability. At the present time, *all* of the data we have support the predictions. None support any alternative position.

4

Nature and Nurture: Bringing Them Together

Arousal and orgasm are perhaps not very impressive phenomena from which to argue that instincts have an influence on complex social behaviors. We might just as well be talking about blood pressure or kidney functioning, which, most of us would agree, are not easy to bring under voluntary control. Sexual arousal happens. We don't even know what causes erections. And no doubt our ignorance in this area is what brings terror to the male who finds that it doesn't happen when it is supposed to. There's not much he can do about such personal disasters. The question now becomes: What does all of this, or any of this, have to do with the complexity of voluntary behaviors surrounding the courtship and mating games?

It is not the purpose of this book to explore in detail theories of motivation, but the nature-nurture controversy is so strong we must take more than a passing look at it. The reader now has a feel for the area and a couple of examples from which to understand the basic arguments in this book. He also no doubt has many reservations and objections. Hence, at this point, I want to suggest a view of motivation and behavior that may answer some of these questions—a view that begins several thousand years ago and continues today. I hope to show that this view has healthy historical precedent, that it runs through most major theories today, that it can encompass both a sociobiological framework as well as data from the "learning" wing of psychology.

Why Do People Have Sex? A Second Look

Let's consider once again, "Why have sex at all?" At the beginning of the previous chapter, I suggested that there are so many costs involved in mating that the process of reproduction appears to be self-defeating. Yet animals do it.

I said we want to copulate because our parents did, and their parents did, and their parents did, on back through thousands of generations. But something is surely lacking from such an "explanation." If you ask a person why he or she has sex, the answer is not likely to be, "I copulate because my parents copulated and their parents copulated and their parents copulated." Of course not. People are more likely to say, "Because it feels good."

There has to be some mechanism to induce animals to action. With all the costs involved in reproduction, there has to be some hedonic value strong enough to overcome the liabilities. And indeed there is. Sex feels good.

Most copulations by people aren't meant for reproduction. A very small percentage of the instances of sexual intercourse occur for purposes of having children. We all know that people go to great lengths to keep the reproduction process from occurring and still be able to copulate. They submit their genitals to the rape of the scalpel—an anxiety-arousing process if ever there was one—and they interrupt their most intimate moments in order to foil the reproductive process by all sorts of contraptions and devices. The hedonic gain has to be something great.

A Thread Running Through Motivation Theory

Many generations before the development of speech, long before we even had a good understanding of why we were doing it, we would have died out if sex had not provided a hedonic trip. We may not know what nerves are firing or what our blood pressure is, but we sure do know a feeling of pain or pleasure when we have it. Those pains and pleasures are the "stuff" of motivation.

Every major motivational theory put forth has incorporated some notion of expected gain to be derived from a particular action. The very word "action" as it is used in modern philosophical discourse connotes a purpose or the desire to bring about some state of affairs. The Greek philosophers Epicurus and Lucretius certainly recognized the effects of "getting rid of pain" and "creating some sense of well-being." Even Socrates saw that "the ideal" would have to involve a state of happiness and that "the pleasant" could not be disassociated from that ideal. Further down the line, eighteenth-century philosopher Jeremy Bentham articulated the basic tenets of the pain-pleasure principle in human motivation about as well as any have said it in recent years.

Freud, the most influential motivational theorist of the past hundred years, incorporated within his instinct theory the notions of satisfaction and removal of disturbing states. Thorndike in the early part of this century had his "satisfying states of affairs" and "annoying states of affairs." Furthermore, in the 1930s and 1940s we find Tolman's "purposive behavior" with its "expectancies" of reward or punishment and Hull's "drive reduction."

In the early 1960s, Hobart Mowrer asked us to think of rats having "hopes" and "disappointments." And even B. F. Skinner, with his desire not to become involved in the organism's head, speaks very freely of animals acting in order to maximize net gains (Skinner, 1969, p. 39). More explicit applications of hedonic principles are seen in the literatures of game theory (Vinacke, 1969), risk-taking (Kogan and Wallach, 1967), social-exchange theory (Thibaut and Kelly, 1959), problem-solving (Edwards, 1954), and social-learning theory (Rotter, 1970).

By the early 1970s, these concepts, often referred to as "cognitive expectancy-value theories," clearly had achieved the upper hand. These theories hold that the order of our preferences for different outcomes relates to our application of affective, or value, scales to all perceived outcomes of a behavior. Nowhere have I found this position more clearly stated than in the following quote from Edwin Megargee, widely known for his work in human aggression:

> Typically, the individual selects the response that appears to offer the maximum satisfactions and the minimum dissatisfactions in that particular situation. This statement conceals a rapid but extremely complex internal bargaining process in which the capacity of a given response to fulfill many different drives and motives is weighted, often unconsciously, against the pain that might result from that response as well as from the postponement of the satisfaction of other competing drives. By means of this internal algebra, which occurs so rapidly the individual is usually unaware of it, the net strength of each possible response is calculated and compared with all other responses and the strongest one selected [Megargee, 1969, p. 1,045].

What does all this mean? It means the majority of psychologists agree that people engage in sex or any other behavior because the value received is enough to offset, from a subjective economic standpoint, the time it takes, the energy it expends, and the risks and costs it entails. The reader is warned, however, not to interpret this statement as indicating a simple decision-making process. Into this "net gain" equation must be fed dozens, perhaps hundreds of bits of information relating to values we attach to physical, emotional, moral, ethical, religious, interpersonal, and material objects or events.

In spite of the complexity of this concept of motivation, it appears to be the best we have. Furthermore, it provides the cornerstone for our attempt to fit together the influences of genetic and environmental variables. The thesis of this chapter is that instincts play an important role in motivation by feeding values—pains and pleasures—into this "net gain" equation. In order to see how they do this, it may be helpful to look briefly again at the role of instincts in recent psychological history.

Nature and Nurture: A Historical Perspective

I mentioned in Chapter 2 that in the latter half of the nine-teenth century and the beginning of the twentieth, the concept of instincts operating in humans was commonly accepted. But that's not the whole story. This view was more than commonly accepted—it was strongly accepted, so much so that almost any desirable behavior was thought to be the result of good genes and almost any undesirable behavior the result of bad genes. The effects of learning experiences were given little attention.

With the behavioristic revolution, of course, all that was changed. For the larger segment of the psychological world, be-havior was seen as almost totally the result of learning, and ge-netic influences were given little attention.

During the twenties and thirties there were academic scuffles once in a while between the "naturists" and the "nurturists," but by and large, the "nurturists" held a strongly dominant po-sition.

By the late fifties enough information had accumulated on individual differences to convince most psychologists that Wat-son was wrong when he said we are all equal at birth with regard to behavioral potential.

But information had also been amassed to show that dif-ferent learning histories can profoundly affect performance. The solution? Psychologists decided that genes can establish limits within which behaviors may vary depending upon experi-ence. A simple example of this compromise could be that of a man with a genetic anomaly that crippled his legs. This genetic condition may place an upper limit on how fast he could ever run even with the most elaborate training program, but it would not make him run or even walk. The degree of mobility he de-veloped within the limits imposed genetically would be the re-sult of experience.

This view was particularly palatable because it avoided the whole issue of genes somehow encouraging us to behave in cer-tain ways. From this perspective, genes only exercise a veto power—that is, they can keep us from behaving—but the positive thrust for behaving comes from other sources.

Well and good. Genes no doubt do operate in this way. But the view is incomplete because it cannot account for a major puzzle in applied-learning theory.

Why Is a Reinforcer Reinforcing?

That puzzle is, why is a reinforcer reinforcing? During the heyday of learning theories, psychologists generally invoked concepts such as "drive reduction" or "release of tension" or "tissue need" to account for the power of the reinforcers they used in their conditioning experiments. But as our knowledge of reinforcement principles expanded, these concepts were not adequate. We introduced such ideas as "appetitive drives" and "curiosity drives," and in the process succeeded only in relabeling the list of instincts psychologists had told us about at the turn of the century.

Finally, theorists ceased talking about why reinforcers were reinforcing. Many, it appears, sought refuge from such difficult questions by throwing their lot with descriptive behaviorism, which does not advertise itself as theoretical. But even then the haunting questions could not be easily avoided. Once, when B. F. Skinner, the father figure of descriptive behaviorism, was asked why food is reinforcing to a hungry animal, he replied, "I do not know why and I do not care" (see Day, 1969, p. 319). But on other occasions, Skinner has felt strongly enough about the issue to address it. He states that the power of reinforcement must have arisen because there was a selection advantage therein (Skinner, 1969, p. 206). And this is precisely the view that the sociobiologists present. Barash (1976, p. 179) tells us:

> Insofar as animals do something because they enjoy it (or because there is reinforcement value in it), that very enjoyment is interpretable as an evolutionary strategy inducing living things to function in a way that ultimately enhances their fitness.

Apart from descriptive behaviorism, only one other learning "school" seems to have any following today. In that school we find the cognitive or social-learning theorists, who have no trouble at all talking about reinforcers having inherent properties to make people feel good or bad.

The point is this: The advocates of modern learning theory have no quarrel whatever with the view that reinforcing value often derives from inherited physiological structure. The "operant conditioning" psychologists have *used* these reinforcers to make animals and human beings perform marvelous feats. But all they did was *use* the reinforcers to change the behavioral stream. Sometimes they may have even transferred reinforcement value from one stimulus to another (for example, with higher order conditioning), but seldom, if ever, have they created reinforcement value. On the contrary, they began with reinforcement value to make their own valuable contributions.

It appears that more and more investigators are now opting for the position that biological evolution, nature, instincts, whatever you wish to call it, operates on the behavior of an organism by giving many reinforcers their power—that is, by making events or activities feel good or bad. Learning, on the other hand, operates by giving us skills, by teaching us to define events or activities on moral or ethical dimensions, and through such diverse processes as operant and respondent conditioning. Within this framework, our present views of learning and our present views of instinct are entirely compatible.

Are there other possibilities for the integration of the effects of genetic endowment and learning? There certainly are. We live in a multidetermined, very complex world. Several other possibilities have been suggested. As I mentioned in the above section, Skinner acknowledges the role of biological evolution in making reinforcers reinforcing. But he argues even much more strongly that genetics affects our behavior by creating in us the capacity to change as a result of given contingencies (Skinner, 1969)—that is, learning some behaviors more easily than others is the result of genetic endowment.

There is still another possibility. At specified stages in an organism's development, genes may set up a neurological readiness for certain classes of stimuli to be quickly incorporated into that organism's storehouse of eliciting and reinforcing stimuli. This is generally the position that has been strongly taken by the European investigators of instinctive behavior (the ethologists) since the 1930s. More or less specific developmental staging of readiness to learn various things is what "imprinting" is all about (Immelman, 1975; Lorenz, 1970). Although there is not a lot of evidence to go on, it appears that sexual preferences in animals and fetishes in humans may be developed this way, especially during early pubescence (Nyby, Dizinno, and Whitney, 1977).

I have suggested three ways that genes might affect complex behaviors: first, by giving reinforcers their motivating power; second, by giving us differential capacities to learn different tasks; third, by setting the stage for the attachment of value to stimuli. All of these views are compatible with the principles of learning as we now understand them. Furthermore, in contrast to the earlier view that nature only "sets the limits," these views of the influence of genes on behavior have strong implications for what behaviors are likely to occur—a somewhat more exciting role for "instinct" than has been its assignment in the recent past.

Other Current Clinical Perspectives on Nature and Behavior

Behaviorism dominates academic psychology today, and it plays a very strong role in theories of clinical psychology. Furthermore, behaviorism has been seen as the traditional antagonist of "nature." For these reasons, I have given the lion's share of attention to the demonstration that today's behaviorism has recently been reaching out toward the notions of genetic influence. Some attention, however, should also be given to the two other important schools of clinical psychology: existential-humanistic psychology and psychoanalytic psychology.

The existential-humanistic camp clearly champions the idea of following and trusting your deepest, natural inclinations. Abraham Maslow, Rollo May, and Carl Rogers, father figures of this movement, believe our genetic endowment provides us with the noblest of values, motives, and feelings. Certainly, this school finds no conflict with the notion of human instinctive behaviors. Rather, it tells us that the way to fulfillment and self-actualization is to let our instincts direct our lives.

The other major clinical school, psychoanalytic psychology, also has a strong investment in instincts. It has been said that one of Freud's most innovative and important contributions was that of "primary process" (Murphy, 1968, p. 189), a concept clearly based in his notions of biological evolution. The primary process was the instinctive, evolutionary source of the stream of conscious activity and as such it shaped the nature of our conscious perception of needs, desires, and wants. The primary process provided motivation and direction for the behaving organism by making certain activities feel good and others feel bad.

In summary, it appears that there is no current psychological theory that comes into conflict with the notion of instincts affecting complex human behaviors. Behaviorism—even descriptive behaviorism—humanistic-existential psychology, and psychoanalytic psychology all deal at one level or another with the question of biology and behavior. None of these positions is incompatible with the view that genes can exert an effect on our behaviors. Apparently objections to such a view come not from scientific persuasion but from personal prejudice.

"Feelings": The Stuff of Genetic Influence

In the first section of this chapter, I suggested that theories of motivation have always huddled around a thread variously construed as "hedonic value" or "net gain" or more simply put, "what feels good or bad." In the following section, we saw that psychologists used fancy jargon in their attempt to disguise the instinctive underpinnings of motivational theory but they have been constantly pushed back toward it. Their theories of behavior were incomplete without some notion of inherent dispositions. Then I suggested that there is nothing in current psychological theory that has any quarrel with the idea of genetic influence on complex human behavior. In this section, I want to underscore the action of genes through "feelings."

The view that genes affect behavior through "feelings" they create is not only quite acceptable, but it also precedes any other modern psychological attempt to articulate the "stuff" of genetic influence. Skinner tells us that it is "an old theme" that antedates Darwin by at least half a century.

The central idea of this view is that if some mutation were to produce an organism that found particular enjoyment in an activity providing a reproductive advantage, that organism would pass on more of its genes than would its peers who did not find enjoyment in that advantageous activity. In this chapter, I have used coitus as an example. All other factors being equal, the animal for whom coitus was highly enjoyable would be likely to engage in it more often than would the animal for whom coitus was only "so-so." And, of course, the animal that does it more is likely to contribute more heavily to the gene pool of the next generation.

Not only should positive feelings have survival advantage, but negative feelings no doubt also play a major role in genetic survival. Consider the example that behaviorist John Watson gives us:

> The panicky state into which the primitive individual falls when limbs of trees break and crash around him, and when thunder and other loud sounds occur in his presence . . . has a reasonable genetic basis" [Watson, 1924, p. 152].

Fear, an emotion having a genetic basis. How? The primitive organism who ran like crazy when strange noises were heard may have survived longer and produced more offspring than did others of his species who shrugged and went on about their business.

The genes then can be said to "want" immortality in the sense that the successful genes are the ones that create wants, desires, or some other characteristics that lead to successful reproduction.

Throughout this book, I'll often refer to the male wanting the female's egg and occasionally the female wanting the sperm of the male. We all know, don't we, that humans want coitus, not eggs or sperms? At one level, yes, but at a primitive genetic level, it is the genes in our bodies that are directing those wants toward a genetic future. The genes don't care a wit about coitus, except as a way of getting into the next gene pool.

To gain a better feel for the theories involved in sociobiology, it is important for the reader to keep this basic principle in mind. And for that reason I'll keep sprinkling phrases about eggs and sperms throughout the book. Some reviewers of this manuscript were offended by such phrases. I don't mean to offend, but I do intend to keep the reader aware of the principle that genes create wants and that the bottom line of their wants is the egg or sperm so important to their immortality.

I did mention several possibilities for the influence of genes on complex behaviors. But for three reasons I will focus on "feelings" as the basis of genetic influence throughout the following chapters of this book. First, the notion of "genetically based feelings" provides a soapbox from which to argue that genes can influence, but they do not necessarily control or determine that array of overt sexual behaviors we commonly call "voluntary." Feelings play a role in our behaviors, a very strong role, but most of the time our experience tells us that we can say "yes" or "no" to those feelings.

The second reason I'll emphasize feelings is that this internal world of ours seems to be the cornerstone of much disagreement and misunderstanding between the sexes. "It's not what he does that bothers me," she says. "It's what he wants to do. How could any normal human being feel that way?"

Or, from the man's position: "Yeah, she let me do it. But she didn't want me to. It made me feel like a crumb. How can anyone be so 'blah' about something that feels so good?" Obviously, many contentions and hurts center around words like "want," "feel," "willing," and "desire."

The third reason for my emphasis on feelings as the link between genes and voluntary behavior is my firm belief that in coming years that will be the point of focus for most theorists who struggle to link genes and complex human behavior.

But How Can Genes Produce Feelings?

It is surprising how suddenly penetrating our questions can become when an idea doesn't agree with our pet theories. Once, while I was discussing hormones and behavior with a colleague, he asked, "But isn't it kind of absurd to assume that hormones can produce desires that we are consciously aware of?"

Of course it is absurd. Absurd because the link between conscious experience and physiology seems beyond even our grandest logical schemes. Absurd because consciousness itself defies all attempts at reduction to more primitive concepts. But no more or less absurd than our common observations that toxic substances introduced into the body can produce feelings of euphoria, depression, or sickness, that injection of insulin can produce feelings of hunger, that eating salt can produce feelings of thirst, that swollen, inflamed tissue can produce feelings of pain, or that scribblings on a page can produce the whole spectrum of human emotions. All of these things are absurd. And hundreds more. Yet we accept them as real. Genes producing enzymes that in turn produce hormones that in turn produce feelings are only some of the marvelous, mysterious absurdities we live with every moment of our lives.

How Do We Study Feelings?

One last comment about feelings. They are very difficult to study scientifically. We can see, measure, and count behavioral events. They are the stuff of empiricism and are available for inspection by the community at large. Cognitive and emotional factors, on the other hand, can be observed only by the individual in whom they occur. From the standpoint of science, or the outside observer, such events must be inferred. And, of course, this lack of access to our data of primary interest presents problems that will come up again and again throughout this book.

Can It Then Be Proved That Genes Influence Our Behavior?

We might as well handle this question now as wait until we have struggled through the evidence. No, we certainly cannot prove that genes influence our behavior. For me to say I intend to prove anything would place me far away from current scientific tradition. Scientists stopped trying to prove points, or verify truth, several decades ago. Today we talk about confirmation, not verification. The older philosophy of science tried to produce "the critical experiment" or "the critical argument" that cut off all competing theories at the waist. We realize now, of course, that rarely if ever are any issues solved with such finality. As science has grown up a little, it has adopted a much more realistic strategy for pitting theory against theory. That strategy involves piling up more and more evidence—confirmation, it is called—until one position becomes more believable than its competitors.

And that is precisely what I intend to do—suggest enough evidence that the burden of proof will shift to the person who tries to maintain that men and women are not programmed to be different sexually.

But Certainly People Prove Points Today

Perhaps in the vernacular, but certainly not formally. That is not to say, of course, that we can't have some very strong opinions. I have some very strong beliefs about innate sex differences. You and I may not share these beliefs, but we certainly do share some strong beliefs in other areas.

Consider, for example, the notion that cigarettes are harmful to your health. You may believe that very strongly, but it certainly hasn't been proved. A very short time ago I heard a tobacco company representative argue long and hard on a television show that "it has not been proved that smoking is harmful to your health." From a formal "philosophy of science" position, of course, he was absolutely right. And no matter what his challengers said, he could always fall back on the statement, "But it hasn't been proved." As I've said before, science no longer claims to prove such things. In this case, however, the evidence is so overwhelming that only a fool or a representative from a tobacco company would care to argue such a position.

Or consider the even more preposterous assertion that the earth is flat. Believe it or not, there exists today a Flat Earth Society, which maintains that it has never been proved that the earth is round. For every piece of evidence one can garner to support the position that the earth is round, this group can come up with some mildly conceivable counterargument. Has the earth been proved round? Not to the satisfaction of the Flat Earth folks.

Some people will probably always maintain that cigarettes are not harmful, that the earth is flat, that masturbation causes hair to grow in the palms of your hands, and that men and women are not programmed to think and feel and act different sexually. People generally believe what fits with their larger view of their particular world. Noted philosophical historian Thomas Kuhn (1970) points out that even the belief systems of most scientists are often not penetrated by the most convincing data in their fields, and many go to their deathbeds holding steadfastly to long-outmoded views.

No, I will not prove my point. No matter how much data I could come up with, some people would challenge me on every statement in order to maintain the integrity of their own views. I've been in science and around scientists long enough to expect this. I expect no more or no less from laymen.

Then Why Not Quit Now?

I said some people, not all. There is a great deal of evidence. There are people who will consider the evidence—if only because they want to believe it—and by so doing they may find their views on the world a little straighter, their lives a little better adjusted, and their feelings about themselves a little more comfortable.

5

Who Wants Sex More?
Who Has More Fun?

After all that talk in the previous chapter about reinforcing value, feelings, pleasure, and the like, it should come as no surprise that I plan to ask if one gender gets more out of sexual activity than the other. We are going to assume that sex, like any other activity competing for our time, must pay its way in terms of hedonic value. Whether that value is derived primarily from the gaining of pleasure or the removal of discomfort, we can't say; it probably involves both. But for the purpose of communication, we'll take at face value the claims people make that sex is fun or that it feels good or that it provides pleasure. And those are the words that will be used throughout this chapter.

I've been courageous—or suicidal—enough to state emphatically that from an inherent biological level men are more often aroused and that they are more orgasmic than are women. Surely, I wouldn't be fool enough to suggest that they also have a stronger sex drive or that they enjoy it more. I wouldn't without ammunition to spare; I can tell you that. This certainly is one of the most controversial of all issues in the "we're all the same" literature. Evidence of the emotional overtones surrounding this question can be seen in the vehement assertions of the feminists that women derive just as much pleasure as men from sex, even more pleasure because "it is woman, not man, who has an unlimited capacity for orgasm" (Billings, 1974, p. 231).

The point of multiple orgasms has been raised by every feminist who has written on the subject. And for good reason. It constitutes the sum total of all the evidence the feminist can raise. But even this lonely argument is crippled in its logic. Sometimes more means better, but I would hate to try to go through life indiscriminately applying such a principle. If indeed women get more pleasure from sex than men do, there are an awful lot of data that have either been fabricated or generated by accident. By the end of this chapter we'll be in a better position to make a judgment about the "multiple orgasm" argument.

In their zeal to expound on female sexual passions, some writers have made themselves look quite foolish. Lonnie Barbach, for example, in her book *For Yourself: The Fulfillment of Female Sexuality,* decries "the erroneous belief . . . that sex is not as necessary for women as it is for men" (Barbach, 1976, p. 10). All well and good, if Dr. Barbach believes that. But just nineteen pages later she says:

> Those of us who decided to go "all the way" before we were married may have had sex to prove our love to a boyfriend, or because we had run out of excuses and, exhausted by male pressure, found it easier to give in than continue to fight [Barbach, 1976, p. 29].

Nowhere does she even suggest that she or her female peers decided to go all the way because of drive, sexual desire, passion, or the seeking of pleasure. Come on now, Dr. Barbach, what do you really believe about female sexuality?

Those who champion the identity of the sexes in pleasure and satisfaction do so not on the basis of any data, but for some other reasons that must remain a little bit mysterious. But then, perhaps there is no more behind these assertions than there is behind the argument of two children over who had the better time at the fair.

Sociobiology and Pleasure

In the last chapter, I pointed out that two of the basic physiological differences between males and females point unequivocally to selection differences on frequency of arousal and orgasmic ability. Those two differences were: (1) the fact that males must be aroused in order to copulate, while females can copulate while unaroused; (2) the fact that males must be orgasmic if they are to pass on their genes, while females may pass on their genes whether they are orgasmic or not.

In this chapter we are going to deal with the hedonic aspect of sex—that is, the pleasure, the satisfactions, the ecstasy, the thrill. These are the emotional components of sex that occur simultaneously with physiological arousal and orgasm. These emotional aspects provide the motivational push. Sex becomes, like food, something of economic value, something worth working for, worth purchasing or even stealing, because it gives us pleasure. It is this value component that leads to a third evolutionary analysis.

Our hypothesis is that males and females will be differentially selected on this value dimension—that is, sex should "feel better" to most males than it does to most females. This difference, like the others we have talked about, is based on an incontrovertible biological difference: The egg of the female can be purchased in what for the seller may be a dull, dry, purely economic transaction. It can also be stolen from an unwilling owner. Sperms, on the other hand, are not subject to sale unless the owner gets turned on. And sperms cannot be stolen from an unwilling owner. Tie this basic fact in with the economic theory of motivation outlined in the previous chapter and we can build a very strong case for differential selection on the pleasure variable.

Following the same strategy we did when discussing arousal, let us assume that at some time in the distant past sex provided equal hedonic value to both males and females. Again, we'll use our hypothetical male and female to whom sex provides great pleasure, and male and female to whom sex is "okay."

The high-pleasure male meets the high-pleasure female. Both remember how much fun sex was the last time—motivational theorists generally agree that we estimate anticipated satisfaction from past satisfaction—so they copulate with equal enthusiasm. Both have a good chance of passing on their genes.

The high-pleasure male meets the "it's okay" female. The male makes his pitch. The female may say, "Fine," or she may say "Don't bother me now, I've got a headache." At that point, it is likely that our high-hedonic-value male will say, "Please, just do it for old times' sake." If that doesn't work, he may say, "I'll give you some coconuts . . . and this pretty shell I just found." To which she may reply, "Throw in the carved stick you have in your hair and you've got a deal." The outcome: Both are likely to pass on their genes.

It may be, however, that the low-hedonic-value female will say, "Get lost with your coconuts and your shell, buddy. There aren't enough coconuts in the world to make me want your body." At which point, our male—to whom sex gives great pleasure—may take some risks, and he may rape the female. I say risks because he may get scratched or bitten, or the female's mate may come around and make him wish he hadn't forced her. Still, he has the option to try to force coitus. And, if he is strong enough and the setting is right, he may succeed. If he does, both individuals have a good chance of passing on their genes.

Now suppose the "it's okay" male meets the high-pleasure female. She is the aggressor because sex is of more value to her than to him. She makes her pitch. He may say, "Fine," or he may say "Don't bother me now, I've got a headache." At that point, the high-hedonic-value female says, "Please, just for old times' sake." The male then faces a dilemma. "For old times' sake" may or may not do the trick. If the last time he had sex it wasn't very much fun—or the last dozen times—he's not likely to become aroused enough, in anticipation of this time, to be very successful. Hence, under the conditions of the male "assenting" the chances are not too good that either he or the female will pass on their genes.

But let's suppose this male says, "No thanks, for old times' sake." At that point, the female could offer him some coconuts and a pretty shell she just found. The male may say to himself,

"Boy, could I use those coconuts. And the shell's not bad, either. She's not much to look at . . . but it's a deal I just can't afford to turn down." So the deal is made and what happens? He may or may not be able to perform. Chances are, if it is purely a money matter, with no sexual interest at all, he won't be successful. The result: Neither is likely to pass on his or her genes.

I don't need to go into the meeting of the low-hedonic-value male and the low-hedonic-value female. The results are the same. The genes of neither have much chance of surviving.

This time I did not use numbers, but I could have. And the results would have shown that the genes of the male to whom sex is a fantastic experience have an advantage over the genes of the male to whom sex is so-so, okay, or even good. The reason, of course, is that those males who prize sex so highly are more likely to buy or steal an occasional egg from a totally uninterested female than are those males to whom sex is less fun. Over many generations, those occasional purchases or rapes will make a difference.

But the genes of the female to whom sex is a wildly ecstatic experience do not have the advantages of those that live within the counterpart male. Furthermore, as long as the male involved does not want sex, her genes have not much advantage, if any, over the genes of females who derive little or no pleasure from sex.

What all this boils down to is that the amount of hedonic value sex provides is very important in the genetic evolution of males, but it is not so important in the genetic evolution of females. Logically, differences should occur. And we should by this time in our development have males to whom sex provides great pleasure. Females should also receive pleasure, but the variability should be greater than that in males, and the mean value should be lower.

The Measurement of Fun

All well and good. The argument sounds convincing, but how can we measure these internal experiences? Zeus and Hera, Ovid wrote, argued about who gained more pleasure from sex, males or females, and they could only answer the question by asking Tiresias, who had been both a man and a woman. Since none of us have ever been two people, that strategy obviously won't work.

Remember the two children at the fair? How would they decide who had more fun? How would two people decide who gains more pleasure out of anything?

Our two children at the fair cannot find any basis on which to settle their argument. Neither can get inside the other. Nor can a third party evaluate appropriately their experiences and settle the issue for them.

Does that mean, then, that behavioral scientists cannot make judgments about emotional states? Not at all. Psychologists do it all the time. We compare people on amounts of anxiety, depression, fear, tranquillity, happiness, and most of the other emotions. My own major emphasis has been the treatment of obesity and specific hungers. Hence, I'll use that area to illustrate how we can measure satisfaction, pleasure, or hedonic value.

The easiest method is to ask people to estimate, perhaps on a scale from -5 to $+5$, the amount of pleasure, or displeasure, they receive from eating a certain food. Although the comparison of two people on such scales would probably not mean much because they might be using quite different anchor points on which to peg "highly pleasurable" or "highly aversive," we can draw some mild conclusions from the responses of groups of people. We assume that the differences in anchor points should be randomly distributed across both, or the several, groups of interest. Hence, the mean values from these groups are likely to reflect true differences in pleasure as subjectively experienced by the members of the groups.

Another perfectly acceptable method of evaluating emotions involves the development of an instrument with many questions, all of which ask for different facets of the emotion. For example, an anxiety questionnaire might ask, "Do you often feel butterflies in your stomach?" or, "Do you have trouble going to sleep at night?" An individual's score is derived from a sum of the items loading heavily on the emotion being measured. Validity is determined by the methods common to the whole enterprise of testing and measuring.

Both these procedures are commonly used, and they are both considered appropriate by the scientific community. There are, however, problems that arise. If people think they are supposed to experience an emotion in a certain way (an "expectancy" variable in psychological research), or if they think the individual collecting the data wants them to answer in a certain way (a "demand" variable), the answers can be systematically biased and may not reflect differences that actually exist. For this reason, researchers usually insist on what are called "behavioral measures."

The behavioral measures fall generally into two categories. First, how often does the individual perform a behavior that should be related to the emotion in question? A food study will again serve as a good illustration, because hunger and the process of eating food are highly analogous to sexual desire and copulation.

Suppose we wanted to evaluate which of several treatments is the most effective in establishing a conditioned aversion to a certain food. As suggested above, we might ask the subjects in the experiment to evaluate, on a palatability scale, how much they like the food before and after the treatment. And, if we had good reason to believe that expectancy or demand factors were not operative, these data from subjective reflection could be quite valuable. However, we would probably also want to throw in a behavioral measure or two. In this case, we would want to see how often the people in this study actually eat the food that has been aversively conditioned. This would be accomplished through some sort of observation or record-keeping techniques. In a closed setting, such as a mental institution or a prison, trained observers would be employed to write down everything eaten by the individual being treated. But when studies such as this are conducted in the community, the data are a little more subject to question because the patients themselves usually keep the records. Some ways of measuring amounts or frequency of behaviors are certainly preferred to others. For example, data gathered by observers are held in higher esteem than are data gathered by the subject. Nevertheless, the point I wish to make is that for the scientific community, all such measures have some acceptance as reasonable reflections of desire.

A second type of behavioral measure involves the assessment of how much effort, expense, or risk an organism will undergo to be allowed to perform the behavior in question. How much pain, for example, will a rat endure in order to reach a rat of the opposite sex? How much work will a monkey put out in order to be allowed to peek out of a window to see the other side of the room? How much will a person pay in order to be able to eat some of the food he likes? How much effort will he expend, or what kind of risks will he take to get that food? If we can build in such assessments, the community of behavioral scientists applauds us, publishes us, promotes us, and says, "Well done." We are told we have done as good a job as can be expected.

My reason for having gone through that tedious discourse on the measurement of subjective value, or pleasure, is this: There are certain established, accepted ways for assessing internal desires, and *all of these measures are available to help us assess the amount of satisfaction or pleasure people derive from sex.* Some of the measures have been employed in a formal way by sociologists conducting field studies, and other measures come to us from informal behavioral observations. All are there, however, in one way or another. From the point of view of a behavioral scientist, the work has been largely done. We need only to study it.

Sexual Satisfaction as Measured by Scales and Questionnaires

SEXUAL DRIVE AND APPETITE

The individual who wades into the sex literature will find repeated many times statements like the following:

> A major component of the ideology of sex in American society of the past was the belief that the male, by nature, had a more imperative and constant need than the female for sexual satisfaction [Wallin and Clark, 1958, p. 247].

Indeed, such statements are made not just to characterize American society but also for all of Western culture. This pervasive belief can be very instructive in our search for evidence relating to differences in sex drive, need, pleasure, or satisfaction, whatever one wishes to call it.

Of particular interest is the fact that these statements are never documented by data. They are simply made. Who says that "a major component . . . was the belief . . . etc."? Where are your data for making this statement? Did you do a survey? Did you ask friends? Did you just pluck this idea out of the air?

None of these things. And for good reason. Social scientists are not asked to document ideas that are very widely accepted. Rather, they can get away with simple statements reflecting broad-based beliefs.

If I were to teach a dog to talk and report it in the literature, I could begin by saying, "It has been commonly believed that dogs cannot learn to talk." I would not have to provide documentation by saying, "I took a survey in the streets of Chicago, and out of 800 people quizzed, 735 responded that they don't believe dogs can learn to talk." Such a survey would not be necessary. My readership would accept my simple statement "It has been commonly believed that dogs cannot learn to talk" because it is indeed commonly believed.

If, however, I were to make an all-inclusive statement about something more controversial, I would be asked to provide data. Suppose I began an article with the statement "It is commonly believed that people who are overweight are that way because of a biological set-point toward which their body constantly strives to adjust." The scientific community would not let me get away with that statement. My colleagues would want to know how I determined that this is commonly believed. Some researchers believe it, true, but do they represent the majority? No, I certainly could not make such an assertion without some data.

Let's return then to the common-belief statement that males have a greater need for sex than do females. The statement appears again and again in the literature without documentation. And this fact itself testifies to the pervasiveness of the belief. Indeed, it *is* commonly believed, even though few, if any, researchers have bothered to gather any data to demonstrate the belief.

So what? Believing it doesn't make it true. Correct. People have clearly been wrong in their beliefs in the past. Nevertheless, any time an idea is very widely, almost universally believed, the very existence of this belief raises some fascinating questions.

If it is a fiction, how do we account for it? People believed the earth was flat for many centuries. How do we account for that belief? Simple. If you look around you, the earth appears to be flat. Furthermore, it is inherently counterintuitive to believe that there are people on the other side of the earth walking around upside down. Ask any child, and you will see how counterintuitive this belief is. Simply put, it made good common sense for people to believe that the earth was flat. The belief squared with their perceptions even though their perceptions were misleading.

Beliefs can also be generated because they serve some function. Consider, for example, the propaganda during the Second World War telling us that the Japanese were vicious, inhuman creatures. Obviously, when one is at war it is highly functional to create a belief that the enemy is not made of the same stuff you are. The Japanese no doubt made use of similar propaganda about the Americans.

The point of this argument is that universal beliefs don't just pop out of nothing. To assert that they do is reminiscent of the spontaneous generation of maggots in Pasteur's day. Beliefs, whether they are true or false, either have some functional basis —that is, they are reinforced because they pay off—or they are adopted because they square with our perceptions of the universe.

It is clear that there is a broad-based belief that men want or need sex more than women do. Can we account for this belief on the basis of function? What possible function can it serve? Where is the payoff for such a belief? Is it an ego trip for the men? Hardly. What is so great about needing or wanting sex? Most of us would rather characterize ourselves as being beyond, and totally in control of, our physical and psychological needs. Does the belief pay off for the women? Not that I can see.

Much more likely, the belief survives because it squares with our perceptions of what goes on inside us and our observations of the behaviors of other people. Seen in this light, the belief certainly does have relevance to our argument concerning sex differences. In essence, the belief provides a very broad observational questionnaire spread across many cultures and many centuries. It is not definitive, by any means. But it is certainly provocative and points in the direction of true differences.

The more formal questionnaire studies point in the same direction. Studying a sample of Norwegian undergraduate students, Larsen (1971) found that females scored lower on test items designed to measure sexual drive, sexual appetite, and arousal. Unlike the broad-scale belief statement that we just got through discussing, the statement concerning what most people think or believe, these data reflect that which an individual himself or herself experiences. The results are the same.

FIRST COITUS

> Mother was lucky. Expecting defloration to be dismal, she gritted her teeth and prayed it would be over quickly. The liberated virgin is supposed to enjoy it, when, in truth, she may feel just like Mother [Meade, 1973, p. 90].

Intending jest, Meade probably captured a great deal more truth than she thought in this quip. The 1972 Playboy Foundation study (Hunt, 1974) did, indeed, find that the majority of females reported that their first coital experience was either neutral or unpleasant. Hessellund (1971) obtained the same results in samples of males and females when such factors as mean age of first coitus, mean age of partner, and mean duration of relationship with partner before the first coitus were controlled. In his sample, only 19 per cent of the females reported that their reaction to their first coital experience was either positive or ambivalent. By contrast, 81 per cent reported that it was negative. Males, on the other hand, presented quite a different picture. Seventy-three per cent of the males said their reaction to their first coitus was positive or ambivalent, and only 28 per cent said it was negative.

CONTINUOUS SEXUAL RELATIONSHIPS

One might counter such data, of course, by saying that for women the first coitus hurts. Obviously it was not going to be pleasant. That may be true. But it is significant to note that even after experience and within the socially sanctioned confines of marriage, a large number of women still report negative reactions toward sexual relationships with their husbands.

In a study by Gupta and Lynn (1972) with ninety-three married couples, 90 per cent of the husbands reported that they enjoyed sex, whereas only 56 per cent of the wives reported enjoying it. Surveying the literature derived from field studies conducted in the United States, Mexico, England, and Puerto Rico, Rainwater (1964) found that among a number of samples taken, the percentage of women giving "very positive" statements about sexual enjoyment ranged from 20 per cent to 54 per cent, depending on the sample. Apparently the truth is as sex therapist Carmen Kerr puts it: "Many women don't enjoy intercourse" (Kerr, 1978, p. 242).

LESBIAN RELATIONSHIPS

But I'm supposed to lie spread-eagled on the bed and enjoy 180 pounds banging away at my crotch. And have an orgasm while I'm at it! [Meade, 1973].

Put that way, the woman's role in coitus certainly doesn't sound very inviting. Maybe Meade has something there. Perhaps the large number of females who apparently do not enjoy sex are being mistreated by rough-and-tumble, insensitive partners. If this is true, we might expect to find much more positive expressions of sexual satisfaction in lesbian relationships. As feminist writer Kerr (1978, p. 105) says, "Women instinctively understand each other's sexual needs; and, in this way, there is less of a sex gap to be bridged."

However, the data suggest that sexual satisfaction, or "unsatisfaction," among lesbians is about the same as it is for women who are heterosexual. Rita Bass-Hass (1968) asked a large number of lesbians about the importance of sex in their lesbian relationships. Forty per cent of the white and 57 per cent of the nonwhite respondents said they were disappointed with their sexual relationships, percentages not at all unlike those found among heterosexual women.

I said above that questionnaire methods are the weakest when it comes to assessing emotions. We don't know if these "reported" different levels of satisfaction or dissatisfaction for males and females really reflect their experiences or not. I also mentioned, however, that social scientists accept such data as providing evidence of a confirmatory, though not conclusive, nature.

Sexual Satisfaction as Measured by Frequency of Participation

As I mentioned earlier in this chapter, the second major method of measuring positive emotions involves counting the number of times people engage in some behavior that should be related to the emotion in question. In evaluating how much people like certain foods, for example, we look at how often they eat those foods. In evaluating how much they like sex, let's look at how frequently they have sex. Sounds perfectly reasonable, doesn't it? The method has credibility with the scientific community for a broad range of questions.

MASTURBATION

It would be foolish to look at differences in absolute frequencies of heterosexual intercourse for males and females. Obviously, there can be none. In other ways, however, it is possible for males and females to differ in frequency of sexual participation. For example, a recent study conducted by the Kinsey Institute reported that homosexual males have sex two or three times as often as lesbians do. But the most dramatic differences are seen in autostimulation, for which there are no constraints imposed by number or gender of partners available. Kinsey (1953, p. 192) made the point that masturbation provides one of the best measures of intrinsic, or biological, sexuality. That's the working assumption of this section.

A quarter of a century ago, Kinsey and his associates (1953, p. 173) presented data showing that about 93 per cent of the males in their study reported that they masturbated, compared to 62 per cent of the females. Then came the "sexual revolution" of the sixties that we referred to before. Sex was popularized. Women were told to throw off the shackles of sexual repression. It is hard to imagine that any woman who could read wouldn't figure that her duty to womanhood dictated that she get into the masturbatory fray.

Arafat and Cotton (1974) tell us that with all the changes in attitudes during the past several decades, especially toward female sexuality, they expected to find changes in patterns of masturbation frequencies. Their large-scale questionnaire study on university students, however (72.5 per cent return), gave them quite a surprise. Reported frequency of masturbation for males was 89.13 per cent and for females was 60.98 per cent, figures that are almost identical to those reported by Kinsey and his colleagues before "sexual liberation." On another sample of college students, very similar data were gathered by Abramson in 1973. Masturbatory frequency: 96 per cent for males and 69 per cent for females. Since the number of people studied was small (eighty-four females and seventy-five males), it is clear that these figures would not differ significantly from Kinsey's. They are, obviously, in the correct ballpark.

Male masturbation appears to be especially stable both across the years and across cultures. Asayama (1975) reports that surveys conducted in Japan in the 1920s showed that 96 per cent of the males masturbated by age twenty-three. In the immediate postwar years, the figure for twenty-one years was 91 per cent. A study on West German workers and students reported a 90 per cent incidence of masturbation for males (Schmidt and Sigusch, 1971), and Finger (1975) more recently found a figure of 95 per cent for a sample of American college males. All of these figures compare exceptionally well with those reported by Kinsey.

For females, the incidence of masturbation in these studies range from a low of 12 per cent in Japanese studies conducted in the 1920s (we can be reasonably sure the survey methods employed in those days were far less sophisticated than those we use today) up to 69 per cent. This wide variation does suggest that within certain limits, for women at least, cultural factors play an important role in self-reports of masturbation. This does not mean, however, that the entire variance between sexes is accountable by culture. Indeed, the stability of the data gathered in the United States throughout the past thirty years argues for something in addition to culture. Even in a study specifically addressed to the issue of cultural differences (class differences vs. sex differences) in masturbation, sex differences were found to override class differences (Schmidt and Sigusch, 1971).

The same results are obtained when one confines his study to homosexual populations. Schafer (1977) found that fewer lesbians than homosexual males masturbate at all. Furthermore, "among those who do masturbate, the males masturbate four times more often" (Schafer, 1977, p. 359).

All of these studies, of course, are available to everyone, and they are fairly widely known. How does the advocate of an androgynous model deal with them?

First, one might raise the objection that masturbation is not a good index of sex drive or sex interest. Maybe men are just lazier or less creative than women and they more quickly run out of things to do. Perhaps masturbation is just a diversionary matter for them. The data argue the opposite. Abramson (1973) found that masturbatory frequency for males and for females correlates significantly with sex drive and interests as measured by the Thorne Sex Inventory. The correlations held when data for each sex were analyzed separately. From what data we do have, it appears that masturbation is indeed an index of sex drive and interest.

A second "cultural" attempt to account for the observed differences in frequency of masturbation has long been in the literature. Shuttleworth (1959) suggested the learning implications of having a penis hang out vs. not having one hang out, long before sociologists and feminists made this argument a standard cartridge in guns with which they hunt down biological sexists. The substance of the position says that little boys get lots of masturbatory practice every time they urinate because they have to handle their genitals, while little girls have to "discover" genital pleasure apart from the process of relieving themselves.

I'll concede that this may be a valid point, albeit weak. It is weak because it does not take into consideration the fact that little girls wipe, or rub, their genitals every time they urinate. And they are taught to do this as early in life as little boys are taught to handle their penises while urinating. Furthermore, the actions involved when a girl wipes her genitals are much more similar in topography to masturbation (see Hite, 1977) than are the behaviors of a boy shaking several last drops out of a limp penis. Overall, I find the argument quite unconvincing.

The most popular method of maintaining a "learned differences" approach to masturbation is put this way by a woman sex therapist:

> Somewhere, either directly or indirectly, we got the message that we shouldn't touch our genitals, and so, when we did, we felt ashamed and confused. Boys were praised for handling their penis when they were toilet trained, whereas girls were diverted from direct genital contact [Barbach, 1976, p. 21].

Before we tackle this desperation attempt head-on, we should in passing note Harry Harlow's comments about masturbation frequency in subhuman primates: "The masturbatory machination is bisexual, although more common in the male than in the female" (Harlow, 1975, p. 81).

If, as the radical feminists say, little boys and little girls are born with the same predispositions toward sexual activity, we should have no good reason to believe that monkeys are any different, should we? Don't the same laws of evolutionary selection operate for both species? Of course, we don't know much about monkey talk, but extrapolating from the "learning" view just presented for human differences, it would seem most reasonable to assume that parent monkeys make a big thing out of teaching their daughters not to play with themselves but praise their sons for handling their penises. Such a state of affairs is not very likely. I mention this because there are some people who believe the earth is flat, and they might find such an argument compelling.

But I think the best answer to the assertion that parents taught boys to play with themselves and girls not to is "Nonsense!" No evidence is ever presented for this assertion. The inability of Barbach to provide any evidence is clearly seen in her phrase: "Somewhere, either directly or indirectly, we got the message . . ."

Furthermore, it seems reasonable to suppose that if we were to look carefully at child-rearing practices we might even find evidence to support the opposite view: that it is the boys who are most often reprimanded for touching their genitals. I mentioned above that girls certainly do have manual contact with their genitals regularly, for which they receive praise just like the little boys. In addition, it appears to me, at least from having raised a boy and a girl, it is the little boy who runs around holding onto his penis and embarrassing his parents in front of company. Think a little. The scene is familiar to most of us. The three-year-old boy is holding onto his crotch and his mother or dad is trying to quietly but firmly get him to put his hand down, at least while he is in the living room with Aunt Clara.

It seems perfectly reasonable to argue that it is the boy, not the girl, who is told over and over not to run around with his hand "down there." Just in terms of frequency of reprimand, the boy should develop stronger inhibitions about manual-genital contact than should the girl.

If you are thinking while reading this, you may well be challenging me to answer the question: If, indeed, boys get more reprimands—that is, they are more often told not to hold onto their genitals—why in the world do they do it? Doesn't that violate the assumed laws of learning?

Not necessarily. Because of the reduced blood supply in a nonerect penis, it often gets cold. And, when some member of your body is cold, you often put your hand on it to warm it up.

It could be that little boys persist in hanging onto their penises because they are cold. Parents, however, usually interpret this gesture as indicating some bizarre preoccupation with sex.

But then again, it may be sexual. Who is to say? All we know is that from an early age male genitals seem to get an awful lot of attention from their owners. Meade (1973, p. 78) was probably correct when she observed:

> In one respect or another, men appear to be obsessed with their penises almost every minute of the day. . . .

Then she punctuates her claim by giving us a few examples of "oral graffiti of female oglers":

> When I see guys adjusting their jock straps on the street or subway, I think, 'Come on, buddy, nobody's balls could be that big! . . .' There's the man who takes up two seats on the bus because he has to spread his legs. He thinks his peter is so big that he can't possibly close his thighs. . . . The ones I love are the scratchers. They never seem to itch anywhere but between their legs. Like they suffered from diaper rash. . . . A salesman, for example, will be standing talking to you and then you notice his hands in his pockets, fondling his pee-pee. Men are constantly touching themselves [Meade, 1973, p. 87].

Yes, from the time they are little boys right through old age, they persist in this type of socially "frowned on" activity. Yet they persist. Obviously there is some kind of value in it for them.

Now, let's stop this nonsense for a few moments. Do I really believe all that I have said about penises being cold, and little boys holding onto them, and getting reprimanded more often than little girls? Do I really believe men are always fondling, scratching, and adjusting their genitals? Do I have any data to support such statements? Of course I don't. No more data than come quickly to memory from some common, everyday observations. I certainly can't provide any substantive support for these views. And I'm not even sure I believe them.

To be sure, I'm poking fun. But far more, I've thrown in these ideas to show that in the absence of data, either informal or formal, almost any view can be supported. The feminists have their view that "somewhere . . . somehow . . . we learned differently." That's fine. It fits with what they want to believe. But the average person should not pay much attention to statements that are plucked out of thin air in order to make a point.

The reports we have on masturbation are highly consistent. Arafat and Cotton (1974) conclude from a broad-scale review of the literature that all research findings indicate that masturbation occurs less frequently among females than males. Billings (1974, p. 228) did her homework also and found that "far lower numbers of women masturbate than do men." From a cross-cultural standpoint, Margaret Mead (1949, p. 216) states that ". . . the lesser frequency of masturbation among young females that is reported for our own society . . . [is] . . . characteristic of all the South Seas societies I have studied. . . ." Frank Beach (1976), who certainly could qualify for the title "dean of sex research," tells us that these differences in auto-stimulation among males and females are reported with great "cross-cultural consistency." Furthermore, both Beach (1976) and Kinsey et al. (1953) remind us that masturbation occurs widely among the males of most infrahuman mammals, but that it is much less frequent among the females.

In summary, our argument has been this: If males derive more pleasure out of sexual activity than do females, we would expect them to have more sexual activity. From the data we have, it seems clear that they do.

What is not clear, however, is the reason, or reasons, for such differences. The stability of the data over time and across cultures, along with observations we make on lower animals, argue in favor of some inherent, biological differences. We don't have a closed case against the "cultural learning" view. But then not one bit of data gathered during the past sixty years supports the view that we are all born alike. If females, with their marvelous capacity for multiple orgasms, are capable of getting more satisfaction out of sex than are men, why do they so seldom make use of this ability? I'm unconvinced.

SWINGING

It is estimated that one to two million American men and women have been involved within the past decade in conglomerate sexual activities, referred to under the various titles of group sex, social sex, swinging, mate-swapping, and couple-hopping (Colton, 1972, p. 156). Of these activities, swinging (the word irritates some; the term "comarital sex" is often preferred by married people) provides us with one of the best opportunities to evaluate the sexual proclivities of the "liberated" female.

Swinging, as most readers undoubtedly know, generally involves attending a party where sex with multiple partners is encouraged and expected. Given what we know about American society, it should come as no surprise to us that it is predominantly the man, not the woman, who suggests that the couple get involved in swinging. Henshel (1973) reports that among married couples, husbands were the initiators (into swinging) six times more often than wives.

However, once involved, is there any particular reason why either males or females should be more likely to drop out? It has been suggested that swinging opens the doors to sexual equality (Denfeld and Gordon, 1970). Specifically, women, after they "get their feet wet," should enjoy swinging more than men (Denfeld, 1974, p. 47). These arguments certainly have merit based on the great advantage women have over men in such a setting. Women can swing all night, having multiple partners and multiple orgasms. Men, on the other hand, are limited in number of orgasms and also face the potential embarrassment of not even being able to obtain an erection at the proper moment. We hear from the "sexually repressed" contingent of the feminist movement: "If society will just give us a chance, we'll be as sexually liberated as males!"

If anything does, swinging provides that chance. What have women done with it? The sociological data we have (for example, Fang, 1976) suggest that swinging is dying—or has already died in many parts of the country—largely because not enough women supported it. Denfeld (1974), for example, conducted a large-scale survey of former swingers and found that women strongly predominated as the partner who insisted on dropping out of the swinging routine. These data provide no surprise to most of the female readers because they know they wouldn't enjoy it in the first place. As with the masturbation literature, the swinging movement shows us that raw, bald sex for the sake of sex simply isn't all that much fun for women. At least it is not enough fun to do much of it.

Sexual Pleasure or Satisfaction as Measured by What People Will Do to Get It

We have talked about two accepted ways of assessing levels of pleasure. First, the questionnaire method asks people to rate that pleasure or perhaps to answer a number of questions relating to its value. Second, we looked at frequency of behaviors associated with the pleasurable state as a measure of amount of pleasure. In this section we will focus on the assessment of pleasure by observing what people are willing to do to get it.

Such dependent measures are rooted in the economic principles of motivation outlined early in the preceding chapter. Pleasure has value to the organism. Pleasure has market value. And the best way to determine that value is to place access to that pleasure on the market and see how much people are willing to pay for it. If they are not willing to pay much, we assume the activity is not very valuable. If they are willing to take great risks, expend huge amounts of energy, or pay great sums, we assume the activity must have great hedonic value.

One of the reasons why Columbus' famous trip was underwritten was because of the great value people in Europe placed on exotic foods that were not easily obtainable. The restaurant in town with the reputation of providing culinary delights is likely to be one of the most expensive. Go to the meat counter in the supermarket and you will find that price generally correlates with your own scale of palatability.

Indeed, market value provides an acceptable way of evaluating pleasure. There is one other factor we must consider, however: The market value of an item is a function not only of hedonic value; that value is also determined by scarcity.

The air we breathe is absolutely essential if we are to stay alive. Obviously it has great value. But it doesn't have much market value because it is free to everyone. Let that air become scarce, however, as in the case of two scuba divers who are lost in an underwater cave, and the value becomes enormous. Divers have been known to kill their friends in order to obtain that last bit of air remaining in a single tank.

With sex, of course, there is theoretically an unlimited supply from females. It is very clear, however, that females have limited this supply and in so doing have created quite a market value for their services. For sex, men pay millions of dollars every year to women with whom they have no social or romantic connection at all. So high is the market value of sex that men regularly risk their physical safety (through fights), their social standing, even their positions in public office in order to obtain it.

As Brownmiller (1975, p. 25) points out, throughout history "fighting to secure women was on a par with fighting to secure food among ancient primitive tribes." Indeed, there are few inducements that can compare in motivating power for the average man. Lobbyists, salesmen, and Kings throughout history all have used the power of sexual reward to get men to jump through hoops.

In order to make history more palatable to children and morally sensitive adults, the contingent use of raw sex as a motivator frequently was obscured; hence, we may tend to underestimate how important this motivator has been. In his book *Sex in History,* Taylor makes this point clear:

> In Christianized versions of early folk-tales, the knight or hero is often offered the hand of the King's daughter in marriage if he performs the allotted task; but in the original versions the question of marriage rarely arises. Thus, in the Chanson de Doon de Nanteuil, the warriors are promised that if they "hit the enemy in the bowels they might take their choice of the fairest ladies in the court." The knight who loves the chatelaine of Couci exclaims

simply: "Jesus, that I might hold her naked in my arms!" And this is precisely the reward which the ladies themselves frankly provided [Taylor, 1954, p. 24].

Apparently, humans are not unique in this respect:

In general, males are the high rollers in the sex game. They take greater risks than females (death in combat over a female, exclusion from breeding by a stronger male) [*Time,* August 1, 1977, p. 63].

Barash (1977, p. 159) says: "In nearly all vertebrates, males compete for access to females, and are the sexual aggressors." Charles Darwin (1859, p. 212) said the same thing over a hundred years earlier:

It is certain that amongst almost all animals there is a struggle between the males for the possession of the female. This is a fact so notorious that it would be superfluous to give instances.

WHO WILL PAY FOR IT?

The best evidence for the high market value that men place on sex comes from a look at prostitution, an apparent economist's dream for pegging sexual values for men and women.

The historical pervasiveness of prostitution is without question. Archaeologists find clear evidence of prostitution in Mesopotamia in 3000 B.C. (Bullough, 1971). In Ancient Rome, it was an accepted social custom (Kiefer, 1935). So ingrained was the institution in Aquinas' time that the famous Church scholar said that prostitution was as necessary for society as a cesspool is for a palace. A hundred and twenty-five years ago, in a fat treatise called *The History of Prostitution,* William Sanger told us in colorful Victorian style:

. . . prostitution is coeval with society. It stains the earliest mythological records. It is constantly assumed as an existing fact in Biblical history. We can trace it from earliest twilight in which history dawns to the clear daylight of today, without a pause or moment of obscurity [Sanger, 1859/1972, p. 35].

One hundred years later, a vastly expanded mass-communications technology and several generations of cultural anthropologists had not changed the picture. Kinsey et al. (1953, p. 323) surveyed the evidence available to them in the mid-twentieth century and concluded: ". . . the age-old institution of heterosexual prostitution has been widely accepted throughout history and in most parts of the world."

From our sociobiological analysis, the pervasiveness and tenacity of prostitution should come as no surprise. As we showed earlier, those males who cared enough to purchase sex ended up also passing on their genes more frequently than those men for whom the economic value of sex wasn't high enough to make them dig into their pockets. Logic tells us that men must have been selected on this variable. Hence, men should still be purchasing sex today. Clearly, they are.

The phenomenon is even seen in other animals. Male chimpanzees will give a female chimpanzee in estrus more than her share of the food in order to gain sexual access in exchange (*Time,* August 1, 1977, p. 63). Even the hummingbird uses what economic muscle he has to purchase sex:

> Hummingbirds forage especially at flowers and they compete among themselves for possession of feeding territories that include flowers, a preferred source of food. Because the males are more aggressive, they usually end up with most of the available flowers, forcing the females to make do on other foods. Outside the breeding season, males respond aggressively to any other hummingbird that intrudes upon their hard-fought, flower-rich territories. But in at least one species, males tolerate the presence of females who are even permitted to feed from their precious flowers . . . *provided* the females copulate with them! [Barash, 1977, p. 159].

These examples remind me of Marion Meade's comment (1973, p. 88): "Eating has always meant more to us than screwing, although most of us still have to do one to get the other." In that sense, perhaps females of many species have something in common.

WILL FEMALES BUY SEX?

Our sociobiological analysis also tells us to expect that few, if any, women will purchase sex from men. Indeed, that is the case.

Most resources on prostitution don't even refer to the purchase of sex by females. For example, in Sanger's (1859/1972) 676 pages on *The History of Prostitution,* not even a sentence is devoted to this subject. Those writers who do mention males selling sexual favors to women quickly dismiss the topic with oblique references like "Occasionally males are paid a fee by women for sexual purposes; but this is rare. . . ." (Esselstyn, 1972, p. 121) or "Males prostituting themselves for females has never been common. . . ." (Denfeld and Gordon, 1970, p. 88). Even the voluminous work of Kinsey and his associates, which is in one sense a masterpiece in redundancy, presents no data whatever on this subject. The sum total of Kinsey's treatment of the topic is this: "There is . . . heterosexual prostitution in which females pay males for sexual relations, but this situation is not common" (Kinsey et al., 1948, p. 596).

It is anybody's guess why we have no access to statistics on heterosexual prostitution by males. Possibly the phenomenon exists only in rumors or secondhand stories. It does appear that women will pay for escort services of males; possibly these incidences hold the promise to researchers of the purchase of sex by females, but when pursued this promise is unrealized. More likely, the phenomenon does exist somewhere, but it is so rare it has not been quantified.

Homosexual males frequently purchase sex from other males. Might we expect homosexual females to do the same? It appears that this is not the case. The purchase of female sex partners by homosexual females is also so rare that statistical data are unavailable. At least this writer has not been able to uncover any. Kinsey says, "The street and institutionalized homosexual prostitution which is everywhere available for males, in all parts of the world, is rarely available for females, any-where in the world" (Kinsey et al., 1953, p. 476).

BUYING SEX IS NOT RARE FOR MEN

The study of prostitution shows us clearly that the pur-chasers are males while the sellers may be males or females. And, when the market gets tight enough, males will line up like hungry people in a bread line. Brownmiller reports that during World War II, after the Italian capitulation, "Italian women would perform any service for a can of food." And for these services, American troops "waited in line. As soon as one man came out, another went in" (Brownmiller, 1975, p. 75).

Some people may cluck: "My, my . . . those naughty boys!" Nonsense! They represented the statistical norm. Studying sol-diers in Viet Nam, Hart (1975) found that 72 per cent of the single soldiers and 50 per cent of the married soldiers *admitted* that they had intercourse with prostitutes. How many more did not admit it?

Clearly, buying sex is not rare for men. And clearly, it is men who keep the business going. I searched the social-science liter-ature and the popular literature in vain for even one report of a female purchasing sexual services from a male. Suppose I had found one. Would my point have been destroyed? Hardly. Kin-sey (1948) estimates that about 69 per cent of the total white male population ultimately has some experience with prosti-tutes. That means that more than sixty million males in the United States either have paid or will pay for sex. Compared to that staggering figure, what difference would one or two, or a dozen, instances of female "purchasers" make? Buying sex is overwhelmingly a male activity.

A RADICAL FEMINIST'S ABSURD VIEW OF PROSTITUTION

Some readers will certainly object to my assertion that pros-titution is in any way tied in with the hedonic value of sex. In *Woman Hating,* for example, Andrea Dworkin sees the purchase of a prostitute's services as motivated by the desire to possess, not the desire for sex:

> The prostitute, the woman as object, is defined by the usage to which the possessor puts her. Her subjugation is the signet of his power. Prostitution means for the woman the carnal annihilation of will and choice, but for the men it once again signifies an increase in power, pure and simple [Dworkin, 1974, p. 60].

Pure and simple gibberish. This view illustrates even more clearly the differences between men and women. Here is a woman who for the life of her cannot imagine how anyone could want sex so much that they are willing to pay for it. Since she judges the world's experience by her own, she has to fabricate a nonsensical explanation and force it upon males. If power is the issue, why don't females, especially the radical feminists, bring men to their knees by hiring them as prostitutes?

But lest I be too hard on one of the feminists, I should also point out that the same kind of gibberish is found in our professional journals. Gokhale, Master, and Master (1962) began a study from a similar framework, assuming that clients of prostitutes must have some psychological hangups. After interviewing 167 such persons, they concluded that factors that caused these men to visit prostitutes were: lack of proper sex education; deep-seated anxieties; frustrations; emotional insecurity; repressed hatred for one or both parents; an unconscious desire to spite the parent; physical handicaps; and a subnormal intelligence. Of these "reasons," only the last two make any sense at all. Sex feels good to retarded and handicapped people, and since sexual opportunities are less often available to such individuals, they may indeed be more likely to seek out prostitutes.

But the other reasons are mostly nonsense. Nowhere do these "investigators" acknowledge that sex might feel good and that's why people buy it.

In the social sciences, one comes upon such absurdities with regularity. I'm reminded of an experience a colleague had several years ago in an assessment practicum for psychology graduate students. One of the students presented the results and interpretation of a psychological assessment he had done for the local courts. The individual being assessed in this case was a seventeen-year-old male who had been caught smoking pot. The court had requested a psychological evaluation to assist in determining what disposition of the case would be in the best interests of the youth.

The student immersed himself in psychological data gathered from several hours of interview and testing and then surfaced to tell us why the young man had been smoking pot. As I recall, the reason had to do with early oral fixations coupled with the avoidance of strong intrapsychic conflicts.

Finally, my colleague said, "Scott, I notice you are smoking a cigarette. You've told us why this young man smokes pot. Can you tell us why you smoke cigarettes?"

The student shrugged and then slowly answered, "I've never really thought much about it. I guess I smoke because it feels good."

"Did you consider," the professor continued, "that this young man might smoke pot because it feels good? Because he gets pleasure out of it?"

"No," the student answered, with what I believe was complete honesty. "I never thought about that. But it sounds perfectly reasonable."

Of course he wouldn't consider such a simplistic explanation. We do not teach our students such things. Where would our profession be if we sent back to the judge a report saying, "This kid smokes pot because it makes him feel good"? Heaven help the social sciences if we ever start using common sense. We'll rapidly be put out of business.

Perhaps a hundred years ago, our social sciences were not prostituting themselves to gain the illusion of profundity as much as they are today. And that may be why William Acton, who in 1857 wrote the book *Prostitution*, could say so simply:

> Supply . . . is regulated by demand, and demand is the practical expression of an ascertained want. . . . The desire of the male [for the prostitute] is the want that produces the demand. . . . [Acton, 1857/1968, p. 114].

Almost one hundred years later, Kinsey was one of the rare social scientists who had the courage to say the same thing:

> Throughout history, there have been few social institutions which have been objects of as continuous condemnation and concentrated attack as the institution of heterosexual prostitution, [yet] prostitution continues to exist, and one may well ask why men continue to go to prostitutes. It is probably that prostitution is no exception to the economic laws, and it continues to exist because there is a sufficient demand for what it offers [Kinsey et al., 1948, p. 606].

The data seem clear. The male places a much higher market value on sex than does the female. But do such data prove our point about males getting more pleasure from sex than females? Of course not. We have gone through quite a few pages since I told my readers that in the science game we don't ever prove anything. Perhaps a reminder at this point is in order.

It is conceivable that certain differences in socialization for males and females are responsible for the behavior we see. It is possible that throughout the past five thousand years of recorded history (we don't have access to information on prostitution earlier) and across many cultures, most of which had no contact with each other until recently, these "traditions" just happened to always occur. It is "possible" that these same "traditions" are maintained in the socialization of hummingbirds and chimpanzees. Possible, yes. But is it probable? Obviously not. The probability of such historical and cross-cultural and cross-species consistency is phenomenally small. Only a desperate individual would ignore such a very strong data base.

WHO WILL TAKE RISKS FOR IT?

I suggested that there are at least two ways of determining the market value of a product. The first is to see what people are willing to pay for it—or whether they are willing to pay anything—and the second is to see what kinds of risks they will take to get it.

Stealing always involves taking risks. By its very definition, stealing is taking something someone else does not want you to take. Consequently, whatever protective measures, sanctions, or retributions can be meted out by the victim of the theft constitute a whole network of risks for the thief.

And the nature of the risk can usually be seen as a measure of the value of the item stolen. Indeed, during the past decade, a sizable literature has been developed on risk-taking. And economic principles provide the foundation for the literature.

Males, throughout our evolutionary history, have been able to force sex and in the process steal those precious eggs upon which the survival of their genes depended. It is only reasonable to suppose that those to whom sex had great hedonic value were more likely to take the risks incurred in forcing sex than were those to whom sex did not provide much of a trip (certainly it would make no sense to argue the opposite). Some were successful, and some, no doubt, got chewed apart by a female they underestimated (or her mate). Nevertheless, it seems reasonable to assume that those males who took the risks and stole the eggs passed on more genes than those who played the game conservatively. Accordingly, we should see the same phenomenon occurring today. Males should be prone to steal sex when the perceived risk is low enough.

As I pointed out before, females could not, and still cannot, steal sperms. Those who wanted to or tried had no genetic advantage over those who did not. Hence, there is no reason to believe that risk-taking for sex was selected into females in the same way that it was selected into males, and we should be surprised if we saw much of it in females today.

Risks with the law. Stealing ova today is called rape. And there are all kinds of risks associated with it. Everywhere in the Western world it is considered a crime. In many states in the United States rape can draw a life sentence, and before the 1972 U. S. Supreme Court ruling on capital punishment, a number of states set the penalty at death. Because of the risks, rape provides for us an excellent opportunity to judge values placed on sex by males and females.

I am intact enough to know, however, that because of some of the myths surrounding crime, and rape in particular, we cannot launch into an examination of rape statistics without first attending to some groundwork.

Myth No. 1: The risk of punishment plays no role in criminal behavior.

This myth has its roots in two rat studies conducted by B. F. Skinner in 1938. From these, Skinner concluded that punishment did not have much effect on behavior. The idea was picked up by social philosophers who wished to build a case against the punishment of criminals and somehow became so popularized that when the laboratory data on punishment finally became clear, no one was interested in it.

Today, the information is very clear. Punishment, or the threat thereof (which constitutes the subjectively perceived "risk" we are talking about), is as powerful as, and in some cases even more powerful than, positive reinforcement. Indeed, conditioned avoidance learning seems to be the most permanent of all types of conditioning procedures used on laboratory animals. After making a review of thirty years of punishment literature, Azrin and Holz (1968, p. 399) said, ". . . it appears appropriate to describe punishment as a process similar to positive reinforcement in terms of its determinants, but opposite in terms of the direction of behavioral change." It is safe to say that no psychologist today who is familiar with the literature on punishment would make the foolish statement that punishment is not effective.

Why, then, does punishment not cut down crime? There are two answers to this question. First, we don't know how much punishment *has* cut down crime because we have never tried doing away with it. There are some criminologists who believe that our present system of punishment is doing quite a respectable job. True, it hasn't cut *out* crime. But whether or not it has cut down crime is simply not known.

Second, in order for punishment to be highly effective, certain requirements must be met. Jeremy Bentham, about whom we spoke earlier, told us a hundred years ago that in order for punishment to be effective, it has to be swift, certain, and severe. So far, no one has been able to improve on that prescription. The laboratory data we have show that he was cor-

rect. If the time between the act of transgression and the
punishment is short (swift), if the probability of the punishment given the transgression is quite high (certain), and if the
value of the punishment is very negative (severe), punishment
will be extremely effective. You can count on that.

But if even one of these requirements severely breaks down,
punishment, or the threat of punishment (with humans we are
talking about the *perceived* or *expected* swiftness, surety, and
severity), ceases to be effective. For example, I occasionally fly
in small airplanes. The punishing consequences of flying can be
very severe (death) and quite swift (unless you are "lucky"
enough to linger until you starve or die from loss of blood).
Why do I do such foolish things? Obviously, the threat of punishment has little effect on my behavior. Obviously wrong. The
one parameter that has broken down is the probability (certainty) of an airplane crash. Not long ago, I read the statistics
on engine failure in single-engine aircraft. If I fly a hundred
hours a year, which I rarely do, I can expect one engine failure
every *eight hundred years*. Or, put another way, for each hour I
fly, there is one chance in eighty thousand that the engine will
quit. Am I so foolish? Does the threat of punishment have an
effect? Not with such odds against it.

In reality, the odds against a criminal getting caught, successfully prosecuted, sentenced, and actually serving time are very,
very small. With appeals, one can often stay out of jail almost
indefinitely. And, once in prison, many prisoners—especially in
the federal prisons—report that life really isn't half bad. Hence,
it can be said that punishment for crime, as it is commonly conducted, is not certain, it is not swift, and it is not severe. Is it
any wonder that its deterrent effect has been questioned?

Yet, in spite of such characteristics, consideration of the risk
of punishment by the criminal does appear to enter into almost
all crimes. The criminal almost invariably conducts the crime in
such a way as to minimize the chances of getting caught. He
does not rob the liquor store if a police car is parked in front of
it. Quite to the contrary, crimes generally are conducted under
the protection of darkness, isolation, or swiftness of exit. Many
criminals are not stupid. They know something about the probabilities, and they play them to the hilt. Obviously, criminals do

consider risks, and they take appropriate cautions. That information in itself is enough to establish that the threat of punishment has an effect on behavior.

Myth No. 2: Punishment may have an effect on some criminal behavior, but crimes of violence or passion, like rape, are in a separate category.

Nonsense! The rapist doesn't perform his act in front of the local police station. Nor does he perform it if the female has a large muscular escort. If the chances of getting caught are obviously great, the potential rapist goes home and takes a cold shower. Rarely are crimes of passion performed without some planning, some effort to minimize the risk of getting caught. One of the reasons some rape victims are killed is so that the probability of the rapist getting caught will be minimized. Rape, like the vast majority of other human behaviors, involves an assessment of the positive and negative outcomes, the attachment of values to these outcomes, and the calculation of the probabilities of these outcomes. If the pleasure, the fun, the hedonic value of the act itself is seen as worth the risk of potential punishers, and if little or no moral dilemma is created, rape is likely to be the behavior of choice.

Myth No. 3: Rape has nothing to do with sex; it is an act of violence and of domination.

I am perfectly aware that there are many writers who say that rape has nothing to do with sex. On the back cover of Susan Brownmiller's book *Against Our Will,* in bold letters, is the statement: "It is not a crime of lust but of violence and power." Such a view is *silly.*

From the information available, it appears that in the great majority of rape cases, physical injury, other than that which might be related to penetration, is not done to the victim (for example, Brownmiller, 1975, p. 216; Burgess and Holmstrom, 1973). And generally, there is no injury at all. If violence is what the rapist is after, he's not very good at it. Certainly he has the victim in a position from which he could do all kinds of physical damage.

Why do social scientists come up with such notions? There

are probably many reasons. First, and perhaps the most important, is this: Who is going to listen to you if you write a book or publish an article saying that rapists are after sex? That's as simplistic as saying people go fishing to catch fish or that they smoke pot because it feels good. No, if you are going to become famous, or even published, you have to be much more esoteric than that. Saying the rapist is not after sex but after violence is one way to get professional attention.

There is yet another possible reason people have stretched their imaginations so in trying to account for rape. This reason itself involves a certain stretch of the imagination. But since our topic is biological evolution, it makes sense to ask ourselves whether or not there should be some evolutionary reason for esoteric explanations of rape.

Both men and women have an extremely negative reaction to rape. I share this reaction. But from a coldly logical standpoint, our reaction appears to be all out of proportion to the actual damage done. How could one, for example, reasonably argue for the death penalty for rape when the penalty for beating another person within an inch of his life is far less? Yet this type of apparent inconsistency has long existed. On a simply additive bruise-for-bruise basis, rape seems far less damaging than a host of other types of assaultive crimes.

The average person is likely not to be able to give you a good reason for his or her extreme abhorrence of rape. The answer I have most often received is: "Rape is the ultimate violation of one's internal space." I'm not sure I know what that means. Nor am I sure that those who offer this reason know what they mean by it. The thrust of a knife in my side is certainly a violation of my internal space. Shooting a bullet into my guts is a violation of my internal space. Yet assuming I lived, for none of these acts would most people get as upset as they would about rape. Stories abound in which the raped individual and her family members have had nervous breakdowns as a result of rape. We do not expect that to happen when a person gets shot.

Futhermore, our response to the rape of men is not nearly of the magnitude of our response to the rape of women. Rape in men's prisons generates from administrators a certain amount of foot-shuffling and embarrassed expressions of, "We just can't do anything about it," but on the whole, it appears that rape on men is winked at and ignored. Both Brownmiller (1975) and Davis (1970) tell us that prison guards turn their backs and walk away during the rape of male prisoners.

Why such a difference in attitudes? Is it really because "nothing can be done" about rapes in prisons? Probably not. If prisons wanted to get serious about rape, some measures could no doubt be taken to reduce the incidence of it.

Something very strange is going on here. The strangeness is that our guts tell us the rape of a woman is far more serious than just the shoving of a piece of flesh inside her vagina. But we can't exactly put our finger on the reason why.

From an evolutionary viewpoint, something far more serious really is going on. For the mate of that female, that precious egg may be stolen. And if that happens, from the standpoint of evolutionary success of the mate, that egg has been murdered. His female has very few of these eggs to give him. If some of them slip by, he loses out genetically to males whose mates were not raped. If even one of those eggs is successfully captured by the rapist, the genes of the mate—if he is a faithful, monogamous mate—are locked out for quite a few months. And, in addition, he may eventually be asked to invest time and energy providing for a child whose genes are not his own.

All of these factors take on critical magnitude in a primitive environment where the mortality rate of infants is high and the average lifespan of the adult may not extend much beyond the midtwenties. It should be obvious that the male who is really complacent about the rape of his mate may not pass on any of his genes at all.

From the female's standpoint, rape also has a number of serious evolutionary consequences, perhaps even more serious than for the male. It is true that if she is impregnated by the rapist, she still owns half of the fetus genetically. However, several disadvantages result.

If unmated, the female faces the obvious disadvantage that the rapist is not going to be around to help care for her and protect her during her pregnancy, and he won't be around to provide for and protect the child when it is born.

Second, if the female has a mate, possibly a carefully chosen one—one with strength, agility, attractiveness, and all the other qualities that would put good genes into her offspring—that mate may devalue his spouse after she has been raped, to the point that he will leave and find another female who is not as likely to be carrying someone else's child.

Third, the female has no idea what kind of genes that rapist brings to the union. He may be a first-class loser. Not only is the female stuck with raising the offspring—she is tied to it because of her large investment in it—but she may also be wasting time with a potential failure because she had no choice over the father. The female is clearly in a lose-lose game if she is raped, and she faces severe consequences.

The substance of what I'm saying is this: Creatures who "happened" to develop abhorrence toward the rape of themselves or their own had a genetic advantage over creatures of their own species who did not develop such feelings. It was the consequences of the feelings themselves that provided the genetic advantage. Logic, or formal explanation, did not have to be involved.

According to this view, we experience these feelings today, but we find it difficult to tie them together with a logic that really works, and we come up with weak attempts like: "Rape is so horrible because it is the ultimate violation of one's internal space." Or perhaps we say things like, "It has nothing to do with sex; it is a crime of violence." All of us are sexual creatures to one degree or another, but we don't consider ourselves to be violent. By removing rape from the arena of our own experience, we think we have successfully explained our own abhorrence to it.

In summary, I believe that rape, like most other acts of sex or violence, is an attempt to produce some state of affairs that has value to the rapist. Gladys Shultz (1965, p. 132) acknowledges that many rapists are motivated by "sex desire only." I agree. The sexual pleasure may be heightened considerably by the accompaniments of force or dominance, but sex remains the central motivating factor. This kind of sex does involve risks, and an evaluation of the risks can help us in evaluating the hedonic value of the act.

You may disagree with me about rape. That's fine. We don't need to agree on everything. You can just skip this section and go on to the next. The data supporting the basic thesis of this chapter are so voluminous that we can easily leave out the rape data and probably not miss it. For those readers who do think rape might have some relevance to our topic, however, I'll follow the idea through.

The prevalence of rape. I never had much of a feel for the pervasiveness of rape until I read Susan Brownmiller's book *Against Our Will: Men, Women and Rape.* If we can believe her data—and I have no reason to think the data are inaccurate—men have throughout history raped at the drop of a hat under any circumstances precluding social, legal, or physical sanctions.

Rape was known, and often proscribed, in the most ancient of our written documents. The Mosaic law dealt with it. Hammurabi condemned it. The ancient Assyrians permitted a rape in kind. Throughout the history of man's struggles to codify behavior, rape has always asserted itself as an issue to be addressed.

According to Brownmiller, rape has always been one of the spoils of war—wars of religion, wars of revolution, wars of territorial conquest. So common has the act been that in modern times nations have outlawed it as a criminal act under the international rules of war. Yet rape during wartime persists as a very common act. Commanding officers expect it and ignore it; foot soldiers see it and participate in it so often that it goes unreported. One can only conclude from Brownmiller's book that most men, if presented with the opportunity during wartime, will participate in rapes.

Among prisoners, the findings are the same. After a two-year study of Philadelphia area prisons containing sixty thousand inmates, Davis (1970, pp. 108–9) concluded:

> . . . sexual assaults in the Philadelphia prison system are epidemic. As Superintendent Hendrick and three of the wardens admitted, virtually every slightly built young man committed by the courts is sexually approached

within a day or two after his admission to prison. Many of these young men are repeatedly raped by gangs of inmates. Others, because of the threat of gang rape, seek protection by entering into a homosexual relationship with an individual tormentor. Only the tougher and more hardened young men, and those few so obviously frail that they are immediately locked up for their own protection, escape homosexual rape.

Throughout American history, British soldiers raped colonists, American soldiers raped Indians, Indian warriors raped settlers, slave owners raped blacks, policemen have raped criminals, prisoners have raped each other, and the men on the street have raped all kinds. Rape, apparently, is one of the most solidly documented universals that exists.

And the practice surely is not contained within Western culture. Rapes, especially gang rapes, have been observed in many primitive cultures. Indeed, Hippler (1974) says of the Athabascans of interior Alaska that men are commonly viewed by women as irresponsible potential rapists. Brownmiller suggests that this belief has been pervasive throughout history for all peoples:

> From prehistoric times to the present, I believe, rape has played a critical function. It is nothing more or less than a conscious process of intimidation by which *all men* keep *all women* in a state of fear [Brownmiller, 1975, p. 5].

In spite of protestations to the contrary by feminists who apparently wish to make the human male look lower than the lowest animal, rape has been observed in animals other than *Homo sapiens* (for example, Barash, 1977, p. 67; Abele and Gilchrist, 1977). For example, Brownmiller (1975, p. 3) says, "No zoologist, as far as I know, has ever observed that animals rape in their natural habitat, the wild." But on the very same page of her book, she gives the following example:

> Jane Goodall, studying her wild chimpanzees at the Gomba Stream reserve, noted that the chimps, male and female, were "very promiscuous, but this does not mean

that every female will accept every male that courts her."
She recorded her observations of one female in heat, who
showed the telltale pink swelling of her genital area, who
nevertheless displayed an aversion to one particular male
who pursued her. "Though he once shook her out of the
tree in which she had sought refuge, we never saw him actually 'rape' her," Goodall wrote, adding, however,
"Nonetheless, quite often he managed to get his way
through dogged persistence."

If this isn't rape, I don't think we have a word for it. If after
climbing a tree to escape my sexual advances and then being
shaken out of it a woman finally lets me have sex, it seems that
she would have a pretty good case in court if she wanted to
charge me with rape. Since monkeys don't use knives or guns to
make their victim remain passive, how else might rape take
place among primates? The implication that human males are
the only "animals" who force sex might delight some angry
women, but it doesn't meet the test of observation.

Rape: a male phenomenon. It is clear that rape has been with
us all throughout history, that it cuts across most cultures, and
that it is even seen among lower animals. The striking feature,
however, is that the rapist is almost universally the male.

Statistics on rape by women are unavailable, probably because there are not enough instances to add together. Out of
458 pages on rape, Brownmiller gives only three paragraphs to
rape by women, and in those few instances, it appears that
when rape by women does occur, it generally takes place by females, who along with a gang of males take advantage of another female.

Occasionally, one will read a newspaper report of a "rape"
by a woman on a man, but in these cases, the man and woman
have generally known each other for some time and the rape
has few, if any, of the "raw sexuality" characteristics associated
with male rape. Furthermore, the very fact that a rape by a female in England would make the Associated Press in America
(AP, December 7, 1977) affirms the novelty of such an act.

I can almost hear some defensive female—who has never

raped a man or has had even the slightest desire to do so—state in vigorous protest: "But we females would rape all the time if it were physiologically possible! Hasn't the point been made, in this book, that females can't steal unwilling sperms? Obviously, rape is going to be a male's game even though we women would love to do it."

More nonsense. It is true that a female cannot force intercourse with an unwilling male, but there are many types of sexual assault that do not require intercourse. Davis (1970), for example, in his report of an extensive study of rape in prisons, describes situations in which inmates were forced into performing oral sex and then threatened with harm if they tried to do any damage with their teeth.

It is not a very pretty picture, to be sure, but this kind of sex act is as much within the province of a female as of a male. All sorts of physical stimulation could be forced from a male by one or several females. Furthermore, a female holding a gun or a knife could even make sure he didn't bite. Still, women seldom, if ever, rape men. Why?

Rape in prisons. Perhaps a brief look at rape in prisons will help us. Recently I asked one of my students, who has worked as a psychologist in a men's prison, if he knew anything about rape in women's prisons. He answered that he knew no statistics, but he would guess that it occurs as frequently in one as in the other. And he was well aware of the frequency in the particular prison where he worked. I had been searching, but as yet had not come across any information on rape in women's prisons. I did not know what the answer was. But from an evolutionary standpoint, rape should be practically unknown among women, since males can steal eggs and females can't steal sperms.

As it turns out, the evolutionary prediction was correct. In speaking of mental institutions, women's prisons, and juvenile detention centers, Brownmiller (1975, p. 296) says, "An imitative rape ideology among females is not unknown in the women's institutions, although it nowhere matches the male experience." She apparently was able to find only one account of a lesbian rape, that by a trustee on the women's ward of a state mental hospital back in the 1940s, and two examples of rapes in which young girls assisted gangs of boys in sexual assaults on women. Not much compared to the thousands and thousands of rapes by men she refers to in the remainder of her book.

After a two-year study of the behavior of women at the California Institution for Women, Ward and Kassebaum (1970, p. 126) concluded: "There is a greater amount of homosexuality among female prisoners than among male prisoners—much of it reflected in manners and dress . . . [but] . . . there is no evidence that any of these relationships are coercive in the way that young male prisoners are sometimes pressured into homosexuality."

Ward and Kassebaum tell us that many women prisoners do adopt an inversion of sex role and play the part of the *butch, stud broad,* or *drag.* The woman who adopts such a role ". . . is the counterpart of the male and, ideally, acts in an aggressive manner and is the active sexual partner. Her hair is close-cropped or worn in 'pixie' or 'D.A.' styles; she wears no makeup; her legs are unshaven; she usually wears pedal pushers, or if a dress, the belt is worn low on the hips. Masculine gait, manner or smoking, and other gestures are adopted" (Ward and Kassebaum, 1970, p. 135).

All of this male imitation, but she doesn't coerce anyone into sex. Strange, isn't it? She even adopts an aggressive manner, Ward and Kassebaum tell us. Didn't we hear somewhere that rape is an act of aggression and violence? What better way to play the role of the aggressive male than to force a little sex now and then? Yet women don't do it.

It is tempting to speculate that these women can simulate all of the behaviors of the male—those that don't involve any risks —but sex still isn't valuable enough to make it worth the risks of rape.

Female rape: do we find it anywhere in the world? I mentioned above that rape is commonly reported in many primitive societies, but as is almost always true in Western culture, the instances are male-instigated. I know of only one suggestion in the anthropological literature that there might be female rape in a primitive society, and that example is seriously doubted by its

reporter. In his famous volumes on the Trobrianders of the
South Pacific, Malinowski speaks of the *yausa,* or "orgastic assaults by women upon men." Although Malinowski never observed this custom and was unable to find anyone who had, the
tales he heard conveyed the following information:

> All districts in the Trobriands have the economic cus-
> tom of female communal labour in the weeding of gar-
> dens. Since it is a tedious, monotonous activity, which
> requires little skill and not much attention, and can be
> best enlivened by gossip and company, the women work
> together at each garden in turn, until all the village plots
> are weeded over. As in all other exclusively feminine oc-
> cupations, it is bad form for any man to come near them
> while they are working, or to pay any attention to them
> save on a matter of business.
>
> Now this communal weeding when practiced by women
> of the villages of Okayaulo, Bwaga, Kumilabwaga, Louya,
> Bwadela, or by the villages of Vakuta, gives the weeders a
> curious privilege. If they perceive a stranger, a man from
> any village but their own, passing within sight, they have
> the customary right to attack him, a right which by all ac-
> counts they exercise with zeal and energy.
>
> The man is the fair game of the women for all that sex-
> ual violence, obscene cruelty, filthy pollution, and rough
> handling can do to him. Thus first they pull off and tear
> up his pubic leaf, the protection of his modesty and, to a
> native, the symbol of his manly dignity. Then, by mastur-
> batory practices and exhibitionism, they try to produce an
> erection in their victim and, when their maneuvers have
> brought about the desired result, one of them squats over
> him and inserts his penis into her vagina. After the first
> ejaculation he may be treated in the same manner by an-
> other woman. Worse things are to follow. Some of the
> women will defecate and micturate all over his body, pay-
> ing special attention to his face, which they pollute as
> thoroughly as they can. "A man will vomit, and vomit,
> and vomit," said a sympathetic informant. Sometimes
> these furies rub their genitals against his nose and mouth,

and use his fingers and toes, in fact, any projecting part of his body, for lascivious purposes [Malinowski, 1929, pp. 274–75].

Malinowski was able to find no substantive data for the *yausa,* and concluded: "The most that can be said with certainty is that the *yausa,* if it happened at all, happened extremely rarely. . . . Taking the tradition at its lowest value, it is a standing myth, backed up by lively interest and a strong belief" (Malinowski, 1929, pp. 276–77). Apparently, during the fifty years since Malinowski's report, no one else has been able to provide any substantiating evidence.

My purpose in this discussion has been to argue that men rape because the act has value for them—value that often has to be very great to offset the risks involved—and that the value probably relates to the pleasure they obtain from the act. I'm also suggesting, however, that for men there is a genetic propensity to rape not found in women. If this is true, why then do not all men rape?

The reasons may be many. Fear of getting caught and punished exerts a differential influence across males (some men have more to lose than others). Also, when the hedonic value of stealing sex is thrown into the "net gain" matrix, it may be offset by religious, ethical, or social values that would make the individual very uncomfortable if those values were violated. There is also the possibility that many males are sensitive about "hurting" other human beings and that although they might like to have sex with a woman with or without her permission, their sensitivity to the psychological pain that rape would cause that individual makes the act abhorrent to them.

Rape is well documented throughout history and across many cultures, but it is almost exclusively an act of the male. This is not surprising in view of the biological facts concerning who can steal what from whom. Rape involves risks; it always has. Yet some males are willing to take those risks. When the risks are low, as in the time of war, many males take the risk (remember, even during war, a male can be imprisoned or shot for raping). In prison settings, where the risks are perhaps even lower (if the guy is smaller than you), rape takes on pandemic proportions. Clearly, there is something of value to be obtained from this activity.

Risking professional careers. There is yet one other type of risk men take for sex. It has no doubt drawn my attention because it involves my profession, psychology.

Jean Holroyd and Annette Brodsky (1977) sent out to five hundred male and five hundred female licensed psychologists a questionnaire asking for information on erotic contacts with patients. Their 70 per cent return rate was excellent and argues in favor of the reliability of the results. Among the male therapists, 5.5 per cent reported having had sexual intercourse with patients. By contrast, only 0.6 per cent of the female therapists reported having done so. An additional 2.6 per cent of the male therapists reported having had sexual intercourse with patients within three months after the termination of therapy. The figure was 0.3 per cent for females.

We do not have information on the percentage of female physicians who have intercourse with their patients, but a study by Kardener, Fuller, and Mensh reported in 1973 gives percentages for male physicians and psychiatrists that were almost identical to those obtained for male psychologists (have had sexual intercourse with patients: physicians, 7.2 per cent; psychiatrists, 5.0 per cent).

Why are these data so significant? They are significant because the professionals involved were playing with fire. For years, sexual contact between therapist and patient in both psychiatry and psychology has been clearly considered unethical by both professions. Licenses of practicing professionals have been regularly revoked and students in training have been dismissed from their programs for such behaviors. So clearly understood was the taboo that it was considered unnecessary to include it in the formal ethical codes until recently. Now sexual contact between therapist and client is formally proscribed (American Psychiatric Association, 1973; American Psychological Association, 1977).

From the time a psychologist or psychiatrist begins his college training until he completes his Ph.D. or M.D. and internship, he has usually invested nine or more years of his life. Yet a surprisingly high percentage of men will risk revocation of their license in order to enjoy a little more sexual action.

It has often been said by the "learned differences" writers that men try to sleep with women not because it feels any better to the men, but so they can then go out and tell all their friends about their conquests. Here's an example that demonstrates the poverty of such thinking. We have differences of the magnitude of about ninefold between the percentages of male and female therapists who have sex with their patients. And *neither* gender can go out and brag about their conquests. If they did, they would rapidly jeopardize their professional standing. I know dozens of psychologists who are in practice. Not once in my life have I ever heard one of these people say anything about having had sex with a client or even wanting to have sex with a client. Such talk is *verboten*.

Yet there has to be some reason for taking such risks. The only reason that makes any sense, given the particular circumstances surrounding the therapist-client relationship, is that sex has great motivating properties. And everything we know about economics tells us there must be considerably more value for males than for females.

As good modern sociologists would, Gordon and Shankweiler (1971, p. 462) assert, without any basis whatever, ". . . men and women are equal in sexual desire. . . ." In this chapter, I've asserted the opposite: Men, on the average, are stronger in sexual desire than are women. In defense of this position, I suggested that current evolutionary logic insists on this difference. Furthermore, we have seen that men consistently rate sex as more pleasurable than women do, that men have sex more frequently than women do, that men are willing to pay for sex far more often than women are, and finally, that men will take greater risks for sex than women will. In preparing this chapter, I have looked through dozens of books and articles. Not once have I come across data that would support any other view.

If such diverse, yet consistent, measurement could be brought to bear on most other questions in the social sciences, my colleagues would be jubilant. Usually a jury of scientists requires far less evidence to render a verdict—unless, of course, they are highly prejudiced on the issue.

Obviously, we have an issue on which emotions run high. Hence, I'm not through yet. The next two chapters present additional evidence on this same question of differences in sexual desire.

Not So Fast! Aren't There Some Alternative Explanations?

Of course there are. Almost an infinite number of explanations are possible, and some we should consider. We should also be aware, however, that all explanations are not equally plausible.

In her book *About Men,* Phyllis Chesler (1978) recognizes the differences in male and female sex drive. She does not present a biological explanation. Rather, she suggests that male horniness is a kind of sublimation of the rage, outrage, jealousy, and shame men feel toward other more powerful men. Could be. But I doubt it. There has never been good evidence supporting the notion that sexual activity is the sublimation of anything. But suppose there were. Suppose sexual energy is sublimated from other sources of psychic energy. If the principle of sublimation holds up in the bedroom, why aren't females, who for generations have been subjected to the outrages of discrimination—much more than men have—as aggressive or even more aggressive sexually than males?

And then there is another objection that deserves our attention. Several women who read this manuscript before publication raised the issue of pregnancy and fear of childbirth as important factors in the observed male-female differences in "expressed" desire for involvement in sexual activity. This is an important point and may indeed account for at least some portion of the difference we see. But I think it cannot account for all. In this chapter, for example, we have looked at several sexual behaviors that have nothing to do with pregnancy and that females engage in with less frequency than males. Masturbation won't make you pregnant but women don't do it as much as men. You can't have babies from homosexual relationships either. Still, lesbians will not force sex with other women, they report less pleasure from homosexual encounters than do men, and they engage in homosexual contacts less frequently. Sexy dreams won't make you pregnant either, but women have far fewer than men do.

It is my feeling that the issue of pregnancy is in part, at least, a smoke screen of justification for lack of sexual desire. I'm reminded of a comment made to me by a woman in her late thirties: "It's rough any more to come up with a good excuse for not having sex. When I was young, I could say it was wrong or that I was afraid of getting pregnant. Now I don't consider it wrong and I've had my tubes tied. About all I can think of to say is, 'That's not where my head is,' and the perceptive man knows that's merely another way of saying, 'I just don't want to.'"

And that statement, I think, sums up a great deal. Women just don't want to as much as men do. The next two chapters add more evidence that this lack of "want to" is biologically based.

6

A Naturalistic Experiment

Hard-nosed social scientists might say to me now, "You still haven't shown us that learning isn't responsible for all these differences. Everywhere we look, we see little girls and little boys being taught different attitudes toward sex. Surely those differences could account for any data you could present."

Possibly, by a stretch of the imagination, they could. But let's not forget that what we teach little boys and girls may just as easily be the result of inherent differences between the two sexes. The chicken-and-egg issue concerning cultural traditions and behavioral dispositions has never been solved.

Of course, culture plays a role, but we must keep in mind that it is unlikely that culture can ever be totally independent of our genes. Culture doesn't spring out of nothing. Our rules, prescriptions for living, cherished notions, and the like came about for some reason. They exert powerful effects on our behavior, thoughts, and feelings, but they must show a certain compatibility with what we are like biologically.

We made the rules. And we made them to fit nervous systems, muscles, and sense and sex organs designed and built by the genes. Even our brains, which pride themselves in their capacity for generating the rules, were given their form and power by the genes.

To arbitrarily state that cultural tradition comes first and behavioral dispositions always follow, smacks more of personal prejudice than of science. But for the sake of pushing an argument, let's adopt this narrow position. Let's assume that cultural rules pop out of nowhere. And let's also assume that all the differences between the sexes outlined in previous chapters were the result of those "spontaneously generated" rules.

In order to do this, of course, we must somehow discount the basic laws of evolutionary biology. Few, if any, in the biological sciences will support us. But let's do it anyway. We're being awfully narrow, but at least we're being consistent.

We have discounted Darwin's basic principle of survival of the fittest, and we are assuming that somehow, all throughout history and across many cultures, it has just happened that little girls and little boys were taught different attitudes about sex. And those different attitudes resulted in the internally consistent body of data we have seen in Chapters 3 and 5.

Would it be more convincing if we could design a society in which boys and girls are *not* differentially enculturated concerning sex? Perhaps that would be the ultimate answer.

But the literature on utopias tells us we're not very successful at pulling off such experiments. The next best strategy appears to be trying to find a society in which children are not taught those prejudicial ideas we commonly associate with behavioral sex differences and then making observations to see if these differences occur anyway.

It happens that at least two societies that either meet or approximate such requirements have been studied. During the early part of this century, Malinowski studied the Trobrianders of the South Pacific. Throughout his two-volume, six-hundred-page work describing these people, he points out in many ways the lack of sanctions on the expression and enjoyment of sex by children, adolescents, or adults. In particular, he seems impressed by how sexual socialization differs so strikingly from our own. He says, for example, "It is important to note that there is no interference by older persons in the sexual life of children" (Malinowski, 1929, p. 59). Both girls and boys freely experiment with sex, imitating all of the adult behaviors they witness, including coitus, and they are never censured or reprimanded. Such play is apparently subtly encouraged.

When they reach adolescence, males and females move into a common adolescent house where sexual relations with a variety of partners are expected. Again, for both males and females the same expectations prevail. Malinowski (1929, p. 63) tells us, "When the boy or girl enters upon adolescence the nature of his or her sexual activity becomes more serious. It ceases to be mere child's play and assumes a prominent place among life's interests."

For the feminists who have been complaining so vigorously about Western repression of female sexuality, this fair land sounds like a utopia, indeed. Such conditions should certainly foster equality of initiation and expression in sexual matters. Malinowski draws precisely this conclusion:

> Considering the great freedom of women and their equality with men in all matters, especially that of sex, considering also that the natives fully realize that women are as inclined to intercourse as men, one would expect the sexual relation to be regarded as an exchange of services, in itself reciprocal [Malinowski, 1929, pp. 319–20].

But, alas, this is not to be. Our grand hopes are dashed when we are told that "in the course of every love affair the man has constantly to give small presents to the woman" (p. 319) in exchange for sexual favors. Furthermore, Malinowski points out that the custom "implies that sexual intercourse, even where there is mutual attachment, is a service rendered by the female to the male" (p. 319).

The reader unfamiliar with Malinowski would be tempted to ask what else we might expect from a chauvinistic male looking for support for his own twisted Western attitudes toward females. This is hardly the case. Malinowski's quest was quite the opposite. He made every effort he could to put down the prevailing view concerning the sexual "inferiority" of women. We see his attitude clearly illustrated in the way he attempts to handle the disturbing state he has just described.

In order to get the full impact of Malinowski's dilemma, let's set the stage again. A proponent of "sexuality is all learned" comes across a society in which both sexes are taught, from infancy, to experiment, explore, and enjoy sex to the fullest. Neither males nor females receive discouragement by their elders. Yet "in the course of *every* [my italics] love affair the man has constantly to give small presents to the woman" in exchange for sexual favors.

Malinowski reminds us of the freedom and equality in all matters, especially sex, and tells us that we should certainly expect the sexual relation to be regarded as a reciprocal exchange of services. Then he says,

> But custom, arbitrary and inconsequent here as elsewhere, decrees that it is a service from women to men, and men have to pay [pp. 310–20].

This is another of those incredible examples of scientific myopia that Thomas Kuhn (1970) tells us has been going on since the beginning of science. Here is a forward-looking, liberated anthropologist of the early twentieth century confronted with some difficult facts. He wants to believe that men and women do not differ in sexual predisposition or desire. Yet he observes that in this primitive, permissive society, just as in Western culture, the men are the sexual initiators and aggressors, coming with a gift in one hand and a penis in the other, purchasing sexual favors.

Regrettably, Malinowski's allegiance to his philosophy prevails, and he quickly dismisses, as a phenomenon related only to a custom that is arbitrary and of no consequence, this unusual opportunity to learn something about inherent sex differences.

A similar example, just as striking, comes from Samoa. Of this society, Dr. Margaret Mead tells us, "Among all the peoples I have studied, the Samoans have the sunniest and easiest attitudes towards sex, putting their whole emphasis on the specific interpersonality of the sexual act" (1949, p. 212). "Male sexuality was never defined as aggressiveness that must be curbed, but simply as a pleasure that might be indulged in, at appropriate times, with appropriate partners" (1949, p. 236). We saw what Malinowski said about the Trobrianders. Mead sees Samoa in the same light, and describes these two groups as "two of the best-studied examples of . . . gay pre-marital freedom" (Mead, 1949, p. 202).

Danielsson, speaking of the Polynesian group, in which he included the Samoans, echoes Mead's comments: "As might be expected of a people with so emphatic and appreciative an attitude towards sex life . . . they make no attempt to suppress sexuality in the younger generation; parents, indeed, encouraged their children in free experimentalizing and realistic play . . . childhood and youth were a time of preparation in this respect as in others, and they considered, without doubt rightly, that it was of the greatest importance for everyone to acquire as much sexual knowledge and skill as possible before marriage" (Danielsson, 1956, p. 81).

Again, it appears that this is the kind of society desired by those who decry the Western repression of female sexuality. Perhaps here we will find that males and females play similar roles in the pursuit of sex partners. But this is not the case. In the same paragraph in which Mead reminds us of the "gay pre-marital freedom" of the Samoans, she also tells us:

> In these primitive societies, before marriage, it is the girl who decides whether she will or will not meet her lover under the palm-trees, or receive him with necessary precautions in her house, or in her bed in the young people's house. He may woo and plead, he may send gifts and pretty speeches by an intermediary, but the final choice remains in the hands of the girl. If she does not choose, she does not come, she does not lift the corner of her mat, she does not wait under the palm-trees. A mood, a whim, a slight disinclination, and the boy is disappointed [Mead, 1949, p. 202].

If we did not know better, we might think the writer was describing the typical American scene with all its "learning" hangups. Mead, like Malinowski, is committed to the view that women are as much in need of sexual pleasure as men (Mead, 1949, p. 293); hence, it is likely that this observed discrepancy between training and sexual aggressiveness may have caused her some consternation. But if it did she does not tell us about it.

Nor does it appear that Mead was biased in her reports. We

find precisely the same kind of male pursuit in a delightful account of a dance in Samoa, written at the turn of the century or before, by Kubary, passed on by Shidlot in a 1908 publication, and then reprinted in Danielsson (1956). Although Mead's observations were made well after the Samoans were influenced by Christian missionaries, this older description of male and female roles, codified in a dance, suggests that the same cat-and-mouse games have been played for generations:

Towards the end of the party, during a pause, a male dancer suddenly approached a pretty girl and beckoned at her to come forward. She hesitated, was pushed forward against her will by her girl friends, and the lad had almost to drag her out on to the open dancing floor. She looked almost bashful, standing in the midst of the circle of spectators with downcast eyes, and running her shapely hands over the *lavalava* cloth which she wore on her round hips. When the choir saw that they were ready it struck up a rhythmic song, at first slow and subdued, but gradually becoming livelier and louder. . . .

The male dancer raises his arms, swings them round his head and beats time with his fingers. His feet drum on the ground as if he wanted to leave it. He seems to be moving in higher regions above the earth, for he does not even look at his partner. . . . She too beats time with her fingers and leaps high in the air. . . . Suddenly they notice one another. Their faces and the movements of their bodies express the greatest astonishment. . . . The girl dancer, however, behaves with the arrogance of a goddess, her mein is indifferent and she avoids her partner with a mocking smile on her lips. He is afraid that she will disappear . . . stops, makes gestures of entreaty, stretches his arms out beseechingly and . . . begs and prays.

Deeply influenced by his violent feelings, the pretty girl dancer laughs invitingly. With eyelids half-closed and head thrown back she holds out her hands to him. He hardly believes his eyes. The next moment he rushes toward her in great bounds, with wild grimaces . . . but instead of joyfully embracing her he begins to reproach her bitterly for her former hesitation, raises a finger threateningly, shakes his head and rolls his eyes. . . . When at last he tries to seize her, of course she slips away as lightly as a mist is scattered by the wind and flees with a mocking laugh to the other end of the grass lawn. The spectators enjoy the performance vastly, eagerly applaud the seductive temptress and roar with laughter at the clumsy admirer's misfortunes. . . . He, disappointed and wounded, makes grimaces of despair, but at the same time broods on vengeance.

Again he approaches her, but not this time as a beseeching admirer. Instead, all his gestures express unconcealed hate and merciless scorn, and with his outstretched first finger he threatens to pierce the girl's back. He purses his lips in a sneer, laughs contemptuously and makes fun of her behind her back. She cannot endure this . . . and tries to meet him face to face, but as soon as she turns round she is met by a hail of jeers and insults.

At last the poor girl admits defeat and bows her proud head. . . . This disarms her vindictive persecutor, who now at last repents and begs for forgiveness. The girl's face brightens, and she is no longer averse, even if she still hesitates. Her admirer multiplies his efforts, leaps gracefully round her, gives proof of marvelous agility . . . and tries all the time to persuade her. At last she is seized by his intoxication. They both dance together face to face, filled with the same passion, faster and faster, more furiously, more madly. Their bodies shine . . . and it is hard to distinguish the different limbs. They are like people possessed, and their frenzy infects the spectators, who are soon taking part in the dance as if entranced and forgetful of all earthly cares. Loud shouts of *malie, malei, lelei* (good, good, splendid) and applause drown the voices of the choir, and the dance ends in complete chaos [Danielsson, 1956, pp. 96–98].

Boys and girls, raised to enjoy sex freely, never tainted by the destructive double standard, yet the male "is afraid that she will disappear . . . makes gestures of entreaty, stretches his arms out beseechingly and . . . begs and prays . . . hardly believes his eyes . . . rushes toward her in great bounds, with wild grimaces . . . tries to seize her . . . [is] disappointed and wounded . . ." The female, on the other hand, "avoids her partner . . . slips away . . . and flees with a mocking laugh . . . [finally] admits defeat and bows her proud head."

We've looked at both the Trobrianders and the Samoans. The results are the same. What do we learn from these two societies? We learn that it may be possible to raise children to view sex from the same eyes, but when it comes to who wants whom to do what, it is still going to be the male who wants it more often, who begs, pleads, and sends gifts, while it is the female who sometimes says "yes." The attempt to explain away such strong evidence for biological differences as "arbitrary, inconsequent custom" qualifies as either grandiose personal bigotry or dismal scientific ineptitude.

These two societies come as close as we may ever expect to find in looking for a true experiment. And the data clearly agree with both evolutionary theory and data generated from many other parts of the world. If you still are not convinced that males are inherently more sexually oriented than females, you probably never will be. Nevertheless, there remains yet one other body of evidence that bears on this question: evidence coming from hormonal studies.

7

More Evidence:
Hormones and Sex Drive

Is there anything so bizarre about believing that males and females have differing levels of sex drive? We know that males and females differ in the relative amounts of sex hormones coursing through their arteries and veins. Furthermore, we know that these hormones effect dramatic differences in physical development. Are we to be so bold as to believe that these hormones, which theoretically should permeate every cell in the body, somehow ignore the nervous system?

Certainly not. The potential effects of hormones on moods, desires, cravings, and the like are practically unlimited. Many such effects have been clearly established. In this chapter we shall concern ourselves with only a few of those effects: the ones related particularly to sexual drive or desire.

Shere Hite (1977, p. 465) says we have been led to believe ". . . by some of the most serious social scientists" that sex drive is the product of "cave-man hormones." She also states: "Actually, the information does not warrant such conclusions." I say the information clearly warrants such conclusions. Here are my reasons for disagreeing so strongly with her.

The Sex Hormones: How Much in Whom?

The two major groups of sex hormones are the androgens (male hormones) and the estrogens (female hormones). Money (1973, p. 5) reminds us, however, that "hormonal sexologists laid a trap for the unwary when they named the hormones androgen and estrogen (male and female respectively)" because these hormones are not sex specific. Males have both types of hormones in their bodies, as do females. The difference lies in the relative amounts of hormones for each sex. Males have more of the androgens and females have more of the estrogens.

The reason for these differing quantities of the sex hormones is not difficult to understand. In both sexes, estrogens and androgens are produced by the adrenal cortex and the gonads. However, the testes, the male gonads, produce relatively large quantities of androgens, the principle androgen being testosterone, and the ovaries, the female gonads, produce relatively large quantities of estrogens.

The endocrine glands that produce these hormones become particularly active during pubescence, and it is their action that turns boys into men and girls into women. All those marvelous primary and secondary sex characteristics we value so highly are effected through the sex hormones.

The male can thank the androgens for the dramatic growth of the penis, scrotum, prostate gland, vas deferens, seminiferous tubules, and all the other plumbing that goes with reproductive capacity. While they are at it, the androgens give him a beard, put hair on his chest, lower his voice, broaden his shoulders, make his muscles lumpy and masculine, and sometimes even make the hair fall off his head.

The estrogens, on the other hand, produce a dramatic growth in the genitalia and the internal reproductive organs of the female. And they cause valued physical attributes like breasts, broad hips, and good-looking legs.

Once they have done us such favors, do the sex hormones cease having any function? Indeed, they do not. In particular, the androgens continue to have a great deal to say about sexual arousal, sexual fantasy, drive, potency, and orgasm.

Androgen Studies with Males

It has long been known, Leshner (1978, p. 191) writes, that "castrating adult males leads to an eventual decrease in both sexual performance and sexual desire." Bremer (1959) studied more than two hundred men castrated for sex offenses and found that the majority reported a total loss of sex drive within a year of the operation. Replacement therapy with androgens can generally restore sexual activity to normal levels (Leshner, 1978, p. 191). The same phenomena are observed in nonhuman animals (Daly and Wilson, 1978).

Recent studies have elaborated considerably our knowledge of the effects of male hormones on male sex drive. Consider the following examples.

In the late 1960s, John Money and his colleagues at the Johns Hopkins Hospital and School of Medicine began some fascinating treatment studies with sex offenders. Eight males, all of whom had long histories of the kinds of sexual behavior society does not generally tolerate, were treated with doses of medroxyprogesterone acetate, a synthetic steroid that lowers plasma testosterone levels.

The therapeutic outcome of these cases is fascinating, but of much greater interest to our topic is the effect of this treatment on "normal" sexual functioning:

> . . . the effective dosage . . . radically lowers plasma testosterone levels to those typical of the female, or lower. Concurrently, potency and ejaculation are radically reduced, and may become zero. . . . If this loss of function is not total, then it is nearly so, as for example when erections are reduced from more than one a day to only one every couple of weeks, and then perhaps without ejaculation. . . . Loss of erection and ejaculation is accompanied by a concomitant reduction of the feeling of sexual urge or lust. This change is appreciated cognitively. It may

be reported as loss of drive, or as a lessening of tension and "nervousness." It is not reported as unpleasant or anxiety-producing. . . . Loss of feeling of lust does not entail automatic loss of ability to be attentive to stimuli formerly associated with sexual arousal. It is rather that the frequency of attentiveness is diminished, and the carry-through to behavior is impeded or inhibited. The same may be said of sexual imagination and fantasy [Money, 1970, pp. 167–68].

Money also reports that this effect is reversible—that is, when medroxyprogesterone acetate is no longer given, and testosterone levels return to normal, sexual activities are also restored.

Contrast this study with one Money and his associates did on five males who, because of surgical removal of pituitary tumors in childhood, received exogenous hormonal medication (Money and Clopper, 1975). For all five patients, testosterone injections were required to induce puberty.

The patients all reported that erotically associated erections were directly associated with testosterone therapy. Ejaculation was reported among four of these five young men, but one of the four had not had an ejaculation since age eighteen, when of his own accord, he discontinued testosterone therapy. The same patient reported that wet dreams also ceased when he went off of testosterone therapy. Furthermore, of those who masturbated, "masturbation was, assertedly, not practiced until after initial androgen therapy" (Money and Clopper, 1975, p. 33). Money and Clopper also report that one patient elected to take an androgen considerably weaker than testosterone "apparently because he found life easier without too strong a libido" (p. 26).

The results from these hormone-therapy studies are consistent with investigations that make direct comparisons between testosterone-deficient males and normal males. At the Research Institute of Endocrinology in Prague, Raboch, Mellan, and Starka (1977) studied 106 adult cryptorchids (males whose testes fail to descend into the scrotum). Levels of male hormone for this group were lower than levels in a control group of normal boys and men. Sexual activity, as determined from a questionnaire, revealed that:

> . . . in cryptorchids the first ejaculation is slightly later and . . . the frequency of nocturnal emissions in pubescence is lower. In adulthood the patients with cryptorchidism exhibit fewer signs of high sexual activity such as repeated coitus on the same day or a high frequency of sexual intercourse. Also, there is an earlier appearance of prolonged periods of sexual abstinence [Raboch, Mellan, and Starka, 1977, p. 413].

In still another study, Money (1975) reports that men with 47 XXY syndrome experience sexual apathy, low levels of ejaculate, and poor emission. He attributes these conditions to a hyporesponsiveness of XXY cells to the male hormone, androgen.

All of these studies argue strongly that it is level of testosterone that controls level of sex drive, potency, and orgastic ability in males. And these studies are only examples. Kraemer, Becker, Brodie, Doering, Moos, and Hamburg cite a number of other review and original-research articles showing that "testosterone administration to patients suffering from an androgen deficiency . . . increases libido . . . [while] the administration of cyproterone acetate, which primarily interferes with the action of testosterone, appears to reduce potency and libido in normal males (1976, p. 125).

Androgen Studies with Females

It is of course no surprise that male sex drive is controlled by male hormones. The surprise comes when we look at what controls sex drive in females. Research indicates that female hormones (of which females have plenty) "are not very important to sexual behavior in the human female" (Leshner, 1978, p. 193). Rather, female sex drive is largely, if not totally, a function of male hormones (of which females don't have a great deal).

Admittedly, much work remains to be done on this question,

but at the present time, the data are very compelling. Two decades ago, Sopchak and Sutherland (1960) concluded from their studies of estrogen and androgen treatments with women: "Androgens heighten sexual desire . . . whereas estrogens do not" (p. 531). At that time, John Money, internationally known for his sex research, was able to muster a large amount of clinical evidence to support the hypothesis "that androgen is the libido hormone in both men and women" (Money, 1961, p. 245). Over the years, the conclusion has not changed. Stoller (1968, p. 11) tells us: "Libido is clearly not dependent on estrogens in women but is probably the result of minute amounts of androgens. . . ." And even more recently, Goodman (1976), speaking of both sexes, states: "Studies and clinical observations over the last twenty years have supported the thesis that biological libido, that is, the driving sexual force, is directly correlated with androgen (male hormone) levels."

In order to gain a better idea of what is meant by "libido" or "the driving sexual force," let's look at several examples of research involving the effects of androgens on female sex drive.

In 1951, Foss reported the case histories of a number of females with advanced metastases from breast cancer whom he treated with massive doses of testosterone propionate. In these women, a marked effect was noted on sexual drive:

> A married woman, aged 42 . . . [received] 300 mg daily of testosterone. . . . After 52 days her husband reported that for some while she had lost all her pain and felt much better, but during the last 14 days she had developed an almost insatiable desire for intercourse. Previously she had never been much interested in sex, and on an average intercourse had taken place about once a month; but she now sought sexual gratification at every opportunity. For the first time in her life, she experienced orgasm.
>
> A married woman, aged 51 . . . [received] 200 mg of testosterone. . . . When questioned about any alteration in libido, she said that before her operation, when normally fit, she had usually had intercourse about twice weekly, but during her illness it became infrequent. On her

return from the hospital her desire had so increased that she sought intercourse four or five times a week. She had had a hysterectomy sixteen years before, and orgasm had been rare; but now she obtained full sexual satisfaction.

An unmarried woman, aged 42 . . . said that . . . [after treatment with testosterone] she had noticed very definite sexual cravings she had rigidly to control.

An unmarried woman, aged 53 . . . said that while having the daily doses of 300 mg [of testosterone] she had noticed a sexual craving which she found difficult to understand and which was unusual for her [Foss, 1951, p. 668].

Foss tells us his findings are not anything unusual; rather, he points out that they are similar to those found by a number of investigators who preceded him. More recent studies tell the same story (for example, Sopchak and Sutherland, 1960). Not surprisingly, it has also been reported that testosterone injections have enhanced the treatment of sexual frigidity in women (Burdine, Shipley, Papas, and Delatestryl, 1957). Some of these formerly frigid females grew facial hair and developed much deeper voices, but then if one wants a man's sexual capabilities, she may also have to take on some of his other characteristics too. The following report points this out only too clearly.

Dr. Jerome Goodman of the Columbia University College of Physicians and Surgeons recently published a report of seven hypersexual delinquent girls, all of whom had characteristics typical of females with abnormally high androgen levels. The following is a case-study example:

. . . When she was 14 . . . she found that her sexual longings were intense and began to seek outlets more frequently . . . she often attended dances to pick up boys, and would perform multiple fellatio in order to demonstrate that she could entice a large number of boys in rapid succession. . . . At this time her breasts—which had been full—began to regress in size. . . . Her entire fantasy life, dreams, and many of her activities were devoted to proving herself as a female. She was concurrently battling with hirsutism (hair on the face), diminishing breast size, irregular menses, and other physical signs of dwindling femininity. As her physical femininity seemed to be deserting her, her libido increased, and she began to engage in sexual activities of a polymorphous, perverse nature. . . . The girl's long-winded descriptions of her sexual dreams and memories seemed nonending. She began bragging about clandestine meetings with young men in the early morning hours. Her grandmother brought the matter to the attention of the juvenile court, and the girl was hospitalized. . . .

Endocrinologists and clinical pathologists diagnosed her condition as acquired adrenal hyperplasia (an increase in the number of cells in the adrenal glands, with associated high levels of male hormones). . . . After treatment with steroids, bioassay revealed the expected decrease in adrenal substances, including the androgenic substances testosterone and pregnanetriol (testosterone levels were reduced to less than one third their former level). . . . Her sexual drive moderated. . . . She was no longer driven to prove herself as aggressive and sexually desirable.

Then suddenly, and almost as before, she again became aggressive, rebellious, and very sexually active. She began courting neighborhood boys and keeping surreptitious rendezvous. She began to engage in more daredevil activities and to use coprolaliac expressions during the treatments sessions. This behavior continued for a period of four weeks; then she admitted that she was not taking the prescribed doses of steroids. When she returned to regular steroid maintenance therapy, her behavior once again changed dramatically. Eventually, almost all sexual material disappeared from the clinical sessions. Even her repetitive dreams of a violent and usually sexual nature again abated [Goodman, 1976, pp. 663–64].

The last example showing the effects of androgens on female sex drive comes from a study of women with polycystic ovary syndrome (POS), a condition characterized by an elevated plasma level of free testosterone. Eleven women who were admitted to an endocrine-metabolic medical service for hirsutism and menstrual disturbances were diagnosed as having polycystic ovary syndrome. In order to study the psychosexual characteristics of these women, two control groups were selected, accordto the investigators, "specifically so as to be biased in directions that would tend to minimize the significance of possible positive findings in the patient group" (Gorzynski and Katz, 1977, p. 217). These groups were made up of career women or athletically oriented housewives.

Data were gathered by having these women complete a self-rating questionnaire between days fourteen and twenty-one of their menstrual cycles. Of six different psychosexual categories isolated from this questionnaire, the only one that showed significant differences among the groups was that involving sexual initiative and aggressiveness. The POS women were significantly more sexually aggressive than both of the control groups:

> Thus, whereas eight of eight career women and eight of nine athletic housewives stated that they rarely or never were the ones who initiated sexual activity and that they tended not to be the aggressive, pace-setting participants in the sexual act, eight of eleven women with POS reported that they almost invariably initiated sex and were aware of a definite, almost aggressive drive to push and dominate sexual activity. As one woman described it: "I just cannot wait for my partner to start . . . I feel an urgency to initiate it myself" [Gorzynski and Katz, 1977, p. 220].

Evidence from Lower Animals

The research above on humans is backed up by similar findings on other animals. For example, male mice engage in intense "courtship singing" (ultrasonic) when first exposed to females. Castration reduces androgens and eliminates the courtship behavior. Give them a shot of testosterone and courtship is resumed. Female mice, on the other hand, who do not have these high levels of testosterone, do not normally exhibit male-typical courtship behavior. But give the females testosterone and they show the same "sex crazy" singing as the males (Dizinno and Whitney, 1977; Nyby, Dizinno, and Whitney, 1977).

Complex but Compelling

Have I oversimplified the issue? Of course. To complicate things, there is evidence that testosterone can be converted into estrogen and vice versa. Furthermore, it appears that in both sexes estrogens must be present for androgens to be effective (Greep and Astwood, 1975, p. 502). A complete treatment of the questions raised in this chapter would fill far more pages than are in this book. But the basic statement that androgens are responsible for sex drive receives broad-based agreement throughout the literature.

I must view the evidence as very compelling. Not beyond argument (as I found out when I went through this chapter line by line with a research endocrinologist), but certainly very compelling. Because of the complexity and somewhat primitive state of the research on sex hormones and human behavior, any position put forth is subject to challenge. But clearly, there is more support for the position that testosterone is responsible for sex drive than there is for any competing theory.

Now for the kicker. Males have *ten times more* circulating testosterone than do females (Money, 1970, p. 170; Anderson, 1974, p. 72). Sexually aggressive males? I should certainly expect so! If, as strongly appears to be the case, testosterone is responsible for sex drive, sexual fantasies, sexual arousal, orgasm, and the like, is it any wonder that all the data reviewed so far argue for differences between males and females on these characteristics?

But What About the Light-switch Theory?

The evidence presented above can stand on its own merits; but a view in opposition to the one outlined here is so often raised that we must give some attention to it. A typical example of the view is given by John Gagnon in *Human Sexualities* (1977, p. 114):

> . . . hormones seem to work primarily like a light switch; when there is *enough* chemical the animal is able to perform sexually. Adding more does not cause the animal to become more sexually active or receptive. . . .

At first glance, this view offers some hope for those who wish to maintain a position of "no differences in sex drive"—at all costs. The uncomfortable evidence I have presented says two things: (1) males have much higher androgen levels than females and (2) androgens cause sex drive. Conclusion: Males have a higher sex drive. No, not at all, say Gagnon and his cohorts. By arguing that androgens operate like an off-on switch, they can maintain an equivalence in sex drive in spite of the vastly different hormone levels.

But it won't work. The available evidence also makes a third point very strongly: Increases and decreases in androgen levels are related to increases and decreases in sex drive. For example, in the studies I discussed earlier by Goodman (1976) and Gorzynski and Katz (1977), women with abnormally high testosterone levels showed considerably greater sex drive (as measured by verbal reports of fantasies and desire and by behavior) than did normal women. And in the Foss (1951) study, women who presumably were normal—that is, women whose light switches should have already been turned on—reported that their sex drive was greatly heightened after receiving doses of testosterone.

With males, the same phenomenon is observed. As I mentioned earlier, male adult cryptorchids, who have a lower than normal level of testosterone, exhibit retardation of the first emission of semen, lower frequency of wet dreams, lower levels of sexual activity, and earlier appearance of prolonged periods of sexual abstinence (Raboch, Mellan, and Starka, 1977). These males were not turned off, just turned down. They did function sexually, but with less frequency and less urgency than normal males.

The "horny light switch" does not fit the evidence. More of

the male hormones means more sex drive, and less of the male hormones means less sex drive for both men and women. The same phenomenon has been seen in nonhuman animals (for example, Klein, 1950).

Are These Other Writers Trying to Dupe Us?

No, I don't think they are. Certainly, there has been a lot of pressure to look for information supporting a position that says women and men experience the same levels of sexual desire, but that's not all. Much of the evidence demonstrating a direct relationship between androgen levels and sex drive has been published only during the past few years and hasn't yet been incorporated into textbooks and other secondary sources. One surely could make an honest mistake about the light-switch theory of sexual arousal. Furthermore, there have also been a few studies that seem to provide support for this position.

For example, in 1972, Raboch and Starka studied levels of testosterone and coital frequency in a group of normal men, and they did not find significant differences in testosterone levels between groups of men who reported coitus "once or twice a week" and those who reported coitus "three times and more a week." Furthermore, when they compared normal men over the age of thirty with a group of over-thirty men with a varicocele (a venous disturbance with an associated lower supply of male sex hormones), they found that coital frequencies did not differ. On this basis, the investigators concluded: ". . . we express the opinion that the presence of a certain quantity of testosterone in the blood is indeed a necessary prerequisite of an adequate sexual activity in men but that there is not any marked quantitative relation between the androgen level and the coital activity" (Raboch and Starka, 1972, p. 224).

It would be easy for someone reading only the abstracts of such experiments to conclude: "Oh, sex drive doesn't relate to androgen levels." But such a conclusion is entirely unwarranted. Let's look at some reasons why.

DIFFICULTY WITH THE CRITERION MEASURE

Frequency of coitus probably does relate to male sex drive, but it obviously also relates to many other variables, like available partners, willingness of mate, working hours, work load, living conditions, emotional relationships, etc. One would be surprised if a measure with such a questionable validity would show any differences at all within restricted ranges of androgen levels. Differences in levels of sexual drive would have to be very pronounced to show up on such a gross measure. If one selects a poor enough measure, he can be quite sure that he will not show differences between groups on anything.

Sopchak and Sutherland (1960) provide us with a good example of the difficulties of using frequency of coitus as a dependent measure. These investigators found that women receiving androgen therapy for cancer reported increased sexual desire but not increased frequency of intercourse. Sopchak and Sutherland suggest that this discrepancy between change in desire and change in behavior may have been related to such factors as physical discomfort, anxiety, other psychological inhibitions, or the absence of a suitable sexual partner.

NEGATIVE RESULTS EXTREMELY DIFFICULT TO INTERPRET

It is far more difficult to interpret negative results than positive ones. For example, where differences between two groups really do exist, a failure to find these differences can easily result from unreliable or from invalid measures (as mentioned above). Spurious positive results are not so easily obtained; hence, positive results lend themselves more readily to interpretation.

WE MUST LOOK AT THE WHOLE STUDY

Raboch and Starka (1972) *did* find some positive results of great interest. Below the age of thirty, coital frequencies did differ between normal males and males with a varicocele. Normal males had significantly more coitus experiences per week than did the males with the lower androgen levels. It was in the thirty-to-forty age group that this significant difference washed out. In view of the weaknesses in the dependent measure (frequency of coitus), as pointed out above, this positive finding is quite striking—that is, sex-drive differences must have been quite dramatic to have shown through the error created by so gross a dependent measure. Certainly, this difference in the twenty-to-thirty group is easier to interpret than is the lack of a difference in the thirty-to-forty group. Yet the investigators have very little to say about it.

THE PROBLEMS OF A SLICE OF NORMALCY

It was mentioned that Raboch and Starka did not find a relationship between frequency of coitus and level of testosterone within the group of normal men. Any time we take a slice out of a distribution of scores, we seriously reduce our chances of detecting a relationship between those scores and any other set of scores.

For example, do you suppose height is important in basketball? Of course it is. But if we were to correlate the height of centers in the NBA with points scored, we might not see any relationship at all. Why? Because we have so restricted the range of height that the relationship that does exist between height and scoring ability would have a hard time peeking through. Graduate schools have often been criticized for using scores on the Graduate Record Exam as a selection variable because these scores correlate so poorly with success in graduate school. Do these low correlations mean that an individual with a 600 is likely to do as well in graduate school as is a person with a 1,400? They certainly do not. People with 600s rarely get into graduate school; hence, their scores don't figure into the correlation. If graduate schools did accept students with a broad range of GRE scores, it is likely that we would see some very high correlations. Similarly, if some professional basketball teams decided to play some five-nine individuals at center, we would probably see a whopping big correlation between number of points scored and height.

I apologize for this somewhat tedious lesson in data interpretation. But I am constantly amazed at how quickly people who should know better will grasp at the very weakest evidence on this sex-difference thing. There are a few studies around showing no correlation between levels of androgens and some very questionable criterion measure. Because of restricted ranges and poor reliability and/or validity of dependent measures, such negative results present serious problems of interpretation.

And Don't Forget About the Flat Earth Society

After telling a colleague about the above androgen studies and stating what I thought was the best conclusion, I was soundly criticized with: "But you are wrong! Although males possess ten times the level of testosterone that females do and even though testosterone may be the hormone that produces sex drive, it is always possible that some other factors that differentiate males from females enhance or dampen the effects of the hormone in each so that they come out equal in horniness!"

Of course, that's possible. And I suppose I should have upheld the academic tradition by standing there in the hall arguing. I could have reminded him that even the small amounts of testosterone produced by the female are more likely to be bound, and thus biologically inactive, than are similar amounts of testosterone in the male. Anderson (1974) has pointed out that a rise in estrogen will dampen the effects of testosterone by producing a rise in sex-hormone-binding globulin, a blood factor that apparently renders testosterone biologically inactive. A rise in testosterone, on the other hand, will amplify its effect by causing a fall in sex-hormone-binding globulin. If this account is correct, we quite certainly do not have a mechanism for equalizing the effects of testosterone in males and females; rather, in addition to differential production rates of testosterone, other mechanisms serve to push the sexes even farther apart in the amounts that are active. Anderson (1974, p. 90) concludes: "We . . . have a self-servo mechanism whereby a rise in one of these two groups of sex hormones tips the balance further in favour of its own kind. It appears likely that this represents an important mechanism for the maintenance of differentiation of secondary sexual characteristics in the human adult." The same argument can be made that this mechanism also serves to maintain a differentiation of sex drive in the human adult.

Would this answer to my colleague's objection have been adequate? Probably not. Because there is no limit to the "possibilities" he could raise. It is possible that a little invisible man sits outside on top of a telephone pole twisting invisible dials that adjust our sex drives so we are all equal. That's a possibility I cannot present evidence against. Possible? Of course. But not very probable.

In the face of very strong evidence, people will resort to all sorts of intellectual shenanigans to preserve cherished beliefs. I felt sure that's what my good-natured friend was doing. Such arguments violate Lloyd Morgan's long-ago-articulated canon of parsimony that has become standard fare for scientific explanation; nevertheless, they are within the rules of the science game.

I was tired. I didn't feel like playing the science game. I didn't even offer the above rebuttal to my friend's objection. I simply shrugged and told him that his propensity for iconoclastic esoterica would make him an excellent candidate for the Flat Earth Society.

Let's Preserve Our Intellectual Integrity

> By Gis and by Saint Charity
> Alack, and fie for shame!
> Young men will do't, if they come to't
> By cock, they are to blame.
> *Hamlet;* Ophelia, Act IV

Ophelia said it with Elizabethan elegance. Today, the more crass characterization goes something like: "A man's brain resides in the tip of his penis." Regardless of how it is said, when man and woman meet, he's the one more likely to be ready to go. He's the one who wants sex the more. He's the one who will "do it if he comes to it."

On the question of overall sex drive, including frequency of arousal, orgastic efficiency, intensity of felt need, pleasure, or hedonic value—whatever you want to call it—we've been over a lot of ground. First, and perhaps more convincing than anything else, biological evolution tells us that men and women should be different. Males must be aroused to pass on genes; hence, they will be selected—more so than females—for arousal. Males must have orgasms to pass on genes; hence, they will be selected for orgastic ability. Males can buy or steal eggs; hence, they will be selected—more so than females—for attaching high value to those behaviors that lead to egg collection. Given the biological differences we all agree are true, if one understands Darwin's very basic principles, there is simply no logical train that ever arrives at the station of sexual identity as it is articulated by much of social science and the radical feminists.

In addition to evolutionary logic, we have seen verbal reports and behavioral data stretching across history, across cultures, and across species, all of which lead to the same conclusion: These differences do exist. In looking at the studies of Mead and Malinowski we saw what is probably the closest approximation to a natural experiment that will ever be done. The results are the same: The males are the sexually aggressive ones; the females are the reluctant ones, even after what appears to be an ideally permissive training. A passing glimpse of some of the most recent studies on hormones and sex drive tells us that all this is as it should be because males have such relatively high levels of "the horny hormones."

If, in the face of this mass of evidence, one can still say, "Well, I don't care; I still believe we're all the same," I'm quite sure no amount of evidence will ever convince that individual otherwise.

8

The Promiscuous Male and the Faithful Female

Man's love is of man's life
a thing apart,
'Tis woman's whole existence.
Byron

The setting was a convention of the American Psychological Association. For over an hour, a distinguished panel had given a symposium on homosexuality. Now the floor was opened for questions and comments from the audience.

"I wish to make an observation and a statement. Both are directed at you, Dr. _____," she said, speaking from the floor mike about eight feet in front of me. "First, I find your gutter language offensive. I would think in front of some six hundred people in a meeting of this kind, you would be able to express yourself in a much more professional manner. Second, and more importantly, I object to your treatment of sex as a plaything. Frankly, I am sick of finding that the first thing men want to do when we go out together is have sex. I believe that before people have sex, they should take their time and develop a relationship. Sex without that relationship is cheap and disgusting. You, Dr. _____, speak of sex as fun and games, and I think your attitude is demeaning to the act."

The psychologist to whom she directed her remarks is not only internationally known for his books on sex, he is also one of the quickest wits and sharpest tongues in the business. I wondered how he would respond to this challenge. My guess was that he would chide the questioner for her unusually provocative appearance. For a woman who did not want men to respond to her as a sex object, she had certainly gone to a great deal of effort—consciously or unconsciously—to dress in a manner such as to make even strong men quake. Given the vantage point I had, I remember with great clarity her long blond hair lying on her bare tanned back where the open "V" of her dress extended down to her waist. The dress was as "mini" as any I had ever seen, displaying a full-length view of long, shapely legs. The discrepancy between the words about "relationship" and the sensuous choreography of her appearance certainly seemed to invite a challenge.

The psychologist, however, chose not to attack her in such a vulnerable spot. Instead, he mustered what I think was a courageous assertion of his own sexuality and his unwillingness to have that sexuality judged by the standards the woman had set forth. In spite of the "raw" quality of his retort, I shall try to recall the substance of his words as nearly as I can.

He said, "I want to point out that you are making the very mistake we have been addressing most of the afternoon. You are prescribing the way other people ought to have sex. You have said sex should not be just for fun. Sex should not be a part of casual contacts. Sex should only take place within the context of a relationship. My response is that you can have sex any way you want, but don't tell me and others how we ought to have our sex. If you want to fuck with a relationship, you go right ahead and fuck with a relationship. But me . . . I like to fuck with a relationship. I like to fuck without a relationship. And I'll fuck as often and under whatever circumstances I please. Frankly, honey, I think you are missing out on a lot of fun, but then that's your business."

I have a number of reactions to this interchange. First, I suppose there is the feeling that he really put down this woman. But then, she had quite clearly intended to put him down, so maybe they are even on that score.

What impresses me more is that each was apparently giving quite an honest expression of his and her deep feelings about the place of sex in human relationships. The psychologist shocked us all with his forthrightness. But, surprisingly, when he finished his statement, the audience applauded. I have wondered why. Perhaps it was because they were pleased to finally hear a man say in public what men say or imply all the time in private. But even more impressive was the opportunity to observe an individual who was not threatened by, cowered by, or ashamed of his sexual desires. He was telling us exactly what he felt inside. And he was saying, "This is a part of my manhood. Take it or leave it. This is me. You do what makes you feel good, but don't tell me how I have to feel about sex."

The woman, on the other hand, was also expressing her feelings and, I believe, the feelings of a large number, if not the majority, of women. She really did find his comments offensive because she did find the sex act distasteful when it took place without a close personal relationship. It didn't feel good; it wasn't satisfying; it wasn't right with someone about whom she had no emotional feelings. And as strange as it may seem, even her manner of dress was probably not designed to elicit a sexual response in men. Rather, it was designed to gain attention from men. And I'm sure it did. Because she, like most of us, assumed that other human beings share our feelings about sex, she was constantly perplexed to find that the display of her body was "misinterpreted" by men. I would seriously be surprised if she ever related her seductive appearance to the responses men made of her. Why? Because she never thought of herself as sexually seductive. Rather, she only tried to do those things that from time immemorial have made men very attentive to women.

This story about two people and their less than friendly verbal interchange may tell us about much more than these two people. Women are interested in sex, certainly, but more often than not only after a relationship has been established, only after a little time has gone by and there is something very special between the woman and her lover. Men, on the other hand, usually *begin* with an interest in sex, and an emotional relationship may or may not follow. The male is quick to respond, and, of course, that means he responds at some level to almost everything that walks by. Not only is "the relationship" unnecessary for sexual response, but also males seem to be particularly aroused by variety, a variable antithetical to development of deep relationships.

It is said that William James, who brought psychology to America from Europe, awoke one morning to find that during the night he had written on the pad beside his bed: "Higamus, hogamus, women are monogamous; hogamus, higamus, men are polygamous." Whether or not there is any substance to the story I cannot say, but the ditty certainly captures the common folk belief about men, women, and relationships.

Sociologists Gordon and Shankweiler (1971) scoff at the idea that the female's sexuality is more tied in with emotion and commitment than is the male's. But by and large, in both the popular and professional literature, the view is seldom challenged. As Arafat and Cotton (1974, p. 297) say, "Women are, on the whole, more conscious than men of the emotional aspects of sex." Staples (1973, p. 14) points out that when females engage in premarital sexual activity, "they are more inclined to demand affection as a basis for participation."

Higamus, Hogamus: A Biological Evolutionary Basis

Why should this be? Philanderer males and faithful females—is this another one of those arbitrary, functionless traditions that Malinowski spoke about? Or is there reason to expect such behavioral predispositions from structural differences between the sexes?

From a biological evolutionary basis, these differences are, indeed, predictable, and all relate to two basic biological differences: (1) Males have millions of sperms; females have few eggs. (2) Females, not males, carry the fetus and suckle the infant.

Personally, I feel that the logic of evolutionary biology in this arena is a little more easily challenged than it is on questions of arousal, orgasticity, and sexual drive; nevertheless, the logic is most compelling.

Given the differences mentioned above, what would be the strategy of a male who wanted to maximize the perpetuation of his genes? He should deflower as many females as he can in the shortest time possible. As Dawkins (1976, p. 176) says:

> A male . . . who can produce millions of sperms every day, has everything to gain from as many promiscuous matings as he can snatch. Excess copulations may not actually cost a female much, other than a little lost time and energy, but they do not do her positive good. A male, on the other hand, can never get enough copulations with as many different females as possible: the word excess has no meaning for a male.

Not only does the male have enough sperm to impregnate all the females he can catch, but also biology imposes no other absolute requirements on him once he has been successful. He can disappear into the sunset, strewing his genes along the way, and there is a good chance that many of his little genotypes will spring up and survive without any tending whatever on his part. The strategy for maximum genetic survival is obviously wrapped up in the word "variety."

Of course, as I mentioned earlier, the use of the word "strategy" does not connote a conscious plan on the part of the individual. Rather, in keeping with current sociobiological usage, the term is used metaphorically to indicate a tendency or a predisposition to action that has some functional significance for the organism. That tendency or predisposition is most easily construed in terms of the reinforcement value of events that flow through the life space of the organism.

Let's suppose, for example, that we have two males, one of whom is a dedicated, monogamous, relationship-oriented faithful type and one of whom is a philanderer, hell-bent on variety. Let's assume that both of these individuals act as they do because of genetic predispositions. The genes of the faithful male make sex feel better when it takes place within the context of mutual commitment and monogamy. Said another way, the "reinforcement value" of sex is maximal under monogamous conditions. The genes of the philandering male, on the other hand, do not relate sexual pleasure to commitment; rather, they make newness of partner the variable of primary concern—that is, for the philandering male a new female generates more sexual pleasure than does one he has had previously.

What I'm suggesting is that our Philandering Male and our Faithful Male do what feels best for them at the time. They are completely oblivious of genes and evolution and all the rest. They merely want to live their lives doing what for each of them comes naturally.

Faithful Male settles down with his mate and starts producing children. It so happens that he is a ring-tailed wonder when it comes to sex . . . two or three times a day for forty or fifty years. And, in the process, let's suppose he keeps his mate pregnant the maximum number of days throughout her lifespan. It should be noted that in primitive hunter-gatherer societies, where Faithful Male probably lives, a later age of menarche in combination with long intervals between births caused by suppression of ovulation during breast feeding may have limited maximum possible children per female to around five (May 1978). Nevertheless, for the sake of our example, we'll let the mate of Faithful Male match the world record with sixty-nine. (*Guinness Book of World Records* lists sixty-nine as the world record for live births from one female.)

The reader is probably saying, "If two or three times a day didn't kill her, certainly sixty-nine children would." But since we've fabricated our female, there is nothing to keep us from making her as strong as an ox.

Let's suppose the times are pretty good and all of these children survive. If half of these offspring were males, Faithful Male now has thirty-five boys running around with sex-influenced faithful genes, genes that make these boys tend to desire the same type of monogamous relationship their dad had.

During this thirty years, however, Philandering Male did not sit still. He ran from cave to cave, from community to community spreading his sperm, and his genes, as widely as he could. One time in the sack, and he did not want that female again. Always he had to find a new partner. Since he required such a variety of partners, opportunities for coitus certainly wouldn't be as great in number as they would be for Faithful Male. But even if he hit one new female every three days, he would have almost five thousand new contacts over a course of fifty years. Out of this number, he should manage to capture a large number of eggs. Shall we be fair in our example and let Philandering Male match the world record? (*Guinness Book of World Records* lists 888 as the record number of children sired by one man.) No, our example will stand without a world record for Philandering Male. He could sire only 25 per cent of the world's record, and even so, when compared with Faithful Male, he would have three times the number of male children running around with his promiscuous genes.

I have chosen the extreme, of course, to make a point. The chances are that no male is going to require a new partner every three days, but he might accomplish very much the same result genetically if he had access to only ten females on a regular basis. If he managed to keep them pregnant a good deal of the time, he would still have far more offspring than would Faithful Male.

It should be clear that the more promiscuous a male is, the more likely are his genes to become dominant in the male population. There is no magic here. The simple, uncontested biological basis for this logic is that males produce millions of sperms daily while females produce only about one egg per month. Over a period of many generations, most of the males running around are going to have genes that make "variety" a factor of significance in accounting for the variance in sexual pleasure.

But how about females? What genetic-selection pressures should result from their reproductive characteristics? The female not only has a limited number of eggs, but she also carries the fetus inside her body until that fetus is born. Furthermore, she provides the food source for the infant during its early development. These factors do lead to a strategy for maximizing genetic survival. First, of course, the female must get the egg fertilized. Since most males are capable of copulating quite often, a single, permanent partner can probably handle the job quite well. Once fertilized, however, this egg, or growing fetus, demands from its mother a great deal of nutrition and some care if it is to survive the gestation period. Even more importantly, once that egg is fertilized, the female cannot produce other offspring until the fetus comes out of her body. Furthermore, it is unlikely that she will ovulate again until she stops breast feeding.

By the time the infant is weaned, the mother has invested quite heavily in it. Obviously, the best strategy for the mother is to do what she can to see that her investment has not been wasted—that is, to provide for the needs of that offspring until it is independent.

Raising children is not easy, of course, in the wilds or in today's complex civilized world. But it is especially difficult if one parent has to do it alone. Hence, the female will enhance considerably her genes' chances for survival if she can get someone to help her provide for the kids. Aunt Sara might help, but a male is a particularly wise choice. As Seward (1977) points out, throughout history, prehistoric as well as recent, the superior strength of the male gave him a great advantage as a provider of food, particularly in societies that depended on hunting large animals. Hence, it was to the great advantage of a woman to avail herself and her offspring of the supply of food more likely to accrue from having a man around. As we shall see later, the father of these youngsters is the most likely candidate for the job.

Not only is provision important, but also the female and her infant, born or unborn, are more likely to survive if another individual—preferably unpregnant and as strong as possible—is around to provide protection. In the wilds, the pregnant female would face serious disadvantages on her own. The same would be true of a female with a child hanging on her breast. As in the case of provision, "the superior strength and size of the male no doubt afforded many advantages in defending against predators" (Seward, 1977).

What this all boils down to is that because of the heavy investment of a precious egg, plus time and energy during gestation, the female enhances the survival of her genes by seeing to it that the offspring, which is genetically half hers, survives to maturity. One way she can do this is by using whatever means are at her disposal to get a male to help her raise the offspring. That may mean submitting herself to the dominance of a male in return for his protection and provision. Or it may mean selecting carefully *ahead of time* a male who shows promise of being the type who will stay around. And, of course, it means sticking with this male through thick and thin.

As we noted for the males, we should remind ourselves that we are not talking about a conscious, planned strategy for maximizing genetic survival. We are talking about creatures who knew nothing about evolution or genes, but who did what felt best for them.

Those females who didn't particularly want a man around to help raise children handicapped their genetic survival, while those who were most comfortable, or who felt best, putting themselves in a position to gain the assistance of a male, enhanced their genetic survival. As Thomas (1974, p. 55) says of the female, "The need of protection and assistance in providing for the offspring inclined her toward a permanent union. . . ."

Thus, while the key idea for the male is "variety" in sexual relationships, a key idea for the female is "long-term relationship with a male." Although it is possible for sexual "fetishes" to be independent—for example, you might have a shoe fetish and I might have a basketball fetish—variety and relationship obviously are not independent. The male who wants variety will be interfering with the goals of the female in his life who wants a depth relationship, from the standpoint of economy of time if from nothing else. And the female who attempts to corner most of the male's time "to relate" will be interfering with his goals of variety. Obviously, there is going to be some tension between these two conflicting goals.

Because the two styles are not independent, it is not easy to discuss these styles separately. Nevertheless, for the sake of clarity in interpreting data, I will break them apart as much as possible.

The Promiscuous Male—Is There Any Evidence?

Yes, there is evidence providing support for this position, both verbal-report evidence and behavioral evidence. But before we get to that, let's again consider, as we did before, the value of a common belief.

A University of Bombay psychology professor tells of being asked by a young Indian female, "Why are men more promiscuous than women?" (Kanekar, 1977, p. 974). Not a surprising question from any culture. Kinsey (1953, p. 682) says, "Among all peoples, everywhere in the world, it is understood that the male is more likely than the female to desire sexual relations with a variety of partners."

As I said before, of course, to believe it doesn't make it true. But the person who wishes to challenge the validity of this statement should at least be able to provide some reasonable explanation for how it came to be, how it survived, and how it got to be so widely spread if it is not true. From the analysis of his data on sexual practices, Kinsey was convinced that the statement is true:

> As far as his psychologic responses are concerned, the male in many instances may not be having coitus with the immediate sexual partner, but . . . with the entire genus Female with which he would like to have coitus [Kinsey et al., 1948, p. 684].

VARIETY IN PREMARITAL PETTING, PREMARITAL COITUS, AND HOMOSEXUAL BEHAVIOR

Kinsey based his conclusions about the promiscuous male on data from premarital petting, premarital coitus, and homosexual contacts. In all of these areas, males show much greater variety of partners than do females. Because of the double standard, so clearly evidenced within American culture, it is likely that a greater variety of partners for males in petting and coitus may be largely the result of learning. But patterns of variety among homosexuals are particularly instructive.

During childhood, there exists no formal socialization process for learning how to conduct oneself as a homosexual. The learning that goes on—concerning when, where, and with whom—takes place after one is inducted into the homosexual culture. Although generalization of learning may be a factor, one would certainly expect that patterns of sexual behavior among homosexuals would be less influenced by the broader cultural expectations than would heterosexual petting or coitus. Furthermore, it is reasonable to assume that without the constraints in sexual relationships imposed by a member of the opposite sex, one might see a clearer sifting out of lifestyles related to the natural tendencies of males and females—that is, if our biological evolutionary logic is correct, we should find, in a community of male homosexuals—largely uninfluenced by females—that promiscuity should play a major role in the whole sexual scene. By contrast, females, when away from the influence of males, should be quite monogamous and relationship-oriented.

Indeed, all the data that are available show these expected patterns of behavior to exist. In an ethnographic study of male homosexuals, Sonenschein (1968) found that relationships varied from brief meetings to longer-term "affairs," and he concluded that the "one-night stand" is probably the male homosexual's most frequent sexual relationship.

Kinsey et al. (1953, p. 458) found that more than half of the single females who reported any homosexual experience had not had more than one partner. Only 4 per cent had been involved with more than ten partners. By contrast, the majority of males reporting homosexual experiences had been involved with more than one partner, 22 per cent with more than ten partners, and as Kinsey says, "Some . . . with scores and in many instances with hundreds of different partners."

Twenty-five years after Kinsey's report, homosexual styles remain the same. Alan Bell and Martin Weinbert, both of the Indiana University Kinsey Institute, surveyed fifteen hundred San Francisco Bay area homosexuals and found that as a rule females reported fewer than ten sexual partners while the majority of males claimed they had had from one hundred to five hundred different partners. Twenty-eight per cent of the white males estimated more than one thousand partners, most virtual strangers (see Gelman, 1978).

In a study of thirty-six male homosexuals between the ages of twenty-two and fifty-eight years (middle class), Cotton (1972) found only two pairs of lovers. Furthermore, he states that many of these men indicated that "they are rather disillusioned about ever being able to maintain permanent relationships, much less try to set up living arrangements with a lover" (Cotton, 1972, p. 313). Concerning enduring relationships, one individual said:

> I gave that up long ago. Some people stay together for a long time, but not many. Anything over a couple of years is really the exception; if you keep a lover over six months you're doing well. After a while, you just stop trying because you get to the point where it all seems useless, and you just play the field [Cotton, 1972, p. 313].

In a later study on lesbian relationships, Cotton (1975, p. 146) reports the following as "typical" of the kinds of comments lesbians make about fidelity in gay relationships:

> The gay guys are always fooling around, looking for someone else, even when they're "married." All the ones I know, and I know quite a few, play the field, and so do their lovers. Sometimes they have an "agreement" and sometimes not, but whether they do or not, they still cruise. I don't know why, but they say it's exciting and they get tired of always having sex with the same person. . . . Maybe they're still hung up on proving their masculinity like straight men. Anyway, they do it a lot more than we do; most of us are satisfied to have our lover, and that's it.

In a study of male homosexuality in West Germany, Reiche and Dannecker (1977, pp. 40–41) concluded the following about the role of variety in partners:

> All *promiscuous* homosexuals have a tendency to engage in a stable friendship (at some time) and all *firmly attached* homosexuals have a tendency to be promiscuous. . . . Homosexual men start friendships, if any, because they have had satisfying sexual contacts with each other and they generally separate again without much ado, when the sexual attractiveness within the relationship diminishes. This causes many friendships of homosexuals to be so short—according to heterosexual standards.

The picture among female homosexuals, as indicated by the

above quotes from Kinsey and Cotton, is radically different. In his 1975 study, Cotton found less promiscuity and greater fidelity among lesbians than he had found among males. He reported that many lesbian relationships are quite stable, enduring over years. A study by Hedblon (1973) found essentially the same. Among sixty-five female homosexuals aged eighteen to twenty-five, four out of five had had sex with fewer than eight women.

Schafer (1977) points out that it has long been commonly believed that homosexual males are more promiscuous but, according to him, never before his study had the truth of this belief been "empirically substantiated so clearly":

> . . . homosexual men had had fifteen times as many sex partners during the course of their lives as had lesbians. Eleven times as many homosexual men had had sex with more than fifty partners in the course of their lives than was the case for female homosexuals. During the year preceding the study, the lesbians had had an average of two different sex partners; the homosexual males, by contrast, had an average of sixteen. Only 1 per cent of all lesbians had had sex with more than ten partners during the preceding year, whereas 61 per cent of the male homosexuals had had sex with more than ten partners [Schafer, 1977, pp. 359–60].

The differences in partner frequency for male and female homosexuals is indeed dramatic. We can only conclude that "variety" plays an important role in the sexual life of the male homosexual. Not so for the female.

PROSTITUTION

We saw in Chapter 5 that women do not buy sex in quantities enough to count, if at all; hence, data on customers of prostitution are not going to tell us anything about variety vs. fidelity for females. However, the success of prostitution as a commercial enterprise is apparently related to the fact that it can offer variety of partners for _males._

In the data-oriented books, whenever writers attempt to explain the demand for prostitution, they often refer to the male's desire for variety. Kinsey (1948, p. 606), for example, says, "Many men go to prostitutes to find the variety that sexual experience with a new partner may offer." Kling, in his book *Sexual Behavior and the Law* (1965, p. 187), tells us, "Prostitution . . . satisfies man's craving for sexual variety." And Woolston, in *Prostitution in the United States* (1969, p. 81), concludes, ". . . the desire for variety leads men to seek new consorts. This applies not merely to the unmarried man who seeks various experiences, but also to the married man who tires of his lawful spouse."

I am reminded of an acquaintance who told me her husband had purchased the services of five different prostitutes in one night while he was stationed in Korea. From a purely economic standpoint, he no doubt could have struck a better deal with one girl for five trips to bed. But obviously, economy was not the issue. Variety was.

Since we are dealing in this chapter with the relationship-variety dimension, it is worth noting that, as expected, the male who goes to a prostitute is not interested in a relationship. Kling (1965, p. 188) points out: "With a prostitute, the male obtains mechanical sexual relief but little else. Prostitutes, as a rule, even the high-type ones, offer little or nothing in the way of companionship or affection."

It may be, of course, that one cannot conjure up emotional affection and offer it for sale along with the sex. And therein may lie a hint as to why women do not purchase sex.

POLYGAMY (more than one spouse)

We all know that paying rent is like pouring your money down a rathole. One is much better off to buy. If one happens to live in a polygamous society and has the economic power, why rent prostitutes? Why not purchase, or conquer, a harem, and gain, in addition to sexual variety, the other services women can also perform?

Indeed, this is what males have done throughout history. Polygyny (the practice of having more than one wife or female mate at one time) is very common (Boas, 1938), and it is practiced in almost all parts of the world (Herskovits, 1955). As surprising as it may seem, the majority of human societies are polygynous (Daly and Wilson, 1978). Furthermore, polygyny always seems to be related to wealth (Hoijer and Beals, 1965). The more a man can afford, the more wives he takes on.

King Solomon provides a perfect example. Traditionally viewed as the richest King ever to reign among the ancient Hebrews, he is said to have had seven hundred wives and three hundred concubines. The record, however, may be held by King Mtessa of Uganda, who is reported to have had about seven thousand wives (Bigelow, 1969). Talk about variety! If he cohabited with each wife once a year, he would have had to deal with about nineteen each day.

When I was just beginning to formulate my ideas about this topic, I mentioned to a social psychologist the interesting fact that evolutionary biology predicts "variety" as an important component in sex for males but not for females, and that indeed this prediction seems to be borne out by the practice of polygyny. His response was, "Wait a minute. How do you explain polyandry? That also goes on in some societies." At that time, I had not yet completed my homework so I did not know what to answer.

Let's take a look at polyandry (a female having more than one husband or male mate at one time). It does exist. Does it function as the female counterpart of polygyny? Is it, as suggested by my friend, the Achilles' heel of this particular insistence of biological evolution?

The first thing we should note about polyandry is that it is extremely rare (Linton, 1936; Lowie, 1940; Thomas, 1974). So rare is it, in fact, that the individual researching the subject soon tires of reading the same few examples over and over, particularly the Eskimos of North America; the Todas, a people of southern India; and an obscure group in Tibet. By comparison with the broad-based tradition of polygyny, the practice of polyandry is miniscule.

But of even greater significance is the finding that polyandry, where it is practiced, has nothing at all to do with the sexual desires of women. Rather, it is a custom designed to insure that all the men in the society will get at least a little bit of sex once in a while. Linton (1936, p. 182) points out that polyandry "seems to be rather uniformly correlated with hard economic conditions and a necessity for limiting population." Murdock (1934) reminds us that when infanticide is practiced to limit the population, the little girls are the ones killed. And as a result, polyandry spreads what remaining female sex partners there are among the males. In his book *Sex and Society,* Thomas concludes:

> . . . the fact that polyandry is found almost exclusively in poor countries, coupled with the fact that ethnologists uniformly report a scarcity of women in those countries, permits us to attribute polyandry to a scarcity of women (Thomas, 1974, p. 7).

Those factors accounting for polyandry today have apparently also been the ones responsible for the practice in the past. In his book *History of Sexual Customs,* Lewinsohn (1958, p. 45) gives only one example of polyandry, and that one is clearly economically based:

> . . . in Sparta, whose fertile soil made it one of the richest parts of Greece, the poverty was so abject that several brothers shared a single wife, as among the most primitive peoples. But even polyandry brought no solution. Hunger compelled the limitation of families to a single child.

Females can put away their dreams of being on top by moving to a polyandrous society. More than one husband or lover? Only because one of your mates chooses to "lend" you out to his friends or relatives. And you don't even have any choice concerning your sex partner. The economic conditions under which you would live would be so severe, offspring would impose a survival burden. Thus, few females would be allowed to survive. Those who did would be used in such a way as to maximize the sexual pleasures of men.

It is of interest to note that both polyandry and polygyny are strongly related to economic conditions. Both, however, are decidedly a man's game. When the conditions are bad, men agree to share the little bit of sex that is around. When conditions are good, they try to corner the market by purchasing harems.

I'm quite sure no woman in her right mind would trade the monogamy we see in Western society—even with its double standard—for any of the types of polyandry practiced in the few scattered parts of the world where it is found.

The reader may wonder about societies in which men are ruled by women. Under such conditions, wouldn't the women accumulate husbands and exploit them sexually? Sorry, but such societies do not exist. There are societies in which descent is traced through the women, and there are societies in which residence of a young couple is determined by the bride's kin rather than the groom's. But there are no societies in which women rule men. As Daly and Wilson (1978, p. 269) point out, "The kingdom of the Amazons is a fiction."

Men having more than one wife, women having more than one husband, both practices underscore the tremendous importance males place on having sexual opportunities. There are no societies in which women rule men, but even if there were, there is no suggestion that the women would use their power to gain more sexual opportunities.

In this chapter, I have thus far attempted to build convincing arguments that men desire more variety in their sexual experiences than women do and that women are stronger in their desire for a relationship. We have looked at the data on "the promiscuous male," and we will be taking a more careful look at "the faithful female." But before we go too far, I want to use these two ideas to throw some light on an objection raised by some of my critics in regard to the earlier chapters on "males having the stronger sexual desires."

The objection goes something like this: If, as I have claimed, males want sex more than women do, how do I account for the reports from middle-age marriages in which the woman seems to want sex more than the man?

First, I have to say that apart from hearsay information, we don't seem to have any other data to back up this claim. At least, I have been able to find none. Nevertheless, I have heard it so often I tend to believe that there are quite a few middle-aged wives who are more aggressive about sex than their husbands are. If this is true—even on a very broad scale—there are at least two possible accounts one might give for such a state of affairs without doing violence to the position that men have the stronger sex drive.

First, if, as argued in this chapter, males are especially aroused by variety in sex partners, that propensity for variety must surely interact in some way with the desire for sex with the *same* partner over a period of time. The desire for variety is antithetical to the desire for sameness; hence, it might be expected that the average male would experience a gradual decline in sexual arousal to a regular partner over a period of years. At some point in time, his desire for sex *with that partner* might become less strong than is her desire for sex with him. His overall sex drive, however, particularly with regard to *new* partners, may still remain much stronger than hers.

Distressing, isn't it! Well, there is another possibility. I have also argued in this chapter that the integrity of the relationship between mates is of primary importance to the female. Many people equate sexual desirability with love. At least, sexual desirability is often seen as a barometer of the nature of the relationship. Male sexual aggressiveness does appear to taper off as a function of age, probably as a result of decreased testosterone levels. Could it be that the female sometimes interprets the decreased sexual aggressiveness of her middle-aged partner as a tapering off of his love for her? She then, in an effort to hold on to the "relationship," may become more aggressive sexually herself.

This latter account for what may be a flip-flop in sexual aggressiveness among married couples is certainly less distressing than the former. Its credibility may be enhanced somewhat by the following additional information on the importance females attach to the relationship and how critical this relationship is to their amorous feelings.

The Faithful Female—More Data

INTERPERSONAL FACTORS AND SEXUAL RESPONSIVENESS

When asked what makes sex good or bad for them, women overwhelmingly give primacy to the relationship. Men do not. Women are particularly turned off if the relationship is sour, and men have a hard time understanding this. The average man might say something like: "Okay, so we have had a fight. But you weren't mad at my penis. So why all the frigidity?" Meade (1973, pp. 140–41) answers: "What men don't seem to understand is that, unlike themselves, women have trouble screwing people they don't like." Hite (1977) gives us the following excerpt from the report of one of her subjects: "I have found sex with people I don't really like, or who I'm not certain will really like me, or with people I don't feel I know well, to be very shallow and uncomfortable and physically unsatisfying. I don't believe you have to be 'in love' or married 'till death do us part.' But mind and body are one organism and all tied up together, and it isn't even physically fun unless the people involved really like each other!" (p. 481).

Rare, indeed, would be the man whose psyche sets forth the requirement that a woman should be likable before sexual attraction can take place.

Not only must men be at least decent human beings; most women require also that the relationship include positive aspects. Avery and Ridley (1975), for example, found that college females consistently identified a greater number of interpersonal factors as important for all levels of sexual intimacy when compared to males.

In a similar study, Driscoll and Davis (1971) asked a large number of college students to rate reasons for their restraint from engaging in sexual relationships. Nine possible reasons were suggested for rating: I felt it would have been morally wrong; I would feel ashamed afterward; too great a risk of being caught; would ruin my reputation; afraid of pregnancy; I did not love the person; afraid it would make our relationship worse; couldn't talk the other person into doing it; decision wasn't entirely mine. From what has been said about sexual differences in this chapter, we would certainly predict that males and females would differ dramatically on two items in particular: Males should endorse "couldn't talk the other person into it"; Females should endorse "I did not love the person." Not surprisingly, the differences on these two items were the strongest, with the differences in the predicted directions.

One hundred and six females said that "I did not love the person" was a "very strong" or the "predominant" reason for sexual restraint, while only twenty-six males responded this way. On the other hand, "couldn't talk the other person into doing it" was the "very strong" or "predominant" reason given by thirty-nine males and one female.

It is also interesting to note that in spite of their commitment to inherent "sexual identity," Masters and Johnson clearly recognize that females are more relationship-oriented, and they accommodate to this reality in their treatment programs. Single males who come to them for treatment are provided with partners, but single female patients must bring their own partners. Why such a chauvinistic policy? Because Masters and Johnson notice that men can accept such surrogates but women require more "meaningful" relationships (Robinson, 1977, p. 158).

We should not forget what was said earlier about sexual pleasure or satisfaction being the basic motivator for sexual activity. The data above suggest that for females the act itself would not feel right without certain emotional factors present; hence, when these factors are absent, females are not inclined to involve themselves in sexual intimacy. The same pattern holds when women are asked to rate the adequacy of the sex experience itself.

From a cross-cultural survey of the literature involving married couples in the United States, England, Puerto Rico, and Mexico, Rainwater (1964) found an inverse relationship between statements of sexual satisfaction (by wives) and degree of emotional relationship. Among the lower class, where relationships between husbands and wives were the most disparate, only 20 per cent of the wives made "very positive" statements about sexual enjoyment, and 54 per cent expressed negative attitudes. Many of these unhappy wives would even precipitate arguments with their husbands—so the husbands would stalk off to the corner tavern in a huff—rather than have sexual relations. Rainwater concluded from his survey that in societies where husbands and wives have a high degree of segregation in their role relationships, the wife is not likely to view sexual relations with her husband as gratifying.

Seymour Fisher (1973) sheds some light on why this may be so by suggesting that the female climax is tied in with a woman's belief that her partner has an emotional investment in her. In reviewing the factors that have been "empirically shown to be correlated with a woman's orgasm consistency" (Fisher, 1973, p. 398), he gives primary importance to the following:

> . . . the greater a woman's feeling that love objects are not dependable (that they are easily lost or will disappear) the less likely she is to attain orgasm [Fisher, 1973, p. 398].

In a similar vein, Masters and Johnson also point to examples of women who found their sexual responsiveness to decrease as marital friction increased (Masters and Johnson, 1970, p. 243).

Sex therapist Kerr (1978) tells women, ". . . being unable to have orgasms is not the problem. The problem is finding someone you want to share your orgasms with. . . ." (p. xiv). (Kerr is probably correct in part, but as we saw in Chapter 3, that's not the whole story.) Kerr also suggests that there are several ways to have sex, including intercourse and "making love." Intercourse is defined as "just plain physical sex, with anybody, because you feel hot" (pp. 235–36). "Making love," by contrast, is an expression of deep emotion by two people who love each other. She writes: ". . . women want to make love and men want to have intercourse" (p. 236). A respondent to Hite's questionnaire said it this way: "It's a trade. Like my mother says, men give love for sex, women give sex for love" (Hite, 1977, p. 435).

LESBIAN RELATIONSHIPS

The studies mentioned earlier on lesbians showed that female homosexuals form longer-lasting relationships than do males. From their study of women prisoners, Ward and Kassebaum (1965, p. 155) give us additional light on the emotional factors underlying such relationships:

> . . . the physical, social and psychological attachments which develop in homosexual affairs are intense. Women in prison are infatuated, in love, and jealous of the other women with all the intensity, happiness and pain of heterosexual love.

In addition, Brownmiller (1975, p. 296) tells us that the females' propensity for nest-building with its associated relationships extends far beyond the relationship with a lover.

> The inmate hierarchy in a women's prison . . . expresses itself in an intricate emotional superstructure imitative of an extended family life rather than in raw domination by physical power. Women who remain in prison for any length of time tend to form families consisting of a butch husband, femme wife, and assorted aunts, uncles, brothers, sisters and children.

Thus we see that emotional involvement and factors that lead to the establishment of an enduring relationship are commonly found among lesbians. Not so among male homosexuals.

SEX AND LOVE: WHO CAN SEPARATE THE TWO?

A great deal of the data in the previous sections demonstrate that females do not easily separate sex and love. By contrast, Kephart sees the male's easy separation of sex and love in a variety of male-dominated activities:

> It is self-evident . . . that a large percentage of males have no difficulty in divorcing sex from love. Whistles and wolf-calls, attendance at burlesque shows, patronizing of

callgirls and prostitutes—all of these are probably manifestations of a sexual urge totally or largely bereft of romantic feelings [Kephart, 1966, p. 318].

Could it be that females are not attracted to these activities precisely because such activities are so removed from emotional commitment?

RESPONSE TO PORNOGRAPHY—IMPORTANCE OF ROMANCE

Drakeford and Hamm (1973, p. 141) make a strong case that "sex is divorced from love in pornographic presentations," an argument fitting well with our observation that pornography is a male-oriented enterprise (more on this in Chapter 9). But pornography does not have to be separated from romantic themes, and when it is not, an interesting result is obtained. In a study by Sigusch et al. (1970) conducted on the content of sexually arousing pictures, females generally judged sexy pictures as less arousing and more unfavorably than men did. But "the sex-specific difference . . . decisively depended on the picture theme. In fact, pictures with romantic content were judged by the women as somewhat more arousing and significantly more favorably" (Sigusch et al., 1970, p. 23).

SWINGING

One last piece of information concerning the female's commitment to relationship comes from the study of "swinging." When sexual activities threaten the relationship, apparently there is not much of a contest. Both Denfeld (1974) and Fang (1976) tell us that the large number of women who elect to drop out of the swinging scene generally do so because of fear of losing their mates. By contrast, when the relatively few men are unhappy with swinging, their emphasis is on the difficulties they had in achieving the pleasure they had hoped for.

Whenever data have been collected on what appears to make sex attractive, "relationship" is a key word for the female. Hite

(1977) says: ". . . it is clear that . . . the importance of sex for women is inextricably bound up with love [p. 434]. . . . Overwhelmingly, women wanted sex with feeling [p. 479] . . . the basic value of sex and intercourse for women is closeness and affection. Women liked sex more for feelings involved than for the purely physical sensations of intercourse per se [p. 431]."

Throughout the animal kingdom, the key word to get the male juices flowing is "variety." Here's a clever study on mice to illustrate.

Macrides, Bartke, and Dalterio (1975) set up housekeeping for pairs of males and females for one week. At the end of that week, the testosterone levels in the males were similar to testosterone levels in the males who lived with other males. When strange females were introduced to these males, a dramatic increase in testosterone level was noted. The investigators conclude:

> Elevation of testosterone levels in these males is similar to that in isolated males paired with a female, does not depend on copulation with the strange female, occurs under housing conditions that permit continuous exposure to the odors of other females and males, and does not occur when the resident female is replaced by another male. . . . The elevation thus appears to be a specific endocrine response to an encounter with a strange female [p. 189].

To my knowledge, there is no evidence suggesting that testosterone—the sex-drive hormone—increases in females when strange males are placed with them. Based on the literature we have at the moment, we would have to view this as a male phenomenon.

Not only does variety make the hormones flow; the behavior is also there. In a large number of mammals, males can be induced to copulate again and again if variety of partner is emphasized (Dewsbury and Rethlingshafer, 1973). Commonly called "the Coolidge effect," this phenomenon is so well-documented, researchers don't even bother to study it anymore. A study conducted on prize bulls at Penn State years ago is illustrative (Hafez and Schein, 1962). After a bull began to lose interest in copulating with a cow, mounting could be reinstated by bringing into the pen a *different* cow or by taking the former cow out of the pen and bringing her back in through a *different* gate.

From what we've seen in this chapter, we might surmise, however, that cow bells are not rung by visions of different gates or different bulls. If we let the average female finish—in fantasy—the Penn State study, we would probably have both bull and cow going out the same gate to the ringing of wedding bells.

> Quoth she, "Before you tumbled me,
>   You promised me to wed."
> He answers,
>   "So would I 'a' done, by yonder sun,
> An thou hadst not come to my bed."
>   *Hamlet,* Act IV

9

The Fast, Indiscriminate Male and the Coy, Fussy Female

She is a woman, therefore to be won.
(King) Henry V

That rich, fat, nutritious egg of the female can be purchased with gold or promises of protection, provision, and a marriage license. Or it can be taken by force. But how much sweeter the prize when it is won. Courtship is the name of the game. The tune is called by the female; the dance is performed by the male.

If the male is to enhance his genetic survival, he must woo and win as many females as he can within a limited amount of time. Not only that, he must also be able to poke those genes into a female as soon as she will let him. And that means any female. If his sexual arousal is fussy or discriminate, his genes lose out to the male who carries around a bag just large enough to fit over the average female's head.

The best male strategy is seen in the behavior of the male bullfrog, who will give almost anything the right size a mating clasp—even the toe of a boot (Barash, 1977, p. 148). So what if this fast, indiscriminate bullfrog loses a few million sperms on a boot. He has plenty to waste. That is far better than having missed a chance to capture a few more eggs.

Human males can apparently be just as indiscriminate in

what arouses them. Morris (1978, p. 208) makes this point by quoting the following monolog by Lenny Bruce:

> You put guys on a desert island and they'll do it to mud. *Mud!* If a woman caught her husband with mud, she'd be outraged: "Eeeeekkk. Don't talk to me, you piece of shit, you. Leave me alone. Go with your mud, you, have fun. You want dinner? Get your mud to make dinner for you."

Little doubt that most men prefer women to mud, but they are not very choosy among women. In a study of the sexual practices of a group of almost one thousand Australian soldiers in Viet Nam, Hart (1975) found that 64 per cent had intercourse with prostitutes. Of this number, 52 per cent reported that they were satisfied with any girl they could get.

Other evidence that demonstrates lack of male fussiness comes from the data on sexual contacts humans have with nonhuman animals. Kinsey (1953) found that 8 per cent of males had reached orgasm through contact with animals, whereas only 0.4 per cent of females had done so—that is, the incidence is twenty times greater for males than for females. Furthermore, apart from orgasm, a great many more males than females reported experiencing erotic responses from either visual or physical experience with animals.

Sexual fussiness is certainly antithetical to genetic survival for males of all species. The best strategy is to deposit genes into or onto anything that moves. The toe of a boot? Male humans usually don't quite go that far, but given their powers of discernment so far greater than those of a bullfrog, one has to wonder if perhaps the bullfrog is even a little more picky.

Let's take a look at the female frog. What is her best strategy? She has no extra eggs to waste. They are large and few. They took a lot of energy to produce. Certainly, if she is to maximize her genetic survival she cannot go around handing out eggs to everything that walks, crawls, hops, or rolls by. If she did, few of her genes would be present in the next generation. On the contrary, evolutionary success dictates that she be fussy as, indeed, she is:

> The female [frog] . . . is more discriminating. She will release her precious store of eggs only if stimulated in just the right way, often by sound as well as touch, and by a

male of the right species. The [male frogs] . . . are following a strategy that is most adaptive for them—play fast
and loose. The best female strategy is different. With this
fundamental contrast in optimum male-female mating
strategies in mind, it should . . . be clear why males are
usually the aggressive sexual advertisers while females are
usually the careful comparison shoppers (Barash, 1977, p.
148).

Once again, we need to remind ourselves that we are not talking about a logical, planned strategy for maximizing genetic
survival. No more than the female frog does the human female
say, "Hmmm, I think I'll only become aroused sexually by certain kinds of males." Not at all. She simply *does* only become
aroused sexually by certain kinds of males. Female *Homo sapiens* who in the past were aroused by everything that walked
by may have had a great number of sexual encounters, but the
survival rate of their offspring was probably far less than that
for females whose sexual arousal was more discriminate.

Why Do Females Call the Tune?

Females control the mating game by virtue of the scarcity of
the eggs they possess. Simple economic theory tells us that
when a highly desired commodity is scarce, those who control
that commodity are invested with a great deal of power. Females can demand that males dance, beg, plead, send gifts,
fight, or turn somersaults because they have the power to dis-
pense the more scarce material required for genetic survival.
Our common word for the strategy of withholding the egg until
the dance is performed is called "coyness," but in raw reality,
the word is "control."

I am not implying that the female consciously exploits her
advantage. The female who does not *want* coitus on first meeting is not thinking about her eggs. She may even be on birth-
control pills or have an IUD, which wastes her eggs. Rather,
she is guided by her feelings and her desires. To her, sex would
not feel good too early in the courtship game because it is

through the sexual feelings that the genes have their effect. Males, on the other hand, have been selected genetically for feeling sexual desire early, and the awareness of those feelings is what causes them to pursue the female.

Control, then, becomes a matter of "who wants what more." As we saw in Chapter 5, there is good reason to believe that males want sex much more often than do females, and they want it from almost any female. Females don't have such overwhelming desires. And these differences in sex drive are highly adaptive to the biological structure of each sex. If the female wanted sex just as strongly as the male does, there would be no control of one sex over the other. The greater the difference in hedonic value attached to the sex act, the greater amount of control the one with the lesser desire will be able to exert over the one with the greater desire.

Coyness, then, is not necessarily something the female can take pride in—as if she somehow is exerting more control over herself than the male is. Coyness, or the desire to withhold the egg, simply exists because the female usually doesn't become aroused until she has gotten to know the male. She is doing what feels best for her. The male is doing the same.

So rare is true sexual aggression among women that we even have a special name for it: nymphomania. No counterpart for this "condition" in males deserves such special attention. The word "male" serves quite well in communicating all those sexual qualities for which the female is singled out as a freak.

In spite of the clear picture concerning who pleads and who shuffles feet, occasionally someone will come up with an absolutely bizarre attempt to deny the female the locus of control. By some mental gymnastics, it has even been suggested that men control the sex game and in so doing they require women to be "coy":

> Femininity requires women to limit their sexuality. . . .
> Women are faced with a cruel choice. They can ensure
> themselves of sexual partners by playing the feminine role,
> but they will be limiting their own sexuality and
> fulfillment, as well as that of the man. Or, they can ex-
> press their sexuality and risk losing their sexual partner or

never find one in the first place" [Billings, 1974, pp. 74–75].

Limited sexuality indeed! In today's Western societies? Any female between the age of eighteen and fifty, give or take a few years, can rather quickly find out just how limited her sexuality is by walking around the block and asking the first three men she meets to sleep with her.

This type of nonsense may make good copy for the feminist press and sociology journals, but it is totally removed from the realm of reality. The boundaries exist where opportunity ends. It is obviously the men who face the boundaries. They plead, beg, cajole, and even pay to expand their boundaries, while women are the ones who essentially control the number of heterosexual encounters that take place.

A colleague of mine, now in her early thirties, told me that when she was an undergraduate she and a girl friend used to go to parties and each pick out a male to sleep with. How did they communicate this desire to the male? By walking straight up to him and grabbing his crotch. She reported the not-very-unbelievable result: Not once did the technique ever fail.

Occasionally, women will express anger over the amount of control they possess. They seem to think it is something that has been hung around their necks by males. I'm reminded of a young man who told me his girl resented having to be the one to make the decision.

"Why is the decision always mine?" she said. "Why do women always have the burden of saying 'yes' or 'no'? You're a part of this relationship too!"

To which the young man replied, "I didn't realize it was such a burden for you. I'll be glad to assume the responsibility for the decision. The answer is 'yes.'"

Females may complain from time to time, but they certainly won't give up that control. If they do they can be quite sure of the results. When a woman complains about having to make the decision, what she is really asking is that the man feel the same way she does—that is, she is wishing he were not a man.

Females do control the sex game. That is very clear. But not in a vicious sense. Not even in a "morally selfish" sense. They control the sex game because their large investment in relatively few eggs gave a strong selective advantage to those of their number who withheld copulation until the "right male" came along.

Who Is the Right Male?

THE ONE WHO STAYS AROUND

Certainly one of the most important tasks for females during the 99 per cent of our history when we were scratching and clawing for survival was to discern which males would stay around to help raise the children. Females may not have been any better at this task than they are today, but we would probably all agree that the male who quickly said, "If you're not going to put out, I'll go elsewhere," would not look like as good a potential mate as, for example, Jacob of the Old Testament, who worked fourteen years to win his beloved Rachel.

> Any male who is not patient enough to wait until the female eventually consents to copulate is not likely to be a good bet as a faithful husband. By insisting on a long engagement period, a female weeds out casual suitors, and only finally copulates with a male who has proved his qualities of fidelity and perseverance in advance [Dawkins, 1976, p. 161].

At the common-sense level, at least, it certainly appears that females who held off until the male proved his mettle were more likely to have added protection and provision for their offspring, their only road to genetic survival.

It has also been suggested by sociobiologists (Dawkins, 1976, p. 161) that females (of all species) could enhance the chances of the male staying around by requiring him to make a heavy investment of time and energy during courtship. For some types of birds, the male must help build a nest before he is allowed to copulate. Or he may be required to feed the female large amounts of food. Dawkins (1976, p. 161) suggests: "A male who waits for a coy female eventually to copulate with him is paying a cost; he is foregoing the chance to copulate with other females." Presumably, there is a point of investment of time beyond which the male would face a genetic-survival disadvantage if he were to run off and leave the offspring—that is, if male birds knew something about probabilities and genetic theory, they might say something like this: "I spent all that time building a nest before my genes landed in some eggs. More of my genes might survive if I spend my remaining time in this life helping the wife raise these genes to adulthood rather than absconding and going through the process all over again with some other female."

The above analysis may sound somewhat discrepant with what I said earlier about the name of the game being "variety" for the male. Now I seem to be talking about "faithfulness" being the name of the game. Not at all. I'm saying that variety is the key for male success if he can plant his genes and move on quickly. If, on the other hand, a female wrangles him into investing quite a lot of time before he gets to her egg, and if most or all females play this same game, he may find that the best strategy is to help raise those offspring but still keep a sharp eye out for any other genetic investments he can make on the side.

The game becomes even more complex when we realize that there is also an optimum length of time for courtship from the female's point of view. If she drags the courtship out too long, she is losing precious time during which she could be making babies. On the other hand, if she surrenders her eggs too fast, she may not select out the male who will be a good provider.

The point of all this is that wise investment of time is crucial to reproductive success. The animals who play this game in the optimum benefit-cost manner come out the winners.

THE ONE WHO HAS SURVIVAL CHARACTERISTICS

We've seen that coyness on the part of the female may have functional value in selecting the most faithful of the male suitors. Or the strategy of withholding copulation may cause the male to invest so much time it becomes to his advantage to stay around and help with the offspring. A third reason for the prolonged courtship could involve taking time to select a male on characteristics that would make him a winner even *among* all those who are more or less faithful. Dawkins (1976, p. 169) calls this the "he-man" strategy, and it makes sense for the female to use it whether or not the father of the children helps raise them.

Presumably, the female withholds copulation until she has had a chance to evaluate the male in terms of skills that directly relate to his own survival as well as his potential as a provider and protector. Furthermore, even if he does abscond soon after winning copulation, the offspring are likely to inherit these outstanding characteristics and will, themselves, be more likely to survive to maturity. The female wins either way.

Certainly, no modern theorist can take credit for this bit of evolutionary logic. Before most of us were born, Havelock Ellis (1922, p. 192) wrote:

> . . . natural selection implies that the female shall choose the male who will be the most likely father of strong children and the best protector of his family.

Even Ellis doesn't take credit for the idea; Charles Darwin said the same thing fifty years before Ellis did his work.

PHYSICAL PROWESS

What characteristics does the female select? Obviously, the answer to this question depends on the lifestyle of the organism and what characteristics enhance its survival. Among many mammals, brute strength, co-ordination, and/or agility would be particularly desirable characteristics in the male. Barash (1977, p. 149) says that among many lower animals, "mates rely upon the physical prowess in the partner, as in defending a territory, warding off predators, or obtaining elusive and/or dangerous prey." Barash further suggests that the importance of selecting a mate on the basis of speed and co-ordination may account for "the elaborate aerial courtship of many falcons and eagles . . . during which objects are exchanged in mid-air" (Barash, 1977, p. 149). Better that the female falcon knows if her potential mate is an ace pilot before rather than after she has committed her genes.

It has even been pointed out that in many species of ducks, females will incite their prospective mate to attack a strange male. By picking out a good, tough male, the female may be protecting herself against future rapes (which are common in ducks) and also insuring the quality of her offspring.

Certainly it doesn't take any genius to see the parallel for humans. Strength, co-ordination, and speed, as seen in athletic contests, in particular, have long been valued as desirable qualities in males. Just ask any ninety-eight-pound weakling and you'll find out just how important these qualities are from a sexual standpoint. Recently, I read an article about a university freshman who was named lineman of the week in a regional poll. The player was quoted as having said that athletic fame is great: He has to beat women off with a stick.

Half a century ago, the individual who first put together a large-scale study on human sexuality stated that "women admire a man's strength rather than his beauty" (Ellis, 1922, p. 191). From all that we can tell, the situation has not changed dramatically in today's courtship world.

Germaine Greer wrote for the "Beauty Hints" column in *Women's Realm:* "It would be genuine revolution if women would suddenly stop loving the victors in violent encounters. Why do they admire the image of brutal men? . . . If women were to withdraw from the spectatorship of wrestling matches, the industry would collapse" (quoted in Reyburn, 1972, p. 194).

Ms. Greer's statement both substantiates our proposition that women are attracted to physical prowess and at the same time expresses the wish that some other world existed. Don't hold your breath, Ms. Greer, waiting for women to eschew male violence. If our analysis is correct—and there is at least some likelihood that it is—the females themselves have been somewhat responsible for male athletic competition by rewarding those who competed (and in particular, the victors) with their eggs. Men have been selectively bred for such shenanigans and women have been selectively bred for paying attention.

STATUS AND POWER

There are, however, other male characteristics that could enhance the survival of the female and her offspring. And it should come as no surprise that these qualities seem to have "sexually arousing value" to females. Like physical prowess, these characteristics also relate to status, prestige, or power.

It is said that someone once asked one of our most powerful statesmen why it was that he was such a seeker of power. His reply: "Power is the only well-documented aphrodisiac for women."

Status is vested in those with strength and agility. We've already spoken of that. What other characteristics give status? Certainly wealth. And perhaps also brains. If status itself is the crucial variable, any characteristic that has brought status or shows promise of bringing status should attract females.

Combs and Kenkel (1966) analyzed the stated "desirable qualities in a date" given by five hundred males and five hundred females who participated in a computerized dating service. While males were interested in having a good-looking partner, females specified qualities that "were in keeping with those found in a match that would meet with high social approval" (Combs and Kenkel, 1966, p. 65).

Victoria Billings asks: "Does your man take on added appeal when he tells you he has landed a job with a five-thousand-dollar increase in salary? Do you get sudden throbbing sensations when you walk out to your blind date's car—and it's a Mercedes?" (Billings, 1974, p. 230). Ms. Billings decries this type of "female chauvinism" as the result of bad upbringing and she implores women to "keep sex and money separate" (p. 240).

Like Germaine Greer's comment on the female response to physical violence, Billings' plea for a different world provides additional evidence for the point I'm making: For women, sexual arousal is, indeed, tied in with the power, wealth, and status of the male.

Furthermore, our analysis argues that this condition is not the result of bad upbringing. It appears to be more likely the result of thousands of generations of selective breeding. If so, females are going to have a hard time simply deciding that they will keep sex and money separate. It might be analogous to asking a man to cease being aroused by well-formed breasts and to decide that henceforth he will be aroused by flat-chested women.

I'm reminded of a conversation I had some time ago with a female friend who acknowledged that she is often sexually aroused by men of power. We then speculated on whether or not the opposite is true: that men are aroused by powerful women. Neither of us could think of any examples that would shed light upon the issue. I could only suggest that I'm one man for whom female power seems to be totally unrelated to sexual arousal.

Frankly, I don't know if there are any data available on this question. But from a sociobiological analysis, there is no reason to predict that power in women should be an aphrodisiac for men. In fact, the opposite might be true.

If a male's selective advantage is enhanced by having a large harem, the male might better stay away from aggressive, powerful females who, in pursuing their own advantage by trying to push out other females, would ultimately reduce the male's advantage. Maybe some sociologist should rush out and take a look and see if males are attracted to, repelled by, or neutral about power in females. At the present time, we don't seem to have any data on that question. What data we do have on power, however, are consistent in supporting the proposition that females are turned on by male characteristics that would enhance the viability of their own genetic investments.

Do Females Dance Too?

Indeed they do. The name of the dance is "seduction." If a female is too cold throughout the long, arduous courtship process, the male may simply lose interest and go chase some other female. Hence, the female must continually tantalize the male by reminding him what a great day it will be when he is finally allowed to copulate. Females do this by constantly advertising their sexual wares, but only, of course, to get the male into the store. They do not intend to sell until the prospective buyer has jumped through the required hoops.

The ideal female strategy is seen in the girl at the perfume counter saying to the salesgirl: "I want something that will make me irresistible, but won't get me into trouble" (Ellis, 1954, p. 65). Translated into the kind of thinking genes do: "I want behaviors in my repertoire that will bring lots of suitors around for evaluation . . . and keep them around until the testing is completed . . . but I don't want to make any genetic investments in the process."

Females throughout Western culture use many mannerisms to accentuate their sexuality. Everyone knows what a sensuous female walk involves. And King Solomon reminds men not to be taken in by seductive eyelids (Pr. 6:25). But clearly the most provocative accentuation of sex has been found in female dress styles. Only recently you say? Not at all. The amount of the body that women cover up may change from generation to generation, but the sexuality is clearly there. When Havelock Ellis was collecting his data on sex during the first two decades of this century, neither the miniskirt nor the bikini had yet made their appearance; nevertheless, he commented on the use of bustles and tight bodices, which served to emphasize the body shape males are attracted to.

Early in the previous chapter, I mentioned the shapely blonde who appeared ridiculous standing there in her highly provocative attire, chiding males for responding to her sexually. From the analysis presented here, there is nothing discrepant about her behavior and her appearance. She was doing what females have been selected for doing: keeping all the males attentive but withholding coitus until the proper relationship had been established.

The point of this section is that the seductive female who slices a man off at the waist when he moves too rapidly is quite predictable. Such a strategy has great genetic survival value for females.

Counterstrategies from the Male

The tension between the male who wants to capture the egg as soon as he can and the female who wants to hold onto her ace (pun intended) as long as possible is obvious. The male has a couple of counterstrategies, however, that may work well enough to also be selected.

First, sexual selection might favor males who are good liars:

> Any male who can pass himself off as a good loyal domestic type, but who in reality is concealing a strong tendency towards desertion and unfaithfulness, could have a great advantage. As long as his deserted former wives have any chance of bringing up some of the children, the philanderer stands to pass on more genes than a rival male who is an honest husband and father [Dawkins, 1976, p. 167].

There is some evidence concerning the male propensity to lie and deceive, but it is decidedly weak. A few studies have suggested that boys are more prone to lie than are girls (Maccoby and Jacklin, 1974, pp. 151 and 186), but I would not want to generalize very far from these studies. Somewhat more convincing, though still beset with diagnostic criterion problems, is the evidence we have on antisocial or sociopathic personalities. The sociopath is the classic smooth, convincing deceiver who lies with such facility that he is very hard to detect. Rowe (1975, p. 112) tells us that the sex incidence of sociopaths is predominantly male (five to ten times as many males receive this diagnosis), and Rappeport (1974, p. 261) suggests that although female sociopathic personalities exist, "they are rare and generally not in pure form." The view of the male as the one more prone to deceive must remain highly speculative because we have such little evidence; nevertheless, the evidence we do have is provocative given the evolutionary analysis used above. It has been said of psychopaths that the dumb ones end up in jail and the smart ones end up in Congress. With tongue in cheek, we might even point to the extraordinarily high proportions of men in prisons and politics.

The problem with this counterstrategy—that is, the male being selected for deceptive ability—is as Dawkins points out: ". . . natural selection will tend to favour females who become good at seeing through such deception" (Dawkins, 1976, p. 167). Folklore tells us that females are better at "reading other people," but I know of no empirical evidence one way or the other.

At any rate, a more fruitful strategy might be one that says males should become romantically attached—wildly in love, if you will—very early in the courtship. People are apt to be much more convincing when they really believe something than when they are just acting (Trivers, 1971, p. 50). Furthermore, the ability on the part of the female to see through deception would do no good in weeding out the actors because there would be no deception to see through. The male who feels, believes, and declares his undying love early in the dance is likely to gain some precious time on the male whose romantic inclinations are slower to rise. The sooner the female becomes convinced that "he's really crazy about me," the sooner she should be willing to mate with him.

Again, the data are not overwhelming, but they do support the notion of the male whose passion rises rapidly. In their studies on engagement and marriage, Burgess and Wallin (1953) found that males were more apt to show interest in their partners at the first meeting. Combs and Kenkel (1966) reported the same. In the study mentioned earlier on computer-selected dating partners, these investigators obtained follow-up data on both males and females. They concluded:

> . . . men more often than women experience romantic attraction for their partners. For every measure of partner satisfaction utilized in this study, male participants were more enthusiastic than women. They were more prone to be satisfied with her personality, physical appearance and popularity standing and to think it possible to be happily married to such a person. More often than [females] . . . they desired additional dates. A six-month follow-up study found that while both sexes had lost much of their enthusiasm for the partner, the drop was particularly pro-

nounced for . . . [females] [Combs and Kenkel, 1966, p. 66].

It should be kept in mind that this study did not involve dating partners picked out by the males, as is usually the case. Rather, these partners were computer-matched. Hence, there should be no *a priori* reason to believe that one sex should be any more attracted than the other.

In an earlier study, Kephart (1966) reported similar results:

> . . . irrespective of who falls in love more often, it is almost certainly the male who is *attracted more readily*. In the writer's survey, the question was asked, "Do you think it has been easy or difficult for you to become attracted to persons of the opposite sex?" Almost twice as many males as females checked "very easy" while at the other end of the scale females were more likely than males to check "difficult" [Kephart, 1966, p. 316].

In a questionnaire study with 250 males and 429 females, Kanin, Davidson, and Scheck (1970) concluded that males consistently developed romantic feelings earlier in the relationship. But once the feelings of romance were recognized by both parties, "the female was more apt to experience the stereotypic reactions we normally attribute to romance—the feelings of floating on a cloud, wanting to run, jump and scream, and having trouble concentrating. The general conclusion is that men fall more quickly; women fall more deeply. Kanin and his colleagues cite an unpublished master's thesis that also found males recognizing love earlier than females. Social psychologist Zick Rubin (1973) concluded the same.

Not only must females be cautious and choosy—slow to develop romantic feelings—at the beginning of a relationship, they must also be willing to pull the plug before investing too much time in a mistake. Hill, Rubin, and Peplau (1976) report some evidence supporting this view. In studying college couples who had broken up after a steady relationship, these sociologists found that women were more often the ones who precipitated the breakup. From the standpoint of evolutionary logic, one might conclude as Hill and his colleagues do: "In 'free choice' systems of mate selection . . . the woman must be especially discriminating. She cannot allow herself to fall in love too quickly, nor can she afford to stay in love too long with the wrong person" (p. 163).

The fast, indiscriminate male and the coy, fussy female. For maximum genetic advantage, the male must move rapidly even if it means taking what he can get. If he plays the fussy game, he may lose out altogether. The female, on the other hand, must take her time and choose her mate with care if she is to maximize the survival of her offspring. And she can do this because she owns the more scarce commodity. Males can generate counterstrategies by becoming good deceivers, and females then are selected for their ability to pick out the deceivers. Males then become rapid in their development of passion. Sounds a bit preposterous, doesn't it? And indeed some of it may be. But then again, the data, and the evolutionary logic, impel us to give the ideas serious consideration.

10

Extending Sociobiology and Sexual Behavior

In the previous chapter, I suggested that some of the ideas in this book are daring and not as easily defended as others. In this chapter, some may appear to be quite farfetched. Empirical support for these theories may indeed be scanty. And we should keep in mind that in this complex world, many different elements are involved in a single behavioral pattern. Nonetheless, the ideas in this chapter are generated from evolutionary logic and may reflect reality. At the least, they provide fascinating food for thought, and like all hypotheses, they invite debate.

The Double Standard

"Why should a girl be more restricted than a guy?" he asked.

"If I were in my room and a girl walked in, provided she was not too unattractive, I would sleep with her at the drop of a hat. Why should I, then, expect a girl to behave differently? It is inconsistent."

Another young man, also puzzled about the discrepancy between his logic and his feelings about sexual liberation in females, expressed himself this way:

"I think it is all right for me to go out occasionally with

other girls but I couldn't accept it if my girl friend dated others. Perhaps it is inconsistent, but I just couldn't resolve it."

These two examples appear in *Dilemmas of Masculinity: A Study of College Youth* by Mirra Komarovsky. Both are from interviews with senior males in Ivy League colleges. Moreover, these interviews were not made several generations ago. They come from the sexually liberated seventies! From a study of a large number of these young men, Komarovsky (1976, pp. 89–90) concluded:

> With the exception of a few strict adherents to the single standard, the men, unfaithful to their steady partners, viewed their own transgressions as morally imperfect but to be expected in males. However, they demanded fidelity from their girl friends.

"For the birds!" you say. Yes, indeed for the birds . . . they apparently have a similar double standard (Barash, 1977, pp. 63–66). The male mountain bluebird gets very nasty if he has reason to suspect adultery on the part of his mate (that is, if another male hangs around too much). Sometimes the male attacks the female so vigorously she will leave for good. And "for the elephant seals"! Elephant seals also live with a double standard. It's fine for the head of a harem of elephant seals to play around all he wants and to build as large a harem as he can defend. But let one of his wives look twice at another male and he will beat her up.

The same story occurs throughout the animal kingdom. Males have very different standards for themselves than they do for their mates. Kate Millet probably characterized quite accurately the double standard both from a historical and a cross-species perspective in this statement:

> When chastity is prescribed and adultery severely punished . . . marriage becomes monogamous for women rather than for men [Millet, 1970, p. 122].

What's going on here? Are males merely taking advantage of their power and strength by refusing to allow their mates the same freedom they allow themselves? If so, why? The double standard certainly exists—few doubt that it does—and it no doubt does have an effect on behavior. But why the double standard in the first place? Where did it come from? What functional value has maintained it and spread it all over the earth? And if it is learned, how is it learned and transmitted among so many nonhuman animals?

These questions should cause us to suspect that there is some evolutionary logic behind the double standard. If you remember much from Chapter 7, that logic may be apparent.

Let's consider the mountain bluebird. Because of the high metabolic rate of these creatures and the inordinate amount of food it takes to raise a brood, monogamy, with both parents acting as providers for the young, is the mating strategy that makes the most sense. Furthermore, Barash (1977, p. 63) points out:

> Among monogamous species, the fitness of males would be greatly reduced if their mate copulated with a different male, since there is no evolutionary return in helping to rear another male's offspring.

The word "cuckolded" stems from the behavior of the cuckoo bird, who is noted for laying eggs in the nests of other birds for them to hatch. From an evolutionary standpoint, the cuckoo bird who lays the eggs is not "cuckoo" at all. The strategy of the cuckoo bird is absolutely superb for genetic selection. The real "cuckoo" is the bird who wastes its own energy and time raising someone else's genes.

As I have mentioned in the past, the successful "strategy" of protecting oneself against being cuckolded does not have to have anything to do with plans or foresight or cognition. It can be, and probably is, based on feelings of dissatisfaction about one's mate copulating with someone else. Somewhere in the dim past, the male mountain bluebird, who through some freak genetic trick became very angry when his mate flirted with other males, started producing more offspring than his competitors. This reproductive advantage occurred simply because his disposition wouldn't allow him to be cuckolded as easily as those relatives of his who were quite relaxed about the unfaithfulness of their mates. Eventually, the raging, jealous male mountain bluebird won out genetically and became the prevailing type.

The same goes for the elephant seal. If adultery on the part of one of his wives really turned his guts into a knot, enough so that he did something to keep this from happening, he acquired a selection advantage over his competitors. For the male *Homo sapiens,* it is perfectly reasonable to believe that the same thing happened. Those male humans who kept a watchful eye on their mates were much more likely to raise to maturity their own genes than they were to raise the genes of someone else.

It is significant, I think, to observe, as Komarovsky did, that men can't give a logical explanation for their double-standard beliefs. Somewhere deep inside they have a gnawing, uncomfortable feeling when their mates play the same sexual game they do. They know it doesn't make sense. They know it is not logical. Yet they still feel that way. Genetic predispositions don't have to be logical, except from the standpoint of survival. And obviously, that gnawing discomfort has strong survival value for the male.

The male clearly has good reason to "feel" attracted toward a double standard when it comes to the mate whose offspring he elects to help raise. But what about the female? What should be her attitude toward faithfulness or unfaithfulness of both herself and her mate? As surprising as it seems, there is reason to suppose that the female might also subscribe to the *same* double standard the male does, though perhaps not to the same degree. As we have said before, the female has nothing to gain from promiscuous matings; hence, there is no reason for her to see these as particularly desirable for herself. But there is reason for her to feel at least some attraction toward a male with a roving eye. If she can find a mate who will stay around to help protect and raise the kids, but at the same time might fool around a little on the side, she increases the chances that her sons will do the same. And since her sons are carrying her genes, she then increases the chance that her genes, through her sons, will be sprinkled around the countryside. We can't know what the ideal cost-benefit ratio would be in this rather high-risk game, but there is certainly room for the female also to be selected for a mild version of the male's double standard. If true, females should be titillated by the man who shows promise of faithfulness but has a devilish smile.

As far as we can tell, the double standard is found throughout history. Engles (1902) suggests that the double standard extends at least as far back as the idea of private property. Bullough (1971, p. 196) says it was part of cultural tradition in ancient Mesopotamia (3000–2300 B.C.):

> . . . in married life there was a dual set of standards involved, one for the wife and a different one for the husband. The wife's activities were rigidly circumscribed and adultery was a serious crime for which the punishment could be death. The husband on the other hand was in no way expected to limit his sexual life to his own bedroom and, provided he kept clear of other men's wives, he was quite free to do as he liked.

Barbach reminds us of a bizarre double-standard practice carried out a century ago:

> Clitoridectomies, as various forms of this operation (removing the clitoris) were called, were sometimes performed on young girls in Europe during the late 1800s to inhibit masturbation, and on young women to prevent unfaithfulness. However, nowhere in the literature do we find recommendations that the penis or testicles be removed to curtail the masturbatory activities of boys, or the adulterous activities of men [Barbach, 1976, p. 18].

And lest we be tempted to think that the double standard is the brainchild of Western European chauvinistic males, we should be aware that the Far East has not taken a back seat in this custom. Asayama (1975) observes that before the Second World War virtually all Japanese husbands enjoyed some form of sexual contact outside of marriage. In contrast, sexual infidelity among wives was condemned both morally and legally. Although things have changed somewhat as Japan has become Westernized—the West softened the double standard rather than strengthening it—the change has not been dramatic. Recent surveys show that 75 per cent of all modern Japanese husbands have extramarital intercourse (in the wealthy classes, this figure is 90 per cent), but for women the percentages range from 3 per cent to 7 per cent. By contrast, in the United States, about 55 per cent of the males up to fifty years of age have extramarital sex, as compared to 24 per cent of the females of that age group.

The double standard is seen very clearly not only in expectations within a relationship but also in expectations about sexual activity before the relationship ever began. We see it in many men's desire to marry a virgin. It is fine to go out with the loosest girl in the neighborhood, but when it comes to marriage . . . ahh, that's quite another matter. Interestingly, concerns over male virginity at the time of marriage are not as great.

For men in the United States, Pietropinto and Simenauer (1978) report: "One third of men today still want to marry a virgin. . . . More significant, in this era where it is supposedly perfectly acceptable for people to engage freely in sex for the sheer enjoyment of it, only 2 per cent of men would want to marry a woman who had engaged in relationships with many men" (p. 290).

Our cultural standards in this regard are probably similar to those described by Isichei (1973) concerning a primitive African tribe. Young girls were "required" to be virgins at the time of marriage, but young males were expected at an early age to master the basics of sex through contacts with older women or widows. In the United States, Kinsey (1953, p. 323) found that more than 40 per cent of the males in his study wanted to marry virgins, but only 23 per cent of the females expressed that desire. Furthermore, he concluded that male emotions, and even codified cultural attitudes, on this issue can be very strong:

> Many a male . . . is prone to seek coitus from every available girl, while insisting that the girl he marries should be virgin when he first has coitus with her. It is the male, rather than the female, who imposes this incongruity on the social code. He will defend his right or any other man's right to try to secure coitus from another man's sister or wife, but he may fight or kill the man who attempts to secure coitus from his own sister, fiancée,

daughter, or wife. Interestingly enough, juries and the stat-
ute law in certain parts of the country are still inclined to
grant him the privilege of defending what he now calls his
honor. . . . At common law and in many states . . .
strong evidence of the seduction is considered sufficient
provocation to reduce a killing from murder to man-
slaughter, and to mitigate the sentence or completely excuse mild assault and battery [Kinsey et al., 1953, p.
323].

On the surface, all of this sounds rather foolish, doesn't it?
Kinsey adds to the seeming nonsense we find in this double
standard by telling us that virginity in the female has long been
seen as a very important economic matter:

Sexual activities for the female before marriage were proscribed in ancient codes primarily because they threatened
the male's property rights in the female whom he was taking as a wife. . . . In the ancient Chaldean, Jewish, and
other codes, the prohibitions were directed primarily
against the female's activity after she had become betrothed, and penalties for the violation of her sexual integrity involved the payment of goods equivalent to those
which the fiancé had already turned over to the girl's father. Goods were also demanded as compensation to the
husband, father, or fiancé for the depreciation in value of
his interests in the female. . . . Our moral judgments of
premarital coitus for the female are . . . still affected by
this economic principle which developed among the Chal-
deans and other ancient peoples, three or four thousand
years ago [Kinsey et al., 1953, p. 322].

Now we are really getting silly. Why on earth should a used
vagina be worth less than an unused one? And why should an
unused vagina have so much more value than an unused penis?
Suppose for a few minutes that you were a member of the
Chaldean culture and you had paid a good sum for a woman
promised you in marriage. Then you found out that she was
sleeping with someone else. If you are any sort of businessman,
you go to the father of this unfaithful young lady and say some-

thing like this: "Sir, it has come to my attention that your daughter, to whom I am betrothed, has been bedding down with another man. I have come to demand compensation of an amount equivalent to that which I gave you for the girl in the first place."

Your future father-in-law, also a businessman, decides to approach the issue logically: "I know what the custom is, but let's be reasonable about this. How on earth can it make any difference to you whether she has lost her virginity or not? She is still the same young woman, with all the talents and beauty she ever had. How can her economic value have diminished?"

Your answer is that she might be carrying some other man's child. Your prospective father-in-law counters with: "Then let us place a chastity belt on this young lady and wait for a few months. You will soon know if she has been impregnated. If not, what have you lost?"

This one might slow you down, but if your genes could answer for you, they would surely say, "This female would be fine for you to invest some sperm in, but no maximally successful male can afford the risk of investing time and energy in her and her offspring. If she is, as seems to be the case, a poor player at the female game—that is, if she is either dumb or promiscuous—you run a risk of being cuckolded." Your genes are not going to let you feel comfortable about such a deal.

It seems clear that the permanent devaluation of the deflowered daughter only makes sense from the viewpoint of selfish genes (a term coined by Dawkins, 1976). Only a losing male is going to feel completely comfortable purchasing such used goods.

Kinsey said: "In most cultures, throughout history, everywhere in the world, some sort of distinction has been made between the acceptability of premarital coitus for the male and the acceptability of such coitus for the female" (Kinsey et al., 1953, p. 322). Although some recent investigators have been game enough to suggest that "there appears to be a convergence toward a single behavioral standard" (Wagner, Fujita and Pion, 1973, p. 155), my bet is that it will never be reached. The evidence at this point is on the side of genetic selection.

The Hourglass Figure

The beautiful woman is one endowed, as Chaucer expresses it,

> With buttokes brode and
> brestes rounde and hye.

What man or woman is there who does not understand the nonverbal expression of feminine beauty communicated by a "Coke bottle" movement of the hands? Marks of beauty certainly have a cultural overlay, as indicated by the differences in criteria reflected in various parts of the world. But the hourglass figure of the female is apparently an attractive feature that cuts across all cultures.

In the Western world, we hardly need to point out an emphasis on breasts and hips. Back in 1922, Ellis (p. 164) pointed out that large buttocks and hips have long been simulated by clothing styles:

> . . . the Elizabethan dramatists refer to the "bumroll," which in more recent times has become the bustle, devices which bear witness to what Watts, the painter called "the persistent tendency to suggest that the most beautiful half of humanity is furnished with tails."

Today, the popularity of the phrase "nice ass" demonstrates that the elevation of male attention hasn't changed.

Among primitive societies, one of the most dramatic confirmations of this emphasis on posteriors is seen in Somali, where men customarily were supposed to choose a wife by ranging women in a row and selecting the one who projected farthest *a tergo* (Ellis, 1922, p. 166).

From a broad collection of reports and observations cutting across many cultures, Havelock Ellis concluded:

> Thus we find, among most of the peoples of Europe, Asia and Africa, the chief continents of the world, that the large hips and buttocks of women are commonly regarded as an important feature of beauty [Ellis, 1922, p. 164].

But big breasts and buttocks are not the whole story. After all, measurements of 38, 38, 38 don't sound very enticing. If we examine our tradition more closely, we find that the "buttokes brode" and the "brestes rounde and hye" must be relative to a small waist. Chaucer just forgot to put that part in because it was so clear to him. The bustle and the bumroll Ellis refers to was accompanied by corsets so tight the female could scarcely breathe. Whence comes this strange power of the hourglass woman to effect such vascular changes in the man? It should come as no surprise at this point that I will propose an explanation based on selective advantage.

Let us suppose that many generations ago males could be aroused by a broad spectrum of physical types. Some were aroused by tree-trunk types of females and some were attracted to Coke-bottle types, and perhaps there were all kinds in between. The male who became aroused by the 34, 24, 34 figure and spent his time wooing and winning this type of female stood a pretty good chance of having offspring soon after he copulated. The male who was attracted by the tree trunk, on the other hand, might have gotten a female who could give him offspring, but then again he might have wasted his time wooing and winning one of at least several other types of females who could not immediately produce offspring, perhaps not at all.

First, there is the prepubescent female, who has genitalia adequate for copulation but no ripe eggs. For this female, the marvelous hormonal miracle that transforms a girl into a woman has not yet begun. That miracle involves not only development of the ovarian follicles that lead to fertility but also it involves the growth of breasts, a redistribution of fatty deposits to the buttocks, and a widening of the pelvic girdle to accommodate the development of the internal sex organs and to provide room for the incubation of a child. She'll be fertile someday, but the male who spends time building her a nest before she hits puberty is losing out in the genetic race.

There is a second kind of female who does not have an hourglass figure: the one who is already pregnant. You say, why would a male woo a female who is already pregnant? It is easy to forget that in evolutionary logic, we are dealing with a huge portion of time during which our ancestors probably had no understanding of the relationship between coitus and pregnancy. They did it because it felt good, and that was that. Offspring happened. It is perfectly reasonable to assume that a male who was aroused by thick waists might be trying to plant his genes in a female who was already pregnant. Obviously, he also is losing out in the genetic race.

And then there is another type of female who sometimes loses her hourglass figure: the post-menopausal female. Many women, of course, keep their girlish figures up into old age, but for many there are changes in the contours of the hips, with accompanying thickening of the waist. The male who courted and won a female who was past menopause would also lose out to the male who was courting a still-fertile female.

One other type of narrow-hipped female may be a poor bet for children. She may be the right age and unpregnant, but if her pelvic girdle is too narrow, she might not be able to deliver a healthy child.

The substance of this argument is that males who became sexually aroused by hourglass figures had a great advantage over males whose eyes and penises were wired up in some other way. The genes of those successful males are probably around today setting our standards for feminine sexual attractiveness.

The Visual Male

Of all the male outdoor sports, girl-watching might well qualify as the most popular. Marion Meade (1973, p. 85) voices the universal female complaint:

> From the moment a woman steps foot out of her home alone, she knows that she's on enemy territory. Her only protection against lip-smacks, leers and uncalled-for remarks is a male escort. Otherwise, out on the sidewalks it's open season any time of year.

Another of those functionless, spontaneously generated customs? Perhaps. But a reasonable argument can be made for the evolution of a male eye with unusual preoccupation for the female form.

Recall, from previous chapters, who chases whom and which sex is selected for variety of partner. The male is the sexual aggressor, fertilizing as many eggs as he can. And it stands to reason that the male who is most often aroused and most often in pursuit of females will have a selection advantage, all other factors being equal, of course.

Three males are swapping yarns on a grassy hillside. One becomes aroused only when a female is at arm's length; another becomes aroused at ten yards; and the third becomes aroused at fifty yards. If a female walks by—at any distance—which male is most likely to get up and go after her? Obviously, the one whose sensitivity for arousal extends the greatest distance. The male, for example, who becomes aroused when two hundred feet from a female will have about four times the number of females travel through his arousal milieu than will the male whose sensitivity for arousal extends only a hundred feet. And both of these males will be making far more advances than will the one whose sexual world only extends a few feet.

Crook (1972, p. 251) suggests that we should think of sexual signals in at least four categories: First, there are the long-distance visual signals, which include body form, gait, and such things as "high heels enhancing the provocative body movements of the walking female." Second, there are the middle-distance signals of voice quality and tone and complexion. Third, there are the close visual signals, which include "areolar tumescence, body flush, eye glitter, and pupillary distension." And fourth, there are the contact signals of "epidermal touch quality, breast tumescence, lip feel, genital sensation, and body scent."

Presumably, all of these signals are potentially sexually arousing. But what of the male who only becomes aroused by signals in the last three categories? Let's say he is aroused by a soft, feminine voice, a fair complexion, eye glitter, and lip feel. If while out gathering some nuts he happened to see a female thirty yards away, what signals would motivate him to run over and try to squirt some genes into the next gene pool? He would probably just continue to gather nuts. On the other hand, the male who was aroused by the long-distance visual signals—body form, swing of the hips—might become excited enough to swim across a river to get at that egg.

Shouldn't females also develop distance sensitivity to males? Perhaps for "getting together," but certainly not for raw sexual encounter. The successful female, you recall, should not become sexually aroused until she has scrutinized the male and has found him to be a good genetic bet. She may see the guy across the river and do a little dance to get him to swim across, but only so she can get a better look at him, not so she can have sex with him. Only the male, not the female, can benefit from having eyeballs wired directly to the genital organs.

Kinsey and his collaborators have provided us with most of the quantitative data on lip smacks and leers. From their observations, it does indeed appear that sexual stimulation for the male is heavily visual. And if the male eye can't find anything of interest in its environment, it turns inward to manufacture its own rich fantasy world for stimulation. We'll consider just a few of the illustrative findings of Kinsey's team.

VIEWING MEMBERS OF THE OPPOSITE SEX

Twice as many men as women reported that they were aroused by seeing members of the opposite sex. Furthermore, the responses of these males were often physiological, including erectile responses, and the male often felt led to approach the female for physical contact (Kinsey et al., 1953). In Kinsey's sample, even the relatively few females who did respond to the sight of males did not have marked physiological reactions. Kinsey tells us that this pattern observed in humans is characteristic of responses in infrahuman species of mammals. Males show signs of arousal upon observing potential sexual partners, but females usually show such signs only after physical contact has been made.

OBSERVING GENITALIA

The sight of female genitalia is particularly arousing for most males (Kinsey et al., 1953, p. 655), but Kinsey found that more than half of the females in his sample reported that they had *never* been aroused by observing male genitalia. In fact, "many females are surprised to learn that there is any who finds the observations of male genitalia erotically stimulating. Many females consider that male genitalia are ugly and repulsive in appearance, and the observation of male genitalia may actually inhibit their erotic responses" (Kinsey et al., 1953, p. 655).

A correspondent of Havelock Ellis (1922, p. 190) wrote:

> I have . . . noticed that women do not like looking at my body, when naked, as I like looking at theirs. My wife has, on a few occasions, put her hand over my body, and expressed pleasure at the feeling of my skin. (I have very fair, soft skin.) But I have never seen women exhibit the excitement that is caused in me by the sight of their bodies, which I love to look at, to stroke, to kiss all over.

Again, as in the case of "the general sight of a member of the opposite sex," it appears that the erotic value of female genitalia is strong throughout the animal world:

> Among the infrahuman species of mammals there seem to be something of the same differences between the reactions of females and males to the genitalia of the opposite sex. For instance, a female monkey or ape grooming the body of a male who may become aroused erotically, may pay no attention to the male's erect genitalia. On the other hand, when male apes and monkeys groom females, they usually show considerable interest in the female genitalia, and explore around and within the genital cavity. Male rats, guinea pigs, dogs, raccoons, skunks, porcupines, and many other male animals may similarly explore at considerable length about the genitalia of the female, but the females of these species less often explore about the genitalia of the male [Kinsey et al., 1953, p. 655].

OBSERVING SEXUAL ACTION

Although Kinsey did not find many females who had had the opportunity to observe other persons having intercourse, the few who had rarely reported sympathetic responses. By contrast, males responded quite positively. Again, Kinsey points out the similarity between humans and infrahuman species:

> The males of practically all infrahuman species may become aroused when they observe other animals in sexual activity. Of this fact farmers, animal breeders, scientists experimenting with laboratory animals, and many persons who have kept household pets are abundantly aware. The females of the infrahuman species less often show such sympathetic responses when they observe other animals in sexual activity" [Kinsey et al., 1953, p. 661].

PEEPING AND VOYEURISM

A number of years ago when I was working at a mental health clinic, a social worker came to me very upset because of a report another psychologist had written on a thirteen-year-old male, court-referred because of window peeping. From all the social worker could find out on her own, this boy was well adjusted, a good student, and an obedient, respectful son. Furthermore, he had good peer relationships and showed no signs of any neurotic problems. It had happened that he was standing out in his driveway one night watching the little girl next door undress for bed when he was caught by the girl's father. The father called the police, and the court sent him to us for a psychological evaluation.

After examining the boy, the psychologist reported that he "had deep-seated sexual problems" and was "in need of long-term, depth psychotherapy." The social worker, a bright, concerned individual, complained that the report was tagging the boy as a sex deviate, and she wanted me to comment.

My response was: "If this kid has problems, they probably aren't in the sexual area. If I had a thirteen-year-old son, and he had a chance to watch the little girl next door undress and he didn't, I'd be seriously concerned about his mental state."

This was years before I discovered that Kinsey agreed with me, but I found that agreement comforting. From his studies, Kinsey concluded:

> There are probably very few heterosexual males who

would not take advantage of the opportunity to observe a nude female, or to observe heterosexual activity, particularly if it were possible to do surreptitiously so they would not suffer the social disgrace that the discovery of their behavior might bring. . . . Our data are insufficient for determining what percentage of the male population is ever involved, but Hamilton found some 65 per cent of the males in his study admitted that they had done some peeping. The percentages for the population as a whole are probably higher [Kinsey et al., 1953, p. 665].

Apparently female voyeurs are so rare that data are not quantifiable. And it is doubtful that the law will ever subject the female voyeur to prosecution. Clearly, this is a case where the law comes down hard on the male. If a male is watching a female undress, he is a voyeur; she is a victim. If a woman is watching a man undress, he is an exhibitionist; she is a victim. Sounds quite unfair at first glance. But this interpretation is probably more often right than wrong, given what we know about male sexuality.

PORNOGRAPHY

One of the clearest demonstrations of male and female differences in response to visual stimuli is seen in the pornography trade. Although for a number of reasons the Burt Reynolds centerfold in *Cosmopolitan* a few years ago created a sensation, no magazine publisher in his right mind is going to produce a visually oriented pornographic magazine for the female audience. If there were any market there, someone would have located it years ago.

Kinsey found that males are far more often aroused than females by viewing paintings, drawings, or photographs of the opposite sex in the nude. Furthermore, 77 per cent of males who had seen pictures of sexual action found them erotically arousing, while only 32 per cent of the females had found any erotic arousal in such material. More recent studies, using better controls, have essentially confirmed Kinsey's conclusions

(Sigusch, Schmidt, Reinfeld, and Wiedemann-Sutor, 1970; Steele and Walker, 1974).

I am quite aware, of course, that there are some, especially in the feminist ranks, who think pornography has nothing to do with sexual arousal and certainly does not relate to genetic selection. Andrea Dworkin (1974) suggests that pornography is motivated by the desire to exploit and victimize women. And Susan Brownmiller (1975, p. 443) says "pornography is the undiluted essence of antifemale propaganda."

I say, "Nonsense!" Pornography is valued because men find it sexually arousing. That's it, plain and simple. Ms. Dworkin and Ms. Brownmiller have to try to find some other reason because they evidently do not find pictures of naked men arousing. That's fine. Sexy pictures are not their cup of tea. But to say that a man who buys a skin magazine is doing so in order to dehumanize women is sheer nonsense. How about the man who walks down the beach enjoying the display of female bodies? How about the husband who likes to look at his wife in the nude? Some feminists have asked us males not to write about the female experience because we can't know what it is. And we ask them not to come up with a silly explanation of the male's propensity to look just because they don't like to do the same.

Data overwhelmingly support the proposition that males are more aroused by visual stimuli than are females. Furthermore, there is an evolutionary logic that says why this should be so. I would place my bet on an evolutionary component in there somewhere.

Older Men and Younger Women

Meade (1973) says, "No one will pay for an old whore." And all the data available seem to prove her right. Fast (1972, pp. 83–84) tells us: "There is no market for women over thirty-five though there is a market for men right into their sixties." In ancient Rome, males married girls much younger than themselves (Hopkins, 1965) and wherever field studies have been conducted, it has generally been found that men prefer young women or girls as wives and sexual partners (for example, Bullard, 1974; Mead, 1949). Barash (1977, p. 291) reports: ". . . it is almost universal in human societies that men are older than their mates."

The feminist publication *Women: A Journal of Liberation* clearly recognizes this age "discrimination." Furthermore, its editors tell us that male interest in younger women is something for which men deserve a certain amount of finger-shaking blame: "Men, because of their own problems of aging sexuality, have created the myth that a woman's sexual usefulness is over at fifty" (*Women,* 1974, p. 3).

Is it, as they say, a product of man's problems with his own sexuality? It would seem that the aging, insecure male would go out of his way to avoid the demands of a woman he might not be able to keep up with. Furthermore, how do these feminists explain the female's interest in older men? They may have a point, but there is also the possibility, and a strong one, that the "older man-younger woman" phenomenon has been mysteriously coded into us by generations of selection.

The editors of *Women* tell us that men have created a myth that a woman's sexual usefulness is over at fifty. From the standpoint of those male genes, which want immortality, the woman's sexual usefulness is indeed over at fifty, or thereabouts. That's no myth. That is biological reality. The male whose sexual arousal focuses on women over fifty has a meager genetic future. Over the long haul, who is going to have more offspring? Obviously, the male with a predilection for youth.

Furthermore, a case can be made from evolutionary biology for a female interest in older males. In Chapter 9, we discussed some of the variables on which a discriminating female should choose a male in order to enhance her sexual selection. The control of resources, for example, is likely to be in the hands of older men, and these resources could be of great value in bringing children to maturity. Such resources might include the control of territories or even better development of hunting or defensive skills because of more practice. Dawkins (1976, p. 170) reminds us that whatever the shortcomings of older men, "they have at least proved they can survive," and the female who plays the courtship and mating game with one "is likely to be allying her genes with genes for longevity."

I have mentioned that evolutionary logic can be used in many different ways, but usually on each question there is one way more compelling than its competitors. Can we think of an evolutionary reason why a female should select a male younger than she is? The first thing to come to mind is that for the female over thirty-five or forty, perhaps she would be choosing a stronger, swifter, more agile mate than would be the case if she selected one her age or older. Perhaps true, but in a milieu of constant physical activity, the male of forty might not be much less agile or less strong than the male of twenty-five. It could well be that the other factors, such as added experience or control of resources, would considerably outweigh the slight advantage the younger man would have in strength or swiftness.

A much more important factor is that after thirty-five or so there aren't very many biologically productive years left for a female. The female's best strategy, by far, is to mate as soon after puberty as possible. The earlier she starts producing, the more of her genes are likely to survive. So the more important question is: "Who should the pubescent female choose for a mate?" Certainly, she will lose out if she selects a male younger than she is. He will not even be fertile yet. Even if she should choose a male her same age, because of the earlier puberty of females, she will have to wait a year or two until he can impregnate her. No advantage there either. Clearly, she should choose an older mate.

Let us play the same game with the male. Can we somehow twist evolutionary logic into convincing us that the male should choose an older mate? Perhaps the postpubescent male should go after an older, more experienced female. Her experience both in child-rearing and in living should make her a better provider for his genes, shouldn't it? Probably not. Apart from the likelihood that she is already mated because of what we have said above, if she already has offspring, those offspring—belonging to some other male—will vie with any new offspring for her attention and time. Her added experience as a mother may be more of a liability than an asset to the survival of more recent genes being implanted into her. Furthermore, if she is an older female and doesn't have any offspring, that's a very bad sign. She may not even be fertile. And even if she is fertile, the very fact that she is older than the male means that her sexually productive years are more limited than a female his own age or younger. No matter what way one looks at it, it appears that the young male has nothing to gain and everything to lose by courting an older female.

Now, of course, I have twisted the words of the writer in *Women*. The editorial comment did not refer to genetic or reproductive usefulness at all. It said "sexual usefulness," no doubt meaning usefulness as a sex partner. Indeed, there is no reason a female of fifty or sixty or seventy should not be as good a sex partner as a younger one. Many older women are probably much better sex partners than many younger ones. But our wants and desires don't always follow logic, except, as I've mentioned many times, evolutionary logic. The sometimes observed desire of women for older men and the almost universally observed desire of men for younger women probably do not relate very strongly to logic as we commonly think of it, cultural teachings, or even the male's concern about his waning virility. The preferences are probably encoded in the genetic material we have inherited from our successful ancestors.

The reader may feel that my claim of men preferring younger women is off base given the findings of Pietropinto and Simenauer (1978). I'm aware that in their book *Beyond the Male Myth* these writers interpret their data to show "that men are not as preoccupied with youth as women might tend to think, bombarded as they are with Madison Avenue copy that extols the importance and beauty of youth" (p. 138).

What about this? Have I overstated or misstated the case for male preference of younger women? Or have Pietropinto and Simenauer misinterpreted their data? I believe the latter to be true.

These investigators asked the following question of the men in their survey: "How do you feel about having sex with older women?" Men were asked to check one of these answers (per cent of responses are also given below):

1. Age does not matter at all. 38.2
2. The woman must be my age or younger. 16.4
3. The woman could be five years older, not more. 16.3

4. Age doesn't matter, but she must not look older.   12.8
5. The woman could be ten years older, not more.   11.3
6. Prefer an older woman.   3.5

Let's take a careful look at these choices. My guess is that the most popular answer would have been something like, "I prefer younger women, but I'm not going to turn down an opportunity with one my age or older if she turns me on." Notice that the man who feels this way does not have the chance to express his feelings. He only has the choices listed above, most of which have strong qualifiers.

The conclusion from these data that males are not very preoccupied with youth raises the suspicion that the writers carefully tailored the questionnaire to conform with a point they decided they wanted to make long before the study was conducted. Their questionnaire, data, and conclusions are much like asking Scotch drinkers if they are willing to drink Clan MacGregor, finding that a majority say "yes," and then concluding that they don't prefer Chevis Regal.

From my vantage point, all the data support the position that males, in general, prefer to have sex with young women.

Maternal Behaviors

Motherhood is in trouble, and it ought to be. A rude question is long overdue: Who needs it? The answer used to be (1) society and (2) women. But now, with the impending horrors of overpopulation, society desperately *doesn't* need it. And women don't need it either. Thanks to The Motherhood Myth—the idea that having babies is something that all normal women instinctively want and need and will enjoy doing—they just think they do.

The notion that the maternal wish and the activity of mothering are instinctive or biologically predestined is baloney. Try asking most sociologists, psychologists, psychoanalysts, biologists—many of whom are mothers—about motherhood being instinctive; it's like asking department-store presidents if their Santas are real. "Motherhood—instinctive?" shouts distinguished sociologist/author Dr. Jessie Bernard. "Biological destiny? Forget biology! If it were biology, people would die from not doing it."

"Women don't need to be mothers any more than they need spaghetti," says Dr. Richard Rabkin, a New York psychiatrist. "But if you're in a world where everyone is eating spaghetti, thinking they need it and want it, you will think so too. Romance has really contaminated science. So-called instincts have to do with stimulation. They are not things that well up inside of you" [Rollin, 1972, p. 59].

This kind of screaming militancy may have some value in spite of its pathetic naïveté about biology and psychology. I say it may have value because there are no doubt some females who do not want children, never have dreamed about having them, and do not associate any "personal fulfillment" with them. These women should be able to feel free to make their decision without the traditional pressures exerted on "un-mothered" females. To that extent, I can see something in Betty Rollin's diatribe.

But to characterize the instinctive component of the activity of mothering as biological baloney shows much greater daring than it does scientific sophistication. At the present time, there simply are no data available at all that can allow us to make strong statements about the nonexistence of the "mothering instinct" in humans. Any knowledgeable person will say, "The jury is still out." Furthermore, evolutionary logic and what little data we do have support a view that the activity of mothering *does* have an instinctive component. Certainly, until the jury returns, the safe route is to go with the logic and the data even though they are sketchy.

Whenever investigators have asked people what they prefer or what they think ought to be the case, women overwhelmingly say the female, rather than the male, should be primarily concerned with home and family (for example, Blake, 1974, p. 143). And no one questions the fact that this is, indeed, the way things are the world over. Women play a much greater role in the nurture and care of children than do men (Mead, 1949).

I am, of course, raising the same argument I have before concerning several other issues. When we can make the whole world our laboratory, comparing peoples who have been separated for thousands of years, and we find a universal custom, the onus of argument hangs on the one who claims that this universal custom just happened to be learned.

But for those who find this point of no consequence, there does exist at least one "laboratory type" experiment that seems to provide considerable support to the view of instinctive maternal behavior in humans. Robert Endleman (1977) reported in the *Annals of the New York Academy of Sciences* data that are difficult to interpret any other way.

In the traditional Israeli kibbutzim, established in the early 1900s, children were placed, as infants when they returned from the hospital with their mothers, in collective houses, to be raised by caretakers. These children remained in such collectives right through adolescence. Parents and children, of course, spent special times together and usually had regular visits, once a day, in the parents' apartments. But the nitty-gritty of caring for children was not performed by the parents.

In recent years, however, more and more women (researchers agree that the impetus has not come from men) have pushed for, and obtained, the opportunity to raise their children in their own homes. Endleman points out that paradoxically this means even more work for these mothers, who have the task not only of raising their own children but who also must continue doing their share of the kibbutz work.

One must certainly wonder why this change is coming about. Are these women who want to raise their own children perhaps captives of the "family tradition" because of their early experiences? Hardly. The fact that these women were themselves raised in the collectives argues strongly against the "cultural" view of their present behavior. The women who are now raising their own children—as a result of their own "drive for this change" (Endleman, 1977, p. 609)—never experienced a nuclear family. Many of them were second and third generations of collective child-rearing.

If this example tells us anything about the effects of culture, it tells us that its effects on this particular pattern of behavior are quite weak. Even though the learning history was not there and the present reinforcement system makes it much more work to both raise the kids and do the required work, these women are electing *out* of the collective plan.

It is of some interest to look at the reasons the women give when they are asked "why," but admittedly we don't learn much. Endleman tells us that some of these women claim that the ideological justifications for the communal system were built on "misguided notions of human psychology." Now, what in the world does that mean? Many other young mothers who have their children at home simply say, "It's more natural." Not much help there either.

No, we do not learn much from these responses. But we never do when we ask a person to justify a behavior that is lodged in his guts rather than in his logic. The comments are typical of those we get when we ask people why they have sex, smoke, or eat apple pie: "Because I enjoy it, that's all." By saying "It's more natural" or "It's closer to what human psychology is like," these Israeli women are communicating "I enjoy it more . . . it makes me feel good." As I said early in this book, what makes us feel good is probably often what is encoded in our genes.

The phenomenon outlined here has a remarkable similarity to what animal trainers Keller and Marian Breland found in some of their operant conditioning programs. You may recall from Chapter 2 that these are the people who fought a four-teen-year running battle with instinct until they finally decided to incorporate the concept into their own theories. In their article "The Misbehavior of Organisms," one of their examples is particularly instructive as an analogy to what might be called "instinctive drift" among the kibbutz women. Since this example involves pigs, I am constrained to say that the only analogy I'm referring to is that involving the surfacing of instinctive behaviors.

> . . . a pig was conditioned to pick up large wooden coins and to deposit them in a large "piggybank." The coins were placed several feet from the bank and the pig required to carry them to the bank and deposit them, usually

four or five coins for one reinforcement. . . . Pigs condition very rapidly . . . and in many ways are among the most tractable animals we have worked with. However, this particular problem behavior developed in pig after pig, usually after a period of weeks or months, getting worse every day. At first, the pig would eagerly pick up one dollar, carry it to the bank, run back, get another, carry it rapidly and neatly, and so on, until the ratio was complete. Thereafter, over a period of weeks the behavior would become slower and slower. He might run over eagerly for each dollar, but on the way back, instead of carrying the dollar and depositing it simply and cleanly, he would repeatedly drop it, root it, drop it again, root it along the way, pick it up, toss it up in the air, drop it, root it some more, and so on . . . he finally went through the ratios so slowly that he did not get enough to eat in the course of a day. . . . The patterns to which the animals drift require greater physical output and therefore are a violation of the so-called "law of least effort" [Breland and Breland, 1961, pp. 683–84].

When I was thinking about the kibbutz women, my attention was drawn particularly to the concluding statement in the above quote from the Brelands. From all that we can tell, the Israeli women who chose, even pressured the system, to have their children underfoot were operating in opposition to the "law of least effort." Furthermore, since infancy they had been trained to accept the "easier" system. Yet they still chose to raise their own children "because it's more natural."

Keller and Marian Breland concluded—reluctantly, they say —"that the behavior of *any* [my italics] species cannot be adequately understood, predicted, or controlled without knowledge of its instinctive pattern, evolutionary history, and ecological niche" (1961, p. 684). As card-carrying behaviorists, they found this admission very distressing. Nevertheless, as scientists they saw no other way to interpret the data. I have little doubt that a truly objective scientist (if there exists such a thing) would be pushed toward a similar conclusion concerning the "misbehavior" of the kibbutz mothers.

How does any of this fit into evolutionary biology? Can we see any selective advantage the nurturing and care of children might offer to females that it does not offer to males? Indeed there is.

There is a difference of major importance among mothers and fathers that relates strongly to the survival of offspring. Mothers have breasts that usually keep infant offspring alive during their early months; fathers don't. Again, think back to that 99 per cent of our history before foundling homes, formulas, and like came into existence. In the wild, infant sucklings abandoned by both parents weren't likely to survive at all. Similarly, sucklings abandoned by their mothers would also have it rough, unless, of course, the father could find and persuade some other milk-producing female to provide nourishment for the little one. Infants abandoned by their fathers, however, did not face such serious problems. They may have suffered from the absence of another provider and protector in the family, but they surely wouldn't be as badly off as the infant with no source of food at all.

Furthermore, as I have said before, by the time a baby is born, the female has a far greater investment in that offspring than does the male. Hence, mother-child bonding during nurturance becomes very important if that investment is to be protected. Throughout much of our history, mothers who easily abandoned their offspring allowed their genes an unlikely future. On the other hand, those females who stuck with their offspring through all manner of difficulties enhanced their genetic survival considerably. For reasons mentioned above, males also should invest time in their children, but not so consistently.

Females wanting to care for infants on the basis of genetic selection? Not nearly as preposterous as Betty Rollin would have us believe. Not preposterous at all. Rather, the view squares with evolutionary logic, extensive other-species data, and the limited human data available.

In this chapter, I have suggested that we consider a genetic basis for the double standard, for the male attraction to female curves, for the differences between male and female sexual arousal through vision, for the attraction of older men to younger women and vice versa, and for the desire, especially on the part of females, to invest themselves in the raising of children. Other hypotheses about sex differences have also been suggested in the sociobiological literature, and still more could no doubt be generated by even a cautious imagination. I've presented these because they seem to be among the most reasonable—and provocative.

11

Exceptions, Emotions, and Ethics

But I Know a Woman Who . . .

Yes, and I know a man who . . . Lest the reader miss the point of this book by rolling around in his brain all the counterinstances he can think of, let's address the problem of exceptions. I'll never cease to be surprised when I hear someone attempt to disprove a generality by pointing to an exception.

Shortly after the surgeon general's report concerning the harmful effects of smoking, someone said to me, "How can smoking be harmful? Look at Winston Churchill. All his life he smoked those big cigars and he lived until he was in his eighties." That's the kind of thinking I'm referring to. You know a woman who can't seem to get enough sex. And I know a man who never looks twice at a good-looking pair of legs. What does that prove? Nothing at all. In the social sciences we see all kinds of exceptions to our rules. And these in no way detract from our generalities because we all expect these exceptions to occur.

Rain is forecast for tomorrow. But instead the sun shines. Does that mean we should disband the weather service? Driving while intoxicated causes accidents. But you made it safely home last night when you could hardly keep your eyes focused. Does that exception mean we should wipe from the books all DWI

laws? You know a man who always floors his accelerator on
the highways, and he hasn't been killed yet. Does that mean
whoever said "speed kills" made a mistake?

This all sounds kind of silly, doesn't it? It is the generalities
that guide our lives and keep us out of trouble. If we went by
the exceptions, we probably wouldn't live very long. Years ago
I read of a man who fell from an airplane without a parachute,
and after landing in a freshly plowed field, he lived to tell of his
experience. Only a fool would pattern his life after exceptions.
If I jump out of an airplane, you can be quite sure I'll have a
parachute on.

I could go on and on with examples and still there would be
some people who would attempt to disprove the generalities
stated in the previous chapters of this book by pointing to one,
or a dozen, or several dozen exceptions. That's okay. Truth
doesn't really care whether or not we believe in it. My concern
is that we at least attempt to play the science game by the current rules. And to help the individual who isn't used to this
game, I'll point out some of the reasons for the exceptions we
see.

WHY THE EXCEPTIONS?

Overlapping distributions. Anytime the statement of a rule is
based on overlapping distributions, there will be many individual exceptions. Let's start with a simple example: On the average, men are taller than women. You know a man five-one and
I know a woman six-one. Of course. But on the average men
really are taller than women. The distributions of males and females on height probably look something like this:

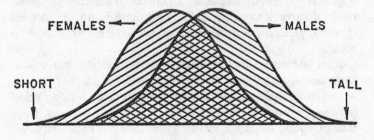

Here's another one: On the average, people who smoke two packs a day don't live as long as people who don't smoke. The distributions may look like this:

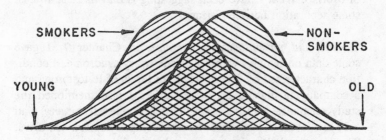

AGE AT DEATH

Obviously, there are a lot of people who smoke and live many years longer than even the *average* person who doesn't smoke. Still the statement of averages holds, and if you smoke and are interested in longevity of life, you will give some serious thought to quitting.

Now back to our topic: human sexual behaviors. Males have a stronger sex drive than females. The distributions might look something like this:

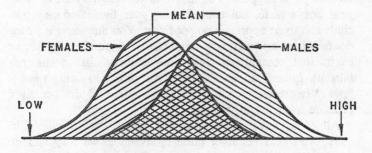

AMOUNT OF DRIVE

If so, some females have more drive than the average male. And some males have a weaker drive than the average female. But the general statement clearly holds.

In summary, overlapping distributions provide exceptions to the rule. The more separation between the distributions, the fewer the exceptions, and the greater the amount of overlap, the greater the number of exceptions. For the sex differences hypothesized in the previous chapters, we don't know the shape of the distribution for either sex, nor do we know the amount of overlap. What I have been suggesting is that there is at least some separation between means.

Genetic and physiological anomalies. In Chapter 7, I gave some data on females with polycystic ovary syndrome, a condition characterized by excessively high levels of testosterone and accompanying high levels of sex drive. I also mentioned the study on males who, as a result of hypopheseal surgery, had very low levels of testosterone and accompanying low sex drive. There are probably dozens of similar conditions, as yet undiscovered, that cause exceptions. But again, these exceptions do not detract from the broad statements that can be made.

Conflicting motivations. As I mentioned in Chapter 4, overt behavior is a function of the interaction of many different motivations. There are males and females who vow celibacy, and many who keep these vows. Does that mean they have no sexual desires? Obviously not. Other factors in their lives outweigh the values they attached to sexual activity; hence, that particular lifestyle is adopted. You may find yourself very attracted to your boss's mate, but concerns for your livelihood may preclude any overt approach on your part. You may have a strong desire for a variety of sex partners, but a moral, religious, or contractual commitment may forever deny that desire fulfillment. In such a case the value you attach to doing what is "right" is greater than the value you attach to the perceived pleasure from sexual variety.

All of us have motivations that create conflict within us daily. And as a result of these motivations, we may end up looking like exceptions to a variety of rules.

Environmental and species-specific pressures. When the environmental pressures are great enough, entire groups will adopt practices that may yield exceptions to the norm as represented by all groups combined. We have seen, for example, that in the vast majority of both human and animal societies, polygyny is practiced. Yet, in some, monogamy is the rule. Why this exception?

Monogamy is practiced by over 90 per cent of the known species of birds (Barash, 1977, p. 160), a fact that might be explained by very high metabolic rate coupled with the relative helplessness of the young at birth. It has been suggested that often one parent could not provide the quantity of food necessary to keep a brood alive; hence, by working together, both parents enhance the survival of their baby genes.

Mammals, on the other hand, are largely polygynous, possibly because the females nourish their young with milk, and the direct involvement of the male with the offspring is less important.

How might we explain monogamous practices in humans. Several ways: First, under some climatic and soil conditions (for example, where food is not plentiful), a monogamous mating with a double standard (additional copulations allowed for the male) might result in the best benefit-cost ratio for human males. Human infants have a long period of helplessness, much longer than that of any other mammals. Hence, their survival may be considerably enhanced under certain conditions by having both parents as providers and protectors.

But there are other possibilities also. Humans are unique among mammals in the extent to which they can use verbalization and tools (weapons). Humans can formulate plans, make contracts, and do all sorts of things nonverbal creatures cannot do. And it may be that this unique ability has often led to a dispersal of power and monogamous mating patterns.

Consider, for example, the langur monkeys in India. In a troop, one dominant male does essentially all of the breeding while the nonbreeding males stay in peripheral groups until the harem master is too old to beat off competitors. When he is defeated, a new male takes over.

If this were a group of humans (even primitive ones), it is not at all difficult to imagine the group of nonbreeding males planning a coup with a contract that they would share the spoils. This idea is reminiscent of Freud's version of the primal horde and the beginning of totemism. Freud suggests that in our primal state, small social groups existed in which a violent, jealous father kept all the females for himself, driving away the growing sons. Then,

> One day the expelled brothers joined forces, slew and ate the father, and thus put an end to the father horde. Together they dared and accomplished what would have remained impossible for them singly. Perhaps some advance in culture, like the use of a new weapon, had given the feeling of superiority [Freud, 1918, p. 183].

It is hard for me to imagine that one or a few males could hold out very long in a human society if they tried to corner *all* of the females for themselves. And, indeed, we do not find this happening. In all human polygynous societies, the majority of the males do have access to females. And the more evenly distributed the political power the more evenly spread are the females.

Mistaken imputations. All of the above possibilities are suggested to explain the exceptions we observe in *behavior patterns*. But overt behaviors are not really the theoretical focus of this book. The sex differences we've mainly been talking about are the internal desires and feelings. And those, of course, we can only measure indirectly.

I have said males generally desire sex more than females do. And one may counter my statement by pointing to a woman who *seeks out and has sex* more often than most males. The behavior we see may or may not reflect sexual desire. It is possible that she is crazy for attention or company and she likes sex about as well, or as poorly, as most other females.

An acquaintance of mine said she invited a single man for dinner and he refused. Her comment was, "Evidently, he doesn't want any sex."

How do we know whether or not he wanted sex? The woman was very attractive. If instead of inviting him to dinner, she had said, "Come over tonight and make love to me," he might have said, "Sure." We don't know what was going through his mind when she invited him to dinner. He may have thought she had wedding bells in her mind and he wanted no part of it.

The point is that we can never judge internal motives by observing single examples of external behavior. Only by observing groups of individuals, across a wide variety of conditions, can we arrive at conclusions about motives.

BUT ISN'T ALL STEREOTYPING BAD?

With all the exceptions we see, and broadly overlapping distributions, isn't it very poor practice to make any statements that will stereotype members of these groups? After all, we can never predict with accuracy for any individual, yet that individual must wear the mantle of the stereotype until it is either proven or disproven.

Are stereotypes all bad? Absolutely not. Stereotypes are the stuff of prediction, without which we would have a very difficult time getting through life. In the inanimate world, we make stereotypic statements all the time: Don't buy a used car; they have a lot of transmission trouble. If you do buy one, of course, you may have no trouble at all. Still you seek this kind of advice. When is the best time to go to Disneyworld? Go in September or October when the crowds are low. Of course, you may show up on the most crowded day in October during the past five years. Still you ask.

As far as behavior is concerned, stereotypes abound. Don't feed the bears. They are likely to bite. A stereotypic statement if ever I heard one. Many bears won't bite. If you see a snake in the woods, don't touch it. Stereotypes. Most snakes won't hurt you.

Suppose you tell a young woman not to go into a certain part of town by herself at night because she is likely to get raped or robbed. And she says, "Shame on you. You are stereotyping all the people in that part of town. I don't believe in stereotypes. I'll go anywhere I please." You would certainly shake your head in disbelief. Yet you may be inclined to shake your finger at me for the stereotypic statements I've made about males and females.

Every day of our lives we make predictions about people based on stereotypes relating to their ages, jobs, cultural background, sex, educational level, and a host of other variables. Graduate schools make a lot of predictions from grade point average and a few test scores. And, of course, they make some mistakes. But don't count on any radical changes. At the present time, these scores provide the most economical ways of predicting success in graduate school. Job applicants of all types are stereotyped based on their aptitude scores. And, of course, these scores don't correlate perfectly with job performance. Mistakes are made. Yet we do it and will continue because it pays off.

Social scientists have convinced us that stereotypes are bad because sometimes they can be very damaging. I certainly would not deny that. But that doesn't mean I'm going to stereotype all stereotypes by calling all stereotypes bad. That would be the height of logical inconsistency.

I said above that stereotypes are the stuff of prediction, without which we would have a tough time getting through life. Sexual stereotypes are no exception. Used correctly, they can save us a great deal of grief. If ignored, they may exact a price. The teen-age girl who hitchhikes alone because she doesn't accept stereotypic warnings about male sexual behavior is likely to learn a lot about stereotypes.

Come up with all the exceptions you can find. Argue that stereotypes are wrong. Still the accepted rules of the science game tell us that the positions that have data to back them up should be preferred over those that don't. Until or unless data can be produced to contradict the sex differences projected in the previous chapters, we cannot easily dismiss them.

But It's Unfair

"It isn't fair that men should be aroused by curves!" a woman with a terrible figure might say.

"It's unfair that men should not want the relationship as much as we do," cries the as-yet-unmarried twenty-year-old female.

And the older woman complains, "Why should those dirty rascals get so turned on by young bodies? We oldsters matter too. It's unfair!"

Of course it's unfair. No denying that. It's also unfair that women should be attracted to men with power or fame. Many men have neither. It's unfair that athletic prowess and muscular build pick up eggs on the beach while the ninety-eight-pound weakling gets only sand kicked in his face.

It's unfair that females should control the mating game and that males should have to do their dance. Because of this control females possess, there are a greater number of males who get left out completely than there are females who do. Among females, the homely, the retarded, the crippled, the handicapped, almost all can have sex if they want it and are allowed the opportunity. Indeed, in institutions for the handicapped (physically, mentally, and emotionally) one of the major problems staff members struggle with is how to keep the females from "being taken advantage of" by sexually aggressive males. Among handicapped males, the story is far different. Rarely does a seriously handicapped male have any heterosexual outlet unless he can rent a prostitute. Barash (1977, p. 156) tells us that the "disparity between the 'haves' and the 'have nots' is usually greater among males than among females" throughout the animal world.

But then whoever said genes care about fairness? It is unfair that children should be born with genetic conditions that cause retardation, and sensory and motor problems. It's unfair that a genetic condition like Huntington's chorea makes men in the prime of their life go crazy and then slowly kills them. And then there are the silly little unfairnesses, like the fact that my genes made my hair fall out while I was in my twenties, while the genes of the guy across the hall left him with a full, thick head of hair.

I agree. It is unfair. Hopefully, some of these things we can change. Some, we probably shall not be able to change. Until we know how to effect the changes, we must no doubt continue to live in an unfair world. Truth may not be fair, but is a lie any easier to live with?

But Can't We Change Things by Practice?

This question needs attention. It has come up many times as I have discussed this manuscript with reviewers.

Yes, we can change "things" by practice. We can change our own behaviors, and by example and education, we can influence the behavior of our children. *But we cannot change genetic material or genetic predispositions by practice.* And that is the issue most reviewers addressed. They wanted to know whether or not by struggling to become more like each other, men and women could eventually produce children who would inherit more compatible traits.

The answer, according to the most widespread genetic theory, is "No." The inheritance of acquired characteristics, proposed by the French scientist Jean Lamarck in the early nineteenth century, once received a lot of attention, but no longer enjoys credibility among biologists. Lamarck's idea was that by practice, animals could pass on genetically what they had acquired—that is, the individual who regularly exercised to develop big muscles would have muscular children.

"Not so," say today's geneticists. Genetic material changes only by mutation (accident) or by recombination of genes from the gene pool. Neither has anything to do with practice. Giraffes did not develop long necks by stretching their necks to reach leaves on trees. Rather, current theory assumes that those giraffes who "happened" to have longer necks were able to survive better during periods when food was scarce, and they were the ones who reproduced. Shorter-necked giraffes didn't survive as well during the scarce times and hence were less likely to pass on their genes.

For sake of a behavioral example, suppose you and I are identical twins, inheriting identical genes. And suppose those genes give us a trait for high levels of activity or energy. We are adopted by two different families. My family is passive, relaxed, and easygoing. Most of my life they encourage me to slow down and enjoy myself. Your family, by contrast, is hard-driving and superproductive. You are always being told to get off the sofa and do something worthwhile. After years of such differential training, it is reasonable to expect that you would be more active than I. But if we both had children, our children are *equally* likely to inherit a tendency toward high levels of activity (ignoring, of course, the genetic contribution of our spouses).

In like manner, African tribes who for generations have stretched their necks with elaborate neck braces continue to have children with normal-sized necks. And generations of foot-binding in the Orient have never produced people who naturally have tiny feet.

Practice will make a difference in the person practicing, but genetically based "predispositions" will only change across generations by genetic accident. Those accidents we cannot yet control.

Ethical Implications

The sociobiologists have really taken their lumps. Unfairly, I think. There are some very angry individuals around who seem to lose all intellectual control when the words "instinct" or "genetic" are mentioned. A cool mind may not need the following comments, and a distraught one is not likely to receive their message. Hence, the words may be wasted. Nevertheless, the *Zeitgeist* compels us to defend ourselves against popular foolishness.

BIOLOGICAL DOESN'T MEAN MORAL OR IMMORAL

Ethical systems attempt to define for us what is good and bad from a moral standpoint. They tell us when we should pat ourselves on the back and when we should browbeat ourselves with guilt. Very important are these systems. It has been suggested that ethical systems form the fragile glue that holds complex social systems together. And that may be true. In a presidential address to the American Psychological Association in 1975, Donald Campbell even suggested that some of the kinds of ethical systems that exist may be around because they play a very important role in the survival of the species. Personally, I subscribe to the view that we can't do without them.

Biology, on the other hand, often tells us what enhances or detracts from our chances of survival, but it doesn't solve ethical dilemmas for us because it doesn't help us determine what is good or bad.

It is true that some scientists have expressed the opinion that our system of ethics should be built on scientific knowledge. But these scientists are quite mistaken. Science only tells us how best to reach a certain goal. It cannot tell us what goal to reach.

But doesn't science tell us what preserves human life? Yes, indeed it does. But before one starts using the tools of science to increase human viability, one must adopt the position that humans are worth it. Science can't tell us that.

Am I being silly? Not at all. When the earth as a whole is considered, one might well argue that our planet would be better off without humans. We are the ones who pollute, build hydrogen bombs, destroy the ozone layer, and the like. Humans may very well bring an end to life on earth well before it would have to end. Is human existence good or bad? Science certainly can't answer such a question. We *begin* by asking and answering that question. Then we use what science knows to help us reach our goal: in this case, to either annihilate human life or to preserve it.

GENETIC DOESN'T MEAN "SHOULD"

Maybe biological science and the other sciences can't help us pin a formal label of moral or immoral, good or bad, ethical or unethical on behaviors. But by saying some behaviors are genetically based, aren't we implying, at least, that people have a right to do these things or that these behaviors should be allowed? For example, if males really do have an instinctive propensity toward "variety" and females have one toward "relationship," doesn't that imply that the double standard is okay? Don't we believe that males and females should be allowed to do what is "natural" for them to do?

No such implication can be made at all. By virtue of their

high androgen levels, males are more aggressive than females—throughout the animal kingdom. By nature, little boys have more "snakes" and "puppy dogs' tails" in them than little girls do. Does that mean we should have different assault laws for males and females? Most of us would say, "No."

While we are on the topic of aggression, it should be pointed out that from an evolutionary standpoint, a certain amount of aggression has great survival value. On the whole, the most passive animals didn't compete very well for the necessities that lead to longevity and many children. From all the logic we can muster, bolstered by the results of much experimentation with lower animals, we would have to say that much of the aggression we see in the world has genetic components. Does the position that aggression is "natural" imply that we should be allowed to beat up or kill our competitors? Of course not. Such an argument is absurd.

Yet this is precisely the argument people make when they say "genetic" implies "should." Calling some behavioral predispositions innate certainly doesn't mean we should condone them. What genetics does tell us about the double standard is that it has been around a very long time, is not superficial, and may be very difficult to wipe out. It does not say we should not try to modify the double standard. Evolutionary biology tells us that males are going to be less happy with monogamous mating than will females, but it does not tell us what should be the cultural standard or even what will bring the most happiness given our present terribly complex world.

GENETIC DOESN'T MEAN DETERMINED

Perhaps you can agree with me on the above points. Having a biological base doesn't mean a behavior is good. Having a biological base doesn't even mean it should be condoned. But shouldn't the behavior at least be excused? After all, if desires are encoded in our genes, doesn't that mean we have no control over our behavior?

No, "genetic" certainly doesn't mean "determined," in spite of the efforts of some highly vocal, politically motivated individuals to argue that it does. A group calling itself "Science for the People" throws the term "biological determinism" around very loosely in attacking sociobiology. Sometimes their statements are simply false. For example, they list the notable sociology writers and then state, "All would have us believe that our behavior is biologically determined and therefore immutable" (*Science for the People,* 1976, p. 9). The truth is that such writers have made it clear that genes account for only part of the variance for any behavior. Our behaviors are not "immutable"; they can be influenced and changed by nonbiological factors.

At other times, these writers show an incredible inability (or unwillingness) to integrate the ideas presented in their own articles. For example, the core members of this group (see Schneider, Boucher, Hansen, Noonan, Risch, and Vandermeer, 1977) admit that "obviously all behaviors have a genetic component" (p. 436). But in the same article, they imply that behaviors cannot have a genetic component because genetic influence equals genetic control (which they don't believe in):

> The old notion that behavior is controlled by genes has been resurrected in new and often subtler forms. No longer is it stated that genes control behavior. Now behavior is limited as a result of "genetic tendencies." The distinction between the two statements is frequently emphasized, but is it really meaningful? [pp. 435–36].

Of course the distinction is meaningful. In Chapter 2, I presented the view that our genes produce certain desires. Genes often tell us what feels good, or what has reinforcing value. Our genes have built us so that when certain conditions occur in our bloodstreams, for example, we want food. That want is clearly biologically based. And it clearly has evolutionary advantage. But that doesn't mean that we have no control or choice about whether or not to eat. Gandhi said "no" to that biological urge many times in order to better the lives of his people. I know of no behavioral scientist who would deny that the basic sexual drive is biologically based. Yet people say "no" to this drive regularly. Some males and females live long, productive lives without having sex at all.

The influence of genes, or "genetic tendencies," does not imply genetic control or biological determinism suggested by Schneider and his colleagues. At the present time, pronouncements from Science for the People are politically, not scientifically, motivated, hopelessly naïve concerning the issue of determinism, and not worth the attention of a serious reader. The group is mentioned here only because they are so vocal on this one issue.

"Genetic" doesn't mean "determined." Nor does "determined" necessarily have anything to do with genetics. It is of interest to note that the most vigorous and outspoken defenders of behavioral determinism today are the behaviorists, not the biological evolutionists. Skinner, who has very little to say about instincts, is the most articulate spokesman for the determinist camp. Even though I consider myself a libertarian and I disagree with Skinner, I applaud his systematic, internally consistent position on behavioral determinism. Unlike the spokesmen for Science for the People, Skinner has done his homework.

The behavioral determinists say our behaviors are totally and completely determined by the interaction of our biological "givens" with our environment, present and past. We have no real choices at any time in our lives. If any position should excuse behaviors, this position should excuse them all. And indeed, it has often been used in courts for just such purposes.

In the famous Leopold and Loeb trial in Chicago in 1924, Clarence Darrow appealed a number of times to the doctrine of determinism as a reasonable defense for the "thrill" slaying of fourteen-year-old Bobby Franks (see Darrow, 1957, pp. 55–80). Later, in speaking to the prisoners at the Cook County Jail, Darrow said:

> I do not believe that people are in jail because they deserve to be. They are in jail simply because they cannot avoid it on account of circumstances which are entirely beyond their control and for which they are in no way responsible. . . . If you will look at the question deeply enough and carefully enough, you will see that there were circumstances that drove you to do exactly the thing which you did. You could not help it any more than we outside

can help taking the positions that we take [quoted in Dworkin, 1970, p. 1].

Darrow was not talking about genes. He was talking about circumstances. He was a thoroughbred behavioral determinist and would be embraced today by behaviorists who have little use for genes, or instincts, or nature.

The point I want to make is that for the past fifty years, determinism has been the fair-haired boy of those who don't have much truck with genetics. Although they also believe in it, the biological evolutionists have never made as much fuss over determinism. And rightly so. Genetics has little if anything to do with the question of "total determinism" as it is argued in the philosophy literature.

Shere Hite (1977) argues, ". . . there is no physically demanding male sex *drive* [Hite's italics] that forces men to pressure women into intercourse" (p. 468). I agree with her totally. Just as there is no physically demanding hunger drive that *forces* people to eat and no thirst drive that *forces* people to drink. Physiological conditions exert tremendous motivational pressures, but they present no major obstacles to the position that the "individual" ultimately decides what he will do.

The arguments of free will vs. determinism are rich and fascinating, but they are quite independent of the issue of nature vs. nurture.

DIFFERENCE DOESN'T NECESSARILY IMPLY INFERIOR OR SUPERIOR

Biological doesn't mean moral or amoral. Natural doesn't mean desirable. And genetic doesn't mean determined. But don't we still run the risk of labeling people inferior by pointing out differences?

Not necessarily. We do the labeling; biology does not. Females have breasts and males don't. Which sex is inferior? Inferior for what? If the task is giving milk to infants, the male is inferior. But if rapid swimming is the task, extra baggage may provide a handicap. Hence, big breasts might make females inferior. Biology doesn't tell us which sex is inferior. It only tells us what the differences are.

I have said loud and clear that males have a stronger sex drive than females do. Which sex is inferior? In a situation where lots of sex is available, the male will probably have more fun. But in a situation where sex is unavailable, the female will probably have an easier time of it. I don't have the foggiest notion about what sex drive has to do with superiority or inferiority.

Some people have larger appetites for food than others. Does that mean that they are superior individuals? We could go on and on with absurd examples. The point is that "different" doesn't necessarily mean better or worse. It means simply "different."

Biological evolution seems to strew our pathway with knotty problems: how to account for exceptions, how to deal with our emotions, how to square what appears to be biological truth with philosophical and ethical issues. But these problems appear only because of our unwillingness to apply to these issues the same kind of careful thinking we used to generate the very hypotheses that worry us.

12

Putting It Together

The Price We Pay

The clear smiling lake woo'd to bathe in its deep,
A boy on its green shore had laid him to sleep;
Then heard he a melody
Flowing and soft,
And sweet as when angels are singing aloft.

And as thrilling with pleasure he wakes from his rest,
The waters are murmuring over his breast;
And a voice from the deep cries,
"With me thou must go, I charm the young shepherd,
I lure him below."

> "Song of the Fisherboy" in *William Tell*
> (translation by Theodore Margin)

Men have never tired of fashioning expressions for this experience: the violent force by which the man feels himself drawn to the woman, and, side by side with his longing, the dread lest through her he might die and be undone. I will mention particularly the moving expression of this dread in Heine's poem of the legendary Lorelei, who sits high on the bank of the Rhine and ensnares the boatman with her beauty.

Here once more it is water (representing, like the other "elements," the primal element "woman") that swallows up the man who succumbs to a woman's enchantment. Ulysses had to bid his seamen bind him to the mast in order to escape the allurement and the danger of the sirens. The riddle of the Sphinx can be solved by few, and most of those who attempt it forfeit their lives. The royal palace in fairy-tales is adorned with the heads of the suitors who have had the hardihood to try to solve the riddles of the king's beautiful daughter. The goddess Kali dances on the corpses of slain men. Samson, whom no man could conquer, is robbed of his strength by Delilah. Judith beheads Holofernes after giving herself to him. Salome carries the head of John the Baptist on a charger. Witches are burnt because male priests fear the work of the devil in them. Wedekind's "Earth Spirit" destroys every man who succumbs to her charm, not because she is particularly evil, but simply because it is her nature to do so. The series of such instances is infinite: always, everywhere the man strives to rid himself of his dread of women by objectifying it: "It is not," he says, "that I dread her; it is that she herself is malignant, capable of any crime, a beast of prey, a vampire, a witch, insatiable in her desires. She is the very personification of what is sinister" [Horney, 1932, pp. 348–49].

Karen Horney's reflections on the anger and dread men have toward women does little to explain it. But as she points out, such feelings have been expressed in poetry, drama, and literature as far back as we care to look. Her mentor, Sigmund Freud, also spoke of man's "innate propensity to disparage and suppress women" (1932, p. 284). Although much of the psychological world today challenges Freud's theories, rarely would one find the suggestion that he was a sloppy observer of human interaction.

Tavris and Offir (1977) begin their book *The Longest War* by asking why there should be such misunderstanding, mistrust, and enmity between the sexes. Brownmiller (1976, p. 24) speaks of man's "contempt for women." Blanchard (1974, p. 17) talks of "hate." Anthropologists describe primitive cultures in which males view females as enemies (for example,

Hippler, 1974). Fast tells us that this fear of women, this anger and distrust, accounts for the importance males attach to the fraternity of a group of their own sex. Men are likely, he points out, to feel that

> Women are dangerous. Women are a race apart. Treat them with respect, and, if you can, screw them, but be sure you can always return to the company of men—a finer, more decent company [Fast, 1972, p. 39].

I know of no one who has taken systematic verbal reports or behavioral measures concerning anger between the sexes, but from all the lore that can be put together we must conclude that negative emotions run pretty high.

Why Such Hostile Feelings on the Part of Men?

"Innocently she may drive men to madness and war" (Greer, 1972, p. 30). Germaine Greer put her finger right on the sore spot: the power of the female over the male. We saw in Chapter 9 that by virtue of her control over the scarcer genetic material, the female comes into the mating game with considerable power. She may not purposely misuse that power. She may not intend to drive men to madness or to war. But if she follows her feelings—that is, if she plays the seduction role that has been genetically advantageous to her and her ancestors—she will have the male on a set of strings, doing a dance that is mixed with excitement and anger.

> They exploit us sexually. They play a neat game of come-on, being flirtatious and warm and yielding, and we're sucked in, and at the last minute when it looks like we've got it made, they draw back. "Who, me? Oh no. Not that" [from Fast, 1972, p. 121].

The above comment by a college male expresses not just the feelings of the younger generation. Recently, a man in his mid-forties told me: "I'm going through an angry stage with women in general. I detest the games they play, especially with sex—

coming on strong and then saying, 'What kind of a girl do you think I am?' when the man makes an advance."

A female psychologist told me that when she became a careful observer she was amazed to see the extent of the power of a beautiful woman over men. She then went on, however, to say that men are more than a little foolish for letting themselves be so controlled. "It is ultimately the male's fault," she said, "for being so sexually oriented."

Not so fast. If I am thirsty and you control the spigot, am I to blame for the power you hold over me? If you haven't had anything to eat for three days, and I am the only one around with food, are you simply "weak" because of your orientation toward me and my food? If a male has a biological drive that says "plant those genes" and the female holds the key to the garden, is he at "fault" because he does whatever seems expedient to gain access to that fertile soil?

Thirst drive, hunger drive, sex drive, all are biologically based. We may be able to get our minds on other things temporarily—for example, we can forget our thirst by losing ourselves for a while in some activity—but ultimately, the nagging discomfort of thirst reasserts itself. Sex is no different. A biological drive can't be eliminated by choice. Males can elect not to dance, but they can't turn off the juices that make them want to. And it is this realization of helplessness that may generate resentfulness and anger toward the female, who does not display such a strong drive.

Even if the female never seduces him, the male still can feel anger. Why? Because he knows she has that power and he would be subject to it if she chose to exert it. This response might be similar to that adolescents often have toward their parents. Adolescent anger is very commonly directed toward parental power, even when parents do not misuse their power. The anger of the student activists during the 1960s was directed toward the power structure, to some degree, at least, merely because it was a power structure. Men are no less resentful of the fact that they are usually the beggars in the sex game.

Some readers, especially those who have never experienced much of a sex drive, may view these paragraphs as giving a comic-book quality to men's sexual desires, as if men are sex-crazed maniacs running around with terminal erections. That's not what I wish to present. But, on the other hand, I do not want to underemphasize the very strong motivating properties of sex, at least for males, that were discussed in Chapter 5. I have met males who on occasions respond to the sexual power of females with all the anger and frustration these words have portrayed. My guess is that most males, at some time in their lives, have had similar experiences.

I want to crawl out on a speculative limb and suggest that this unevenness in sexual power may account for some of the inhumane political status men have placed on women throughout history. If a man is chasing a female, it doesn't do him much good to direct his anger toward that particular female. If he were to do so, he might be cutting himself off from the very reinforcers he's dancing for.

An alternate expression of anger might take place toward the entire class of women. Because of their superior physical strength, males have long held political power—that is, the bottom line says that political power is vested in who can beat up whom. And for thousands of years, men have used that power to scheme, connive, and legislate full human rights away from women.

It is possible that men have elected to counter power with power, paying bruise for bruise. As one particularly distressed young man once said to me: "Make me beg . . . make my insides bunch up in a knot while they so casually shake their heads. . . . I wish I could make them beg. . . . I wish I could make them hurt!"

Certainly, this doesn't paint a very pretty picture of men. There is an evolutionary view of "the exploitation of females," however, that makes men look slightly more noble; hence, some of our male readers may prefer it.

A paper by Hartung (1976) has suggested that both males and females enjoy a greater genetic selection advantage by conferring more social status, power, and wealth onto their sons than onto their daughters. I mentioned earlier that the female's control of the scarcer genetic material makes the selection variance of females smaller than that of males—that is, the difference between the "haves" and the "have nots" is much greater among males than among females. Daughters, by virtue of their few precious eggs, are likely to reproduce up to capacity regardless of their social status. For sons, however, the story is quite different. Sons found undesirable by the fussy females might not get the chance to reproduce at all, whereas desirable sons—wealthy or otherwise powerful sons—might do a great deal of reproducing. The genetically wise parents then, who have any resources to pass on, should not split up those resources and divide them equally among sons and daughters. They have a greater likelihood of sprinkling their own genes plentifully around the next generation by investing power and other resources in their sons. And, indeed, this is the way the game is generally played (Hartung, 1976, p. 612).

Take your choice. The male power trip may have some genetic basis because of evolutionary advantage, or it may simply be an angry "tit for tat." Probably it's some of both.

Do Females Get Angry?

Indeed they do. But when it comes to sex, these feelings could be characterized more as disgust or disappointment than anger.

And that is not surprising. Since females control the heterosexual encounter, they should only get angry about sex if the male tries to take power into his own hands and force coitus. And when that happens, of course, they do. I don't know of an angrier book than that of Brownmiller on the subject of rape. But most of the time, rape doesn't occur. Females remain in control and have little reason to be angry about overt sexual behavior on the part of males.

Their negative feelings, in the form of disgust, seem more directed toward male ideation and desire, which appear to be deviant from prescribed social expectations. Let's face it. As they have been outlined in this book the sexual feelings of the female lie closer to those championed for centuries by Church leaders and moralists as "healthy" than are the feelings I've suggested are common among males. The female has less inclination for sexual arousal and a lower drive. Furthermore, she is more apt to be attracted to only one man and to protect the relationship at all costs. All those characteristics have been applauded in our formal sex ethic. Males, on the other hand, are more aggressive sexually, more rapid in arousal, more promiscuous in their preoccupations, and are responsive to most females. Hardly the picture of sexuality that is held up as an ideal.

As long as a male doesn't communicate his internal sex world, he's in no trouble. But if he expresses his sexuality, he becomes, by comparison with formal standards, some kind of a deviant. The female who sees his sexuality is likely to label him as such. Then she views him with disgust—the same way most of us view socially deviant people.

But there is another possible reason for female disgust. I have listened to females complain that men aren't really the way they pretend to be sexually. Rather, men are only trying to live up to a *macho* image, forcing themselves to act in sexually aggressive ways. Women who view males in this light are likely to be disgusted with them. After all, no one has much respect for an inauthentic person.

Whatever the reasons, women do get angry with men, much as they might get angry with a little boy who has not yet been socialized.

A Hurdle We Cannot Leap

To a large degree, these feelings arise on the part of both sexes because we cannot get into each other's worlds. Why does the sexually honest male seem—to the female—to be struggling to wear *macho* boots that don't fit him? Because the female generally has no idea what his real struggle is like. Don't forget, he has ten times the amount of androgens she has. The likelihood of her ever experiencing the sex drive he feels quite often is slim.

Consider Susan Brownmiller's attempt to explain the escalation of the prostitution business in Viet Nam as a result of the "underlying . . . assumption that men at war required the sexual use of women's bodies" (Brownmiller, 1976, p. 95). What she seems to be suggesting is that the men stationed in Viet

Nam didn't particularly want the services of prostitutes. Rather, higher-level powers assumed men would want the prostitutes and accordingly escalated the business of prostitution. The men who put the cash on the line were only living up to expectations.

Any man would tell you this is absurd. But I think it is reasonable for Ms. Brownmiller to attempt such an account because she is a woman. She probably never in her life has felt the desire for sex to the point that she would seriously consider going out and paying for it. Hence, she cannot conceive of that being the experience of anyone else. She is essentially locked out of the male sexual world.

From his study of the sexual attitudes of thousands of people, Kinsey concluded:

> Most males can immediately understand why most males want extramarital coitus. Although many of them refrain from engaging in such activity because they consider it morally unacceptable or socially undesirable, even such abstinent individuals can usually understand that sexual variety, new situations, and new partners might provide satisfactions which are no longer found in coitus which has been confined for some period of years to a single sexual partner. To most males the desire for variety in sexual activity seems as reasonable as the desire for variety in the books that one reads, the music that one hears, the recreations in which one engages, and the friends with whom one associates socially. On the other hand, many females find it difficult to understand why any male who is happily married should want to have coitus with any female other than his wife. The fact that there are females who ask such questions seems, to most males, the best sort of evidence that there are basic differences between the two sexes [Kinsey et al., 1953, p. 409].

Most females will probably never understand the male experience. But, of course, the converse is also true. Brownmiller (1976, p. 346) suggests that one of the myths most men hold about rape is, "If you're going to be raped, you might as well

relax and enjoy it." That idea, to the average woman, is absurd.
Women tell us that rape is an indescribable trauma.

A man simply can't understand this. He can imagine sexual
intercourse being great, good, so-so, or even neutral. But he
can't imagine it being horrible. To a man, sex is sex, and the
more the better. Bag over the head, stand in line, take turns,
sight unseen. Maybe not ideal, but better than nothing. He certainly cannot understand how or why such an experience would
be psychologically painful. If it became known that there was a
woman in town who periodically raped men, there would be a
crowd outside her door at all times.

A thirty-year-old confirmed-bachelor type once said to me,
"Things have been going well with my latest girl for the past six
months, but now she's starting to talk about marriage. It always
happens. I've never seen it fail. Why does a woman always put
marriage before anything else?" Same old story: He isn't interested in marriage, so he can't understand why she is. From an
evolutionary standpoint, she is interested in a stable, dependa-
ble, long-term relationship because that's where her genetic future lies. She feels it deeply and cannot easily dismiss the desire.

And then there is the male who said to me, "If I had a sore
back and asked for a backrub, she would do that. Why won't
she satisfy my sexual needs?"

First, she probably has no conception of what your sexual
needs feel like. But much more than that, sex for a woman is
not as neutral as giving a backrub. For her to submit to you
when she did not want to could be a very painful experience for
her psychologically. We've talked about the evolutionary reasons for this. The female who didn't feel strongly about protecting that egg until "Mr. Right" came along had a serious selection disadvantage.

A man cannot understand how a woman can smile at him,
laugh with him, want to be with him, tell him he is a fascinating, charming person, but not want to make love to him. He
can understand, of course, that she may feel she *should* not
make love to him—for a variety of social and/or moral reasons
—but he cannot understand how she cannot *want* to make love
to him and still say and do all these other things.

"Surely she is crazy," he thinks. "Or lying. That's it. She's lying. She really doesn't think I'm much of a man. She's just saying so . . . a typical woman's trick . . . perhaps to have a date . . . perhaps so a fawning man will be around enhancing her own ego. All this seductive come-on stuff she gave out all evening. For attention. That's what it was for. Not because she was attracted to me. What a sucker I've been. If she really thought I was neat, surely she would feel the same way I do about sex. Don't ever trust a woman."

By the same token, the woman cannot understand why her company can't be enjoyed for what it is. He has told her she is a fascinating, charming person too. So why not be satisfied with the fascination and the charm? Didn't they have a fun evening? Why isn't that enough? Why does his whole life have to center around sex?

"All this nonsense he gave me about thinking I'm so neat. He likes my ideas. He enjoys my company. The hell he does," she thinks. "He's only had one thing in mind all evening. All the rest were lies. He doesn't like me. He only likes my body. If he were really much of a man, he'd feel the way I do. He would want to get to know me first. Don't ever trust a man."

Disgust at the other person's selfishness, anger over being used, distrust from being duped—all these things are, quite tragically, in our own minds. We do, indeed, use our own experience as the criterion by which others should be tested. If somehow that person's words make no sense within my experience, he or she must be lying, or crazy, or both.

Piling Hurt on Hurt

Like fools bent on destroying what little understanding there might be to salvage, we press the issue and fan the flames. Men often become probing inquisitors, at one level perhaps trying to argue their way into something they want, but at another, honestly confused and exasperated because they can't comprehend how another person can be so inconsistent.

"But why?" the man will ask. "You said you like me and enjoyed being with me. Why won't you have sex with me?"

"I don't know why," responds the woman, perhaps thinking this is as stupid as being asked why she didn't like eggplant when she was a kid. "I just don't want to. There's no particular reason. I just don't want to." Her anger grows because he is unwilling to accept her simple statement that she doesn't want to. Why should she have to defend her feelings? He's not only a savage animal sexually; he hasn't even any social understanding. And so it goes.

Fortunately, there are many people who can accept differences without teasing, cajoling, or disparaging. But there are many who can't. Maybe it relates to our insecurities. The individual who is consistently in need of affirmation of his own worth may not be able to tolerate the presence of someone whose preferences make his own look inauthentic. I don't claim to know the answer. We could probably invent hundreds of hypotheses to explain these behaviors, but regardless of the reasons, the problem remains. Many people simply can't accept others who differ in desires, preferences, or wants. And this rejection is mutually magnified by piling hurt on hurt. Is it any wonder we sometimes end up hating each other?

Straightening a Few Kinks

My basic commitment to psychology is that of a scientist. I am interested in data, the "harder" the better. In most of this book I've attempted to present the best empirical evidence that relates to our sociobiological hypotheses. But when people are hurting, we often can't wait for science to tell us what should be done. This following section is a mixture of hunches, clinical lore, and lessons from personal experience working with people. It is not science, but at the moment, it is the best I have to offer.

ACCEPTING REALITY

In telling about a meeting she had with a business consultant, a client said to me, "He was very helpful and very thorough in his consultation, but I was incensed to find out that he wanted to go to bed with me."

Incensed? Why should she be incensed? Shouldn't it be a compliment that someone thinks you are attractive enough to want to bed you? Wouldn't it be far worse for her to find out that men did *not* become turned on by her? What's going on here?

The best explanation may be that she was incensed, or perhaps disgusted, with the man because of a discrepancy between her expectations and reality. She was not sexually attracted to him. Consequently, she could not understand how or why he should want to sleep with her. Kind of silly, isn't it?

How much better it would be for this woman to take a good look at herself—her physical appearance, her speech, her nonverbal manners—and then decide, "Yes, given the way men have been selected, most men are going to want to have sex with me. Some will let it be known. Some, because of moral, religious, or contractual commitments, will not let it be known. But most will at least want to. I will not be surprised, or incensed, or disgusted, when this happens. Rather, I will accept it as reality, and perhaps even be complimented by it."

Earlier in this chapter, I referred to the man in his midforties who told of his anger at the woman who plays the seduction role and then expresses shock when he makes his move. He interprets the "come-on" as sexual, and that's understandable. But reality tells us that many women will play a flirtatious, seductive role without having genital sex in mind. If this man can do it, he should attempt to recognize this reality and feel complimented that the female thought he was attractive enough to do her little dance for him.

> The possibility of reconciling the different sexual interests and capacities of females and males, the possibility of working out sexual adjustments in marriage, and the possibility of adjusting social concepts to allow for these differences between females and males, will depend upon our willingness to accept the realities which the available data seem to indicate [Kinsey et al., 1953, p. 688].

Twenty-five years ago, Kinsey told us what these realities

were. Rather, he confirmed what we already knew. And I've said nothing new in this book. I've just said it in a different way. The differences between males and females in the sexual arena are real.

In the last chapter I said we are not asked to like them. Here, I shall state that we are not asked to understand them. But we are well advised to accept them if we are to get on with the business of living. A few alternatives are outlined below only because they seem so unpalatable.

We can forget about heterosexual relationships. Because of her inability to accept males as they are, Andrea Dworkin (1974, p. 184) suggests withdrawal from men:

> Intercourse with men as we know them is increasingly impossible. It requires an aborting of creativity and strength, a refusal of responsibility and freedom: a bitter personal death. It means remaining the victim, forever annihilating all self-respect. It means acting out the female role, incorporating the masochism, self-hatred, and passivity which are central to it.

This type of thinking illustrates one possible tragic—I think—solution for people who will not or cannot accept the differences that exist. We would probably all agree with Ms. Dworkin that most of us could escape a lot of hurts if we cut out heterosexual relationships altogether. But for most of us, the hurts we would escape could nowhere near counteract the enjoyment we would be missing.

We can try to live with lies. The most commonly practiced solution, of course, is to just keep our mouths and lives closed. Because their sexual preoccupations are more discrepant with formal sexual ethics, males probably learn to be much more tight-lipped about their own sexual struggles than do females. A great deal of distress has been caused in relationships not because the male's *behavior* was out of line, but because he expressed his *desires*. You wonder why your husband or your boy friend doesn't talk to you about sex? What would happen if he did?

For many people, secrecy may be the answer. I believe firmly in a certain amount of privacy in everybody's mind. If I am your parent, your brother, your spouse, your fiancé, or your boy friend, I have no right to probe areas of your inner world you would rather keep secret. I must respect your privacy. And you must respect mine. But many times, we do share our deepest feelings and desires with those we love. If that happens and our partner is not prepared to accept the reality of differences, a great deal of needless distress may result.

A young woman said while in my office, "He's so jealous about me. He doesn't want me to look at another man, but he looks. And I know damn well what he's thinking too. It makes me feel angry. And it makes me feel hurt and inadequate. He's enough to satisfy me. Why am I not enough to satisfy him?"

Reality says you are not enough, miss. Nor is it likely that you will ever find a man to whom you will be enough. Your mate is carrying genes that won out because they kept a watchful eye on their mate and a lustful eye on the woman next door. Hence, he fences you in while his mind roves the prairie. That's the way the world is. You may find a man who will be totally faithful in his sexual behavior. There are many around. But the chances of finding one faithful in his desires are slim.

In a graduate course in psychotherapy, another professor and I were leading a discussion on marital therapy. The case under consideration was that of a man who often got himself involved in affairs with other women to the detriment of the marriage. The question came up about the nature of the relationship between this husband and his wife. The answer from the case files was that it was not the best.

A young lady in class nodded vigorously and said, "It is obvious the relationship wasn't good. If it were, there is no way he would want to have other sexual relationships."

Some people may see her comment as a bit naïve. That is not the issue. The important point is that she was expressing what she really felt inside. She could not see how she herself could want sex with another man as long as she had a good relationship with her husband. So she figured, as I have said many times, everyone else in the world is made up the same way.

It is of interest that the males in the class made no comments at all. I'm quite sure they couldn't really understand her pronouncement.

As a budding therapist, this young lady will, of course, have to broaden her understanding of the world. But regardless of her professional effectiveness, she may face considerable personal distress if she does not make some cognitive adjustments. It may be that for the rest of her life she will be very comfortable with strong monogamous feelings toward her mate, never even giving a passing thought to sex with other males. But it is highly unlikely that she will find a man who has this same attitude. If her mate learns quickly, and shares very little about his own sexual world, she may continue to live quite comfortably with falsehood. But if he does communicate his world, and she has not learned to accept the difference between her and "most men," she will surely face a lot of heartache, thinking such things as, "He doesn't love me as much as I do him. Why am I not enough to satisfy him if he is enough to satisfy me?" Better that she settle for reality now and not get hurt later.

I am reminded of the somewhat tired words that tumbled out of a graduate student one day in my office: "I've cried buckets . . . I've died a hundred deaths . . . I've gone through the agonies of hell . . . I've gotten so angry I couldn't see straight. In five very close relationships over a ten-year period the words never meant the same for the men that they meant for me. Each time I thought, 'This time it will be different. He really feels what I feel.' But always it has been the same. I've decided that men simply do not put emotions and sex together the way women do. It's evidently a fact of life I'll have to accept."

At the time of my conversation with her, I was just beginning to believe in such differences myself. She helped me along the way. But far more than that, she helped herself along the way. She is struggling to accept the differences, because she knows how desperately miserable the alternative can be.

ACCEPTING YOURSELF

One day not long ago I was discussing with a student the final draft of his dissertation. The student said, "I can't believe this is really over. After years of work, it's finally done."

"What do you plan to do now?" I asked.

"Well," he replied with a shrug, "I'm in a bind. For several years my wife and I have been planning a trip to Europe. We figured when this was all finished we would just travel for six months or so before I get heavily involved in a job."

"Sounds great," I broke in.

"But that's the problem," he went on. "I really don't want to go. I hate sight-seeing. And I'm really interested in what I'm doing here in town. I'd like to really get into my work."

I said, "Have you considered your wife going by herself, or perhaps with a friend? When she got back, you might have an even better marriage."

"Yeah, I could really go for that," he said softly. "But my wife would never do it. She's very protective of our relationship and thinks everything we do has to be done together. You know, it's funny. I really need space. She doesn't seem to need any. And she doesn't want any. It's always togetherness. I don't know whether she's afraid about our relationship, or what. She shouldn't be. We get along real well and love each other. Sometimes I really wonder about myself and feel guilty because I don't want that closeness in everything the way she does."

A somewhat similar problem, but from the female side of the fence, is seen in Margaret Rosoff's (1974) confession of great unhappiness "for years" over her failure to have orgasms in intercourse. Kinsey (1953, pp. 371–72) tells us that it is not at all uncommon for females to define themselves as inferior because of the failure to reach orgasm.

So here we have a man feeling guilty because he judges his inclinations toward romance and relationship by those of his wife. And a woman experiences distress and disappointment in herself because she judges her orgastic ability by that of her partner. How much better it would be if these people could accept themselves, not using others as a measuring stick at all for their own experiences and desires. But alas, that's pie in the sky, isn't it? We are social creatures, and to a very large degree, we cannot escape wanting to be like others. The point I wish to make here is that this problem is compounded when males use females as their criteria and when females stack themselves up against males. The experiences of the two individuals mentioned above are not unusual for their sex, but are unusual for the opposite sex. I'm suggesting that the task of accepting ourselves is made a little bit easier—it is never really easy—by at least using a criterion group in the same ballpark with us. If males understand what male sexuality is like, they will probably judge themselves as less deviant than they would if they compare themselves to the whole population, or just to females. And the same sort of thing is true for females.

RESPECTING YOUR FEELINGS

The female who doesn't have an orgasm easily should not worry about it. She has much feminine company. Many women report pleasure in coitus without orgasm. Enjoy that aspect of sex. Don't define yourself as neurotic. Don't doubt your love for your partner. He may not even be a lousy lover. Do all you can to achieve orgasm—perhaps you might consider sex therapy —but after you've tried all you know, relax and accept yourself.

The woman who has tried out promiscuity, thinking that's what all people should be able to enjoy, and who has found that the whole thing is distasteful to her, should drop out. Don't worry about trying to be something you are not. Accept yourself.

A psychotherapist in private practice recently told me that many women are now coming for counseling because they can't escape the current campaign telling them that the only fulfilled woman is the professional woman and that having and raising babies are definitely out. These women are trying to conform, but deep inside they want to have and raise babies. If that is you, do what makes you feel good. Forget the popular propaganda and accept yourself.

If you are a male who has fallen fast and hard—but your girl hasn't yet declared her love—recognize that this is normal for males. Don't judge yourself as a loser because she hasn't come your way yet. Accept yourself.

If your wife tells you every night that she could never even look at another man, and you know you've been exercising your eyeballs all day, don't feel like you are a piece of slime that slipped out from behind some rock. Just know that you have a lot of male company. Accept yourself.

It may be, of course, that none of the stereotypic things I've mentioned are true of you. You may be a woman who hates babies. Great. Accept yourself and don't have any. You may be a man who can't stand to look at any other woman but your wife. Great. Accept yourself and don't look. It's tough to be a happy deviant, but it is possible. Society can probably only tolerate so much deviance before it crumbles, but in the sexual sphere there is probably still ample room for being what makes us comfortable. I must agree with Lonnie Barbach, who tells us (1976, p. 197):

> Sexual liberation entails acceptance of your own unique sexual responses and sexuality in general, not because it conforms to external standards or solely because it provides pleasure for a partner, but because it is an intimate expression of yourself.

PROTECTING YOURSELF

"All he wants is to make love to me," she complains. "I am not going to be nothing but a sex object. I'm a complete human being. If he is not interested in all of me, including my brain, he can get lost."

"All she wants me for is to take her places and talk to her," he complains. "I am not going to be nothing but a talk object. I'm a complete human being. If she isn't interested in all of me, including my penis, she can get lost."

The common cry of the female is that she is valued only for her body. Males can also feel used, but for different reasons.

A bright professional man once told me he felt he was being intellectually raped. Women loved to spend time talking to him. They would drop by his office and consume hours of his time talking about their problems, asking his advice, and telling him how refreshing it was to be able to talk to someone who really listened and had such good ideas. But if he suggested he wanted more than the talking, he was generally treated with contempt. Intellectual rape? I suppose that's as good a term as any.

Both males and females can get mad if they feel they are being abused. If you feel that you are a sex object and you don't like it, tell your partner how you feel. You may even want to terminate the relationship. Better that than to continue to feel abused. Similarly, if you feel that you are a talk object, and you don't like it, do something about it. When you feel used, you will come to resent that individual anyway and eventually the relationship will crumble.

Let's not forget, of course, that it is possible to enjoy giving. If you can give another person something because you delight in making him or her happy, you don't run the same risk. Some females don't care a wit about sex. But they do enjoy meeting the sexual desires of their mates. Great. Enjoy giving. Again, that's doing what you enjoy doing. Some men like to be by themselves, and they don't care much for conversation. Nevertheless, they sense a need in their partners for sharing ideas. So they talk, at least they try, because of their concern for that other person's needs. Great.

There's a difference between feeling used and feeling the thrill of giving to someone you love. Give if you can, in many ways, to meet the other person's needs. But when you start feeling used, protect yourself. If you don't, you'll pay eventually. And so will the one who used you.

ACCEPTING THE OTHER PERSON

Frankly, I don't know which is more difficult; accepting yourself or accepting someone who is different from you. Both require work. In accepting others, there are several special things we can do that may make our task easier.

Listen. It is very difficult to listen, especially to a person you disagree with. Counselors have special exercises to help us learn to listen, and you may want to avail yourself of some of these. But for starters, just trying to understand what the other person is saying will help. An acquaintance once complained to me about the deterioration of her friendship with a former lover. The interchange we had illustrates, I think, what I mean when I say we often don't even try to listen to each other.

"He can't relate to me anymore on just a friendship basis. He's always thinking about sex," she complained. "Why can't a man just relate to a woman as a friend? Why do they have to think so much about sex?"

"Let me give you an analogy," I began. "I don't think it is ever possible for men and women to really understand what goes on inside the other, but maybe we can approach an understanding. Let's suppose that you stop by my house to visit around dinnertime. You've had a very busy day and had to skip lunch. I invite you in but I'm just sitting down to eat a charbroiled thick steak, baked potato with butter and sour cream, and tossed salad with . . ."

"That's enough," she cut in. "I haven't had much to eat today!"

"Okay, I'll leave out all that good stuff. Let's suppose you are sitting with me while I eat. For some crazy reason I don't offer you any. Maybe I don't have enough. Or maybe I am insensitive enough not to think about it. At any rate, I don't offer you any."

"You're terrible. Why wouldn't you offer me any?"

"Look," I said with mild exasperation, "I'm not offering you any for the sake of the illustration. I'm not that hardhearted, but I want to illustrate a point."

"Okay."

"Now, you are talking to me, and I'm eating all this good food, right? You can see the food and smell it, and you are watching me put it into my mouth. You are at least mildly hungry. Could you easily forget about the food and concentrate only on our conversation?"

"What has that got to do with sex?"

"Answer my question. Would you be aware of the food and your own hunger?"

"Of course. But that doesn't have anything to do with sex. Sex is an entirely different thing. I can talk with an attractive man and completely put sex out of my mind. I think your illustration is dumb!"

"Look, you asked me a question and I'm trying to answer it. If you think my answer is dumb, then forget it. Answer your own question. If you want to listen for a few minutes, I'll try to answer your question."

"What was my question?"

"You said, 'Why do men so often think about sex when they are with a woman?'"

"Oh, okay, go ahead with your answer."

"Now you said you would probably have a hard time just talking with me and not thinking about the food, right?"

"Right, and I also said that doesn't have anything at all to do with sex. Because food and sex are two entirely different things. Anyone who has to think about sex when he's with a woman is weak. We should be able to control our thoughts . . . to compartmentalize . . . to think about sex when the time is right and to think about other things when the time isn't right."

"Why can't you do that with the food?"

"Because food is a different thing."

"Okay, it's a different thing. But why can't you compartmentalize? Why can't you just put it out of your mind and not think about it? Why can't you just completely ignore all that stuff inside you that tells you how hungry you are?"

"I still think your illustration is dumb." She shook her head vigorously. "Sex is sex and food is food. They're two entirely different things."

She was right, of course. Sex is sex and food is food. But she was also very wrong in her assertion that anyone should be able to compartmentalize feelings. Maybe she can, and that's fine. But she was totally unwilling to accept the possibility that there are some perfectly healthy people in the world who can no more ignore sexual tugs than they can hunger pangs. She asked me a question, and I may have been offering an absurd answer. You can be the judge of that. But the distressing part, I found, was her unwillingness to even hear what I was trying to say.

Many of us may not be able to accept differences. We may not be able to understand differences. But if we are not even willing to listen, we don't give understanding or acceptance a chance.

Realize that feelings happen. In the first part of this chapter, I mentioned that thirst, hunger, and sex drive are all biologically based. There are tricks and crutches we can use to put these things out of our minds temporarily, but they come back to nag us. And their persistence no doubt has great survival value for us.

I believe we can control our behavior, and we are responsible for controlling our behavior. But we cannot as easily, perhaps not at all sometimes, control our wishes and desires. If the young lady in the above example were to come to me for help to stop smoking, she would probably be incensed if I gave her some of her own advice: "Well, why don't you just not think about smoking? Just put it out of your mind. We should be able to compartmentalize, to control our thoughts. I can watch someone smoke or smell smoke and not even think about smoking. You should be able to do this too. Anyone who can't do this is weak."

What kind of a therapist would she think I am? A dumb one, obviously. Other illustrations showing the lack of control we have over our desires are almost endless. For about ten years, I have been involved in obesity research, trying to develop procedures to help people lose weight. After a few weeks of hard work, my clients will often say, "You just don't know how hungry I am. I just crave sweets. Why, I could polish off a whole box of chocolates right now."

Maybe I should try responding to these people by saying, "Why don't you just not think about food? Just put it out of your mind. . . . Learn to compartmentalize. . . . Anyone who can't do this is weak. . . ."

From such a restricted view of human desires, the same response would be appropriate to the alcoholic who is successfully struggling to stay on the wagon but is facing a lot of psychological distress: "Just don't think about it. Learn to put it out of your mind."

The whole scene becomes kind of ridiculous, doesn't it? Of course, I do not say such things to my clients. But that is not to say that I understand their experiences. I do not understand and never will understand how people could want to suck cigarette smoke into their lungs. The experience makes me choke, cough, sneeze, and hurt. It is beyond my comprehension why anyone can't just put such things out of mind. As far as alcohol is concerned, too many drinks make me want to go to sleep. That's all. I just become very sleepy. Based on this experience, I can't for the life of me understand why anyone would jeopardize his job, his reputation, and what-have-you by continually getting drunk.

But my lack of understanding does not mean that these people do not have strong urges. And because I can easily put such thoughts out of my mind does not mean that they can.

Desires happen, urges occur, and rarely can we simply turn them off at will. Accepting others means accepting their idiosyncratic cravings as part of them and not blaming them because they are not like us. If we can realize that sexual feelings happen, we may avoid a lot of distress with those we love.

KNOW WHAT HURTS YOU AND WHAT DOESN'T

Most males find it difficult to comprehend why females are not aroused by . . . graphic representations of sexual action, and not infrequently males essay to show such materials to their wives or other female partners, thinking thereby to arouse them prior to their sexual contacts. The wives, on the other hand, are often at a loss to understand why a male who is having satisfactory sexual relations at home should seek additional stimulation in portrayals of sexual action. They are hurt to find that their husbands desire any stimulation in addition to what they, the wives, can provide, and not a few of the wives think of it as a kind of infidelity which offends them. We have seen considerable disturbance in some of the married histories because of such disagreements over the husband's use of erotic objects, and there are cases of wives who instituted divorce proceedings because they had discovered that their husbands possessed photographs or drawings of sexual action" [Kinsey et al., 1953, p. 663].

Most males are aroused by visual stimuli. And we've seen an evolutionary logic as to why this should be so. Does a husband's preoccupation with erotic pictures harm the wife?

"No, it doesn't harm me, but it sure does hurt me," a female may reply.

Strictly speaking, it does not hurt you. You hurt you. Psychology is indebted to Albert Ellis for pointing out to us so clearly the difference between someone doing something that hurts us and someone doing something that we use to hurt ourselves.

A typical example given by Ellis is that of the young man who doesn't ask a girl out because he is afraid she would say "No." Ellis asks his client, "What would happen if she said 'No'?" To which the young man answers, "It would hurt me." Ellis then points out that the young lady saying "No" does no harm to this man. Rather, his thoughts go something like this: "She said 'No,' and that is terrible. That means I'm worthless." It is his interpretation of her action that hurts. It is what he says her action means that hurts.

If your husband or boy friend likes to look at all the women on the beach, does that act hurt you? Of course it does not. You hurt you by saying to yourself, "He likes to look, and that's terrible. That means I'm not worth anything to him." If he looks at the *Playboy* centerfold for longer than the allowed fifteen seconds, that behavior of his does not hurt you.

Males can get caught up in this self-defeating verbal game too. Victoria Billings (1974, p. 230) says:

> It was supposed to be a breakthrough for female sexuality when men learned that women could enjoy sex. But this knowledge has become a new kind of bondage. Men now *demand* that a woman enjoy sex, not in her own way, but in a way a man can understand and feel convinced that he's pleasing her. She is supposed to give a convincing demonstration that she is enjoying herself.

The observation of Ms. Billings is an excellent one. A man gets hurt when his partner doesn't show all the signs of enjoyment he expects. Her behavior, or lack thereof, doesn't hurt him. Rather, he hurts himself by saying, "She's not getting it on. That's terrible. That means I'm worthless." And so he pressures her to try to be something she isn't. For what reason? So he doesn't hurt himself.

How tragically controlling we are, insisting that other people pattern their sex lives after our own. And the main reason is that we are not secure enough to allow those we love to be different. If they are not like us, we shudder at their independence, quite sure their behavior affirms our deepest fears of our own lack of worth. So frightening are these threats to our fragile self-images that we demand, we disparage, we sulk, we threaten. We reach deeply into our bag of manipulation strategies and attempt to get that person to change his or her behavior so *we* can again hide in a false sense of security.

Of course, it is false, and we know it. By manipulating those around us, we achieve a little immediate relief. But manipulation always exacts its price. Slowly the love, the concern, and the spontaneity dry up. By grasping them too closely, we push our loved ones away. By twisting their tails, we bruise their tenderest spots. By making them be like us, we fan the embers of anger. Until there is little left.

Can we allow those so very important to us to do what makes them feel good? Can we ever learn what really hurts us and what does not?

SHOW CONSIDERATION

Because they are generally the aggressors, men have traditionally caught the brunt of appeals to have some consideration. And indeed they should. A man should realize that sex at the wrong time or with the wrong person can cause psychological distress in a woman. Back off and give her a little room. You may be a visual male, but for pity's sake, don't drag your wife to a porn movie if she says she doesn't enjoy it. A little common consideration can enhance your relationship a great deal.

But men don't deserve all the lumps. Women should try to understand the psychological distress their own seduction dances can cause men. As I have said many times in this book, genes make you want to do something, they don't *make* you do it. You can control your behavior just as the male can control his. Become aware of the seductive gestures you throw out and use them only when you really intend to seduce.

And about the pocketbook . . . show a little consideration here too. Meade (1973, pp. 100–1) says, *perhaps* tongue-in-cheek:

> Your average woman, including your average *Cosmo* "girl" wants to get married. In the interim, however, there's no reason why her expeditions in search of a husband shouldn't allow her to enjoy herself once in a while. One of the biggest unmentionables about dating is she gets out of the house at someone else's expense. The hitch is that she needs a man to do it. No woman would be crazy enough to pay for someone else's dinner and movie.

Representing the male side of this hustle, Kinsey (1948, p. 595) says:

> The gifts that are bestowed by males of all social levels upon girls with whom they keep company may be cloaked with fine sentiments, but they are, to a considerable degree, payment for the intercourse that is expected.

Kinsey's comments sound awfully crass, but he was not known to shy away from what he believed to be the truth. In his monumental study of sexual attitudes and practices, Kinsey *personally* conducted some eight thousand interviews, each slightly less than two hours in length (Robinson, 1977, p. 44). I'm of the opinion that his observation about males spending the bucks in hope of sexual consideration is true.

There are many females who do not believe this at all. They say, "He wants to wine and dine me merely because he likes my company." In the rare case, perhaps. But you might as well expect him to make his move sooner or later. Don't then become incensed. He's been making an investment in you. He feels you owe him. And he may get very aggressive about this investment.

The female can help to ward off this situation by refusing to let him make a large investment. You may want his company. It's fun to have an escort. You may enjoy all sorts of sports activities, theater, and other recreation with him, and you may value his conversation. But if it is clear to you that there is no sexual future at all, pay your own way. Going dutch is becoming very common. And the male gets the message quite clearly when the female pays her way. He makes no economic investment. He can make no demands. And he doesn't feel nearly as angry and cheated. That's a great way to build and keep a friendship.

Think about your own behavior. And show a bit of consideration.

Where Have We Been? And How Not to Get There

Popular lore tells us that disgust, anger, and distrust have often been the responses of males and females when they have dealt with each other in a sexual context. There are, no doubt, many reasons for these reactions, but the central one appears to be our tendency to judge the experiences of others by our own. If I don't feel what you seem to be feeling, I have a hard time accepting your experience as authentic. Furthermore, I feel threatened because if you really are not like me, that may mean there is something wrong with me. And if I'm not so sure about me anyway, I may do all sorts of things to deny your feelings or try to make you change them.

I have never met an invulnerable individual yet. Hence, I assume that the vast majority of us will continue to find discomfort when our sexual desires, feelings, and attitudes conflict with those of another person. We can probably never eliminate all the emotional uneasiness and distress. But we can make things easier on ourselves and others. If we can learn to accept ourselves and our feelings, we shall have made a big leap in the right direction. When we like us better, we will find it easier to trust what is inside and do what is necessary to protect ourselves from exploitation.

Accepting ourselves and protecting ourselves are two of the keys to accepting those who differ from us. And we can help along that excursion into interpersonal understanding by trying to listen, by realizing that feelings and desires happen—they often are not under our control—and by learning when it is that people hurt us and when we hurt ourselves. And let's not forget to show a little consideration.

The task I've outlined is made so much easier if we can accept the reality of differences between the sexes. Therein lies the purpose of this book. I've tried to show that men and women differ in a number of remarkable, mysterious, even wonderful ways. The logic of evolutionary biology, research on sex hormones, and observational data from across cultures, across species, and across history provide overwhelming support for these basic, inherited differences. Yet we still have to battle our emotions if we are to accept the direction our knowledge tells us to go.

Throughout history, scientists as well as laymen have found it difficult to lay aside old beliefs—no matter how wrong—and accept new ones. It's a scary and difficult task, but often necessary if we are to make progress in our quest for a peaceful relationship with unrelenting reality. I must agree with one of the staff members of the feminist journal *Women* who wrote: "I'd rather live with a recognized reality than an unrecognized one" (*Women*, 1974, p. 34). That's what this book is all about.

Postscript
A Personal Word

About This Book

It has been fun to write. In addition, I believe its message is important. But I am very much interested in hearing opposing views. Some ideas, especially those in Chapter 10, are quite speculative, even though reasonable from a sociobiological standpoint. If the ideas in this book can be challenged *with any data,* I'll consider the arguments carefully. And who knows? I might change my views. Hopefully, the rest of my life I'll be changing my mind on many things as I become aware of more information. Sociobiology is no more "sacred" than many other beliefs I have.

About Evolution

Although I have now written several hundred pages based on the assumptions of evolution, my personal beliefs are in some ways quite discrepant with those of most evolutionists. My sense of logic makes me very skeptical about the possibility that life could have ever "happened" or that the magnificent complexity of any living organism could have come about purely as the result of a series of accidents.

First, the probability of any naked gene, synthesized by chance, finding itself in a soup of perhaps fifty different highly specialized enzymes required for its replication is so nearly zero (see Monod, 1971) that a great "leap of faith" is required to embrace the theory that life "happened." Second, even if we do accept this improbable view of the beginning of life, it seems to me that the evolution of the several millions of life forms we know today places a great strain on the theory of natural selection. It is estimated that the earth is four and one-half billion years old. Is that enough time for even the human brain with its ten billion neurons interconnected by ten trillion synapses (Popper & Eccles, 1977) to have evolved by chance? That's a growth of two thousand new synapses in the developing brain per year since the earth was formed. And all as the result of genetic accidents that happened to be adaptive? Add to that information the fact that most mutations are not adaptive for the organism and that the brain is only one part of an incredibly complex organism, and we must obviously make another "leap of faith" to accept natural selection as *the* device by which various life forms evolved.

Of course, the alternative position—that a Creator-designer had a hand in all this—also requires a great leap of faith. As far as I'm concerned, neither is more, or less, preposterous than the other; hence, I've chosen—for reasons I probably don't fully comprehend—to leap for the Creator-designer theory. I find it very difficult, perhaps impossible, at this point in my life to embrace evolutionary theory in its entirety. I find it easier to adopt the position that life was created in rather complex forms and then the Creator allowed—perhaps even used—natural selection to change those forms over millions of years.

Sir Karl Popper, the well-known British philosopher of science, is very critical of the explanatory power of natural selection and finds evolutionary theory to be "terribly weak" (Popper & Eccles, 1977, pp. 560, 566); nevertheless, he challenges us to see how far we can go with the theory. Because I believe natural selection plays a very important role—even though not the whole role—in our development, I must agree with him. Hence, in spite of the reservations stated above about evolution, I encourage the kind of speculation found in this book. Furthermore, I find no conflict between any of the points

I have tried to make in this book and the constraints I, along with Popper, must place on evolutionary theory.

In addition to my skepticism concerning the explanatory power of evolutionary principles, I have often struggled with a second problem: the implications of evolutionary theory for my religious system, a system of beliefs that plays a central role in my life. That struggle centers around the nature of the universe as construed by materialistic evolutionists—in particular, around evolution and the nature of human beings. Here are a few of my current thoughts.

The most prevalent metaphysical position in science today is that the universe is composed of only matter, obeying the laws of physics and chemistry. Not only does this position lead inexorably to behavioral determinism, which we touched on earlier (and which I claimed not to believe), but it also forms the basis for "the continuity of the species"—indeed, for the continuity of all matter. Man's position in such a universe is described for us by Bertrand Russell (1956, p. 107):

> That man is the product of causes which had no provision of the end they were achieving; that his origin, his growth, his hopes and fears, his loves and his beliefs, are but the outcome of accidental collocations of atoms; that no fire, no heroism, no intensity of thought and feeling, can preserve an individual life beyond the grave; that all the labour of all the ages, all the devotion, all the noonday brightness of human genius, are destined to extinction in the vast death of the solar system, and that the whole temple of Man's achievement must inevitably be buried beneath the debris of a universe in ruin—all these things, if not quite beyond dispute, are yet so nearly certain, that no philosophy which rejects them can hope to stand.

When Russell wrote these words, science was more cocky concerning its destiny than it is today. Naturalism provided the path toward unlocking all the mysteries of the universe. Nowadays, we have a greater awareness of our finiteness and are less boastful about which metaphysical view is "so nearly certain" and which has no hope of standing.

Hence it is probably easier for me now than it would have

been a quarter or a half century ago to disagree with materialistic monism. And I do. I reject Russell's view of the universe. I believe there is another kind of "stuff" in addition to that which is material. I believe that some part of human beings will continue to exist after the physical universe, as we know it, has either run down or blown itself to bits. That something is the soul, found in a great variety of writings under such aliases as "self," "agent," "homunculous," or "person"—that human imponderable that has baffled philosophers since they first started thinking about themselves.

Such a view, of course, makes humans discontinuous with the rest of matter. And it places me somewhat apart from the evolutional traditionalists. It does not, however, imply that the principles of biological evolution through genetic selection do not apply to humans. If one wishes to take the position, for example, that God performed a special creative act when he formed man and woman and gave them a soul, that discontinuity from other species does not mean that within the species *Homo sapiens* evolution has not been active throughout the thousands of years since that "divine intervention." There are also religious people who believe that we did evolve from lower forms of life and that at some point God gave humans some eternal essence. Obviously, that position has no grudge against evolutionary change in our species.

I'm sure I was prompted to mention this topic because of the many religious people who choke on the word "evolution." Religious individuals may benefit from the message of this book too. The evolutionary claims that have been outlined have no conflict with a great array of religious positions.

About Feminism

In the first chapter of this book, I threw good-sized rocks at the radical feminists. I don't apologize for this. I think their position on inherent psychosexual identity of men and women is gibberish. But lest I be found guilty of implying that all feminists live in the same intellectual swamp, let me say here, quite emphatically, that I believe my position is probably not very different from that of many—perhaps most—actively involved in the woman's movement.

Juliet Mitchell, in her Marie Stopes Memorial Lecture entitled "Female Sexuality," expressed precisely the view of sexual differences that this book is intended to portray:

> . . . since the growth of popular sociology, it has become fashionable to view the characteristics of "femininity" and "masculinity" as largely the products of relatively superficial indoctrination . . . this argument suggests that we teach girls to become girls by giving them dolls, baby ironing boards and cookers, forbidding them to get dirty, to be rough or climb trees; and boys to become boys by the obverse process. In other words, at school, in the home, through books, advertisements and the television we socialize girls into sugar and spice and everything nice and boys into toads and snails and puppy dogs' tails. This type of popular sociological explanation is no more adequate than the earlier rigidities of biological determinism [Mitchell, 1973, p. 129].

Where I might disagree with Ms. Mitchell, I suppose, is on how much of which does what. But essentially, we have no quarrel at all about the interactive nature of genetic endowment and environment.

The woman's movement has much in its favor. For too long women have been on the short end of the economic stick. They have been systematically denied education, employment, and political opportunities. The feminists have done a great deal toward righting some of those wrongs. And even though they sometimes mistakenly told us what we *must* do in order to be fulfilled, more often than not they encouraged us to live peaceably with our own inclinations. Many of us owe the movement a great debt.

But pendulums often swing too far. In their rush for equality of opportunity, some of the more radical feminists tried to obliterate all differences in inherent tendencies between the sexes. This dismal mistake should not, however, cause us to forget the valuable contributions made even by the most zealous feminists.

From a highly personal standpoint, the reality of my life is that I am a man, and as such I have many of the characteristics common to men. I am not ashamed of these characteristics. They are mine by birthright. A recognition of what I perceive to be "truth" and the use of labels, or stereotypes, have been helpful in coming to terms with my masculinity.

But I am also an individual, and it is in accepting my individuality that I feel the greatest debt to feminism. I have many characteristics society commonly associates with females. I am desperately in love with my children. I enjoy holding, cuddling, and comforting them. When they were little, I enjoyed changing, feeding, and soothing them. I like to cook. And I cry more easily than most women do—reading books, watching movies, looking at people I love, hearing or giving a tender word; these things and many more can immobilize me with great, marvelous emotions.

As the feminists have said, it's tough to accept our characteristics that do not meet role expectations. Perhaps it was no accident that several feminist friends recognized my personal struggle to accept these aspects of my individuality and encouraged me to be me. I'm happier with me. Thanks.

What do I think about the feminist movement? It has been a mixed bag. Mostly good, mostly helpful.

About Human Beings

Even in the helping professions, it is sometimes considered melodramatic to say, "I care about human hurts." But I do. Maybe that's why I'm in clinical psychology. I am perhaps allowed the opportunity to view more problems than I would if I earned my living in some other way. In addition, I catch glimpses of the reasons people hurt, and I often wish their worlds were different.

During the past fifty years, psychologists, sociologists, anthropologists, and finally the radical feminists ganged up with a myth that has caused much pain. They told us there was something wrong with us if our sexuality differed from that of our mates. And so we tried desperately to be the same. It didn't work. Human beings matter. Human hurts matter. That myth has got to go. The pendulum has already begun to swing back to a more acceptable moderation. I'm trying to give it another nudge.

References

Abele, L. G. and Gilchrist, S. Homosexual rape and sexual selection in Acanthocephalan worms, *Science* (1977), 197, 81–83.

Abramson, P. R. The relationship of the frequency of masturbation to several aspects of personality and behavior, *Journal of Sex Research* (1973), 9, 2, 132–42.

Acton, W. *Prostitution*. New York: Frederick A. Praeger, Inc., 1857/1968.

American Psychiatric Association. The principles of medical ethics with annotations especially applicable to psychiatry, *American Journal of Psychiatry* (1973), 130, 1,057–64.

American Psychological Association. Ethical standards of psychologists, *APA Monitor* (March 1977), 22–23.

Anderson, D. C. Sex-hormone-binding globulin, *Clinical Endocrinology* (1974), 2, 69–96.

Arafat, I. S. and Cotton, W. L. Masturbation practices of males and females, *Journal of Sex Research* (1974), 10, 4, 293–307.

Asayama, S. Adolescent sex development and adult sex behavior in Japan, *Journal of Sex Research* (1975), 11, 2, 91–112.

Avery, A. W. and Ridley, C. A. Sexual intimacy among college students: A look at interpersonal relationship, *College Student Journal* (1975), 9, 3, 199–205.

Azrin, N. H. and Holz, W. C. Punishment. In W. K. Honig (ed.), *Operant behavior: areas of research and application*. New York: Appleton-Century-Crofts (1966), 380–447.

Barash, D. P. *Sociobiology and behavior*. New York: Elsevier (1977).

Barbach, L. G. *For yourself: the fulfillment of female sexuality*. Garden City, N.Y.: Anchor Books (1976).

Barrett, J. C. and Marshall, J. The risk of conception on different days of the menstrual cycle, *Population Studies* (1969), 23, 3, 455–62.

Bass-Hass, R. The lesbian dyad, *Journal of Sex Research* (1968), 4, 2, 108–26.

Beach, F. A. Cross-species comparisons and the human heritage, *Archives of Sexual Behavior* (1976), 5, 5, 469–85.

Bigelow, R. *The dawn warriors.* Boston: Little, Brown & Company (1969).

Billings, V. *The woman's book.* Greenwich, Conn.: Fawcett Publications, Inc. (1974).

Blake, J. The changing status of women in developed countries, *Scientific American* (1974), 231, 136–47.

Blanchard, M. The man in me, *Women* (1974), 4, 1, 16–22.

Boas, F. *General Anthropology.* New York: Heath & Company (1938).

Bolton, R. Aggression and hypoglycemia among the Qolla: A study in psychobiological anthropology, *Ethnology* (1973), 12, 3, 227–57.

Breland, K. and Breland, M. The misbehavior of organisms, *American Psychologist* (1961), 16, 681–84.

Bremer, J. *Asexualization: a follow-up study of two hundred forty-four cases.* New York: Macmillan (1959).

Brownmiller, S. *Against our will: men, women and rape.* New York: Simon & Schuster (1975) (Bantam edition, 1976).

Bullard, M. K. Hide and secrete: Women's sexual magic in Belize, *Journal of Sexual Research* (1974), 10, 4, 259–65.

Bullough, V. L. Attitudes toward deviant sex in ancient Mesopotamia, *Journal of Sex Research* (1971), 7, 3, 184–203.

Burdine, W. E.; Shipley, T. E.; and Papas, A. T. Delatestryl, a long-acting androgenic hormone: Its use as an adjunct in the treatment of women with sexual frigidity, *Fertility and Sterility* (1957), 8, 255–59.

Burgess, A. W. and Holmstrom, L. L. The rape victim in the emergency ward, *American Journal of Nursing* (1973), 10, 1,741–45.

Burgess, E. W. and Wallin, P. *Engagement and marriage.* Philadelphia: J. B. Lippincott Co. (1953).

Chesler, P. *About men.* New York: Simon & Schuster (1978).

Clavan, S. Changing female sexual behavior and future family structure, *Pacific Sociological Review* (1972), 15, 3, 295–308.

Colton, H. *Sex after the sexual revolution.* New York: Association Press (1972).

Combs, R. H. and Kenkel, W. F. Sex differences in dating aspirations and satisfaction with computer-selected partners, *Journal of Marriage and the Family* (1966), 28, 62–66.

Cotton, W. L. Role-playing substitutions among homosexuals, *Journal of Sex Research* (1972), 8, 4, 310–23.

———. Social and sexual relationships of lesbians, *Journal of Sex Research* (1975), 11, 2, 139–48.

Crook, J. H. Sexual selection in the primates. In B. Campbell (ed.), *Sexual selection and the descent of man.* Chicago: Aldine Publishing Co. (1972), 231–81.

Daly, M. and Wilson, M. *Sex, evolution and behavior.* North Scituate, Mass.: Duxbury Press (1978).

Danielsson, B. *Love in the South Seas* (1954), tr. F. H. Lyon. New York: Reynal & Co. (1956).

Darrow, C. The crime of compulsion: Leopold and Loeb (Chicago, 1924). In A. Weinberg (ed.), *Attorney for the Damned.* New York: Simon & Schuster (1957), 16–88.

Darwin, C. *On the origin of species by means of natural selection, or the preservation of favoured races in the struggle for life.* London: John Murray (1859).

Davis, A. J. Sexual assaults in the Philadelphia prison system. In J. H. Gagnon and W. Simon (eds.), *The sexual scene.* Chicago: Aldine Publishing Co. (1970), 107–24.

Dawkins, R. *The selfish gene.* New York: Oxford University Press (1976).

Day, W. F. Radical behaviorism in reconciliation with phenomenology, *Journal of the Experimental Analysis of Behavior* (1969), 12, 315–28.

Denfeld, D. Dropouts from swinging, *The Family Coordinator* (1974), 23, 1, 45–49.

———. Dropouts from swinging: The marriage counselor as informant. In J. R. Smith and L. G. Smith (eds.), *Beyond monogamy: Recent studies of sexual alternatives in marriage.* Baltimore: The Johns Hopkins University Press (1974), 260–67.

Denfeld, D. and Gordon, M. The sociology of mate swapping: Or the family that swings together clings together, *Journal of Sex Research* (1970), 6, 2, 85–100.

Dewsbury, D. A. and Rethlingshafer, D. A. *Comparative psychology: A modern survey.* New York: McGraw-Hill Book Company (1973).

Dizinno, G. and Whitney, G. Androgen influence on male mouse ultrasounds during courtship, *Hormones and Behavior* (1977), 8, 188–92.

Drakeford, J. W. and Hamm, J. *Pornography: The sexual mirage.* New York: Thomas Nelson, Inc. (1973).

Driscoll, R. H. and Davis, K. E. Sexual restraints: A comparison of perceived and self-reported reasons for college students, *Journal of Sex Research* (1971), 7, 4, 253–62.

Dworkin, A. *Woman hating.* New York: E. P. Dutton & Co. (1974).

———. *Our blood.* New York: Harper & Row (1976).

Dworkin, G. *Determinism, freewill and moral responsibility.* Englewood Cliffs, N.J.: Prentice-Hall (1970).

Ellis, A. *The American sexual tragedy.* New York: Twayne Publishers (1954).

Ellis, H. *Studies in the psychology of sex: Sexual selection in man.* Philadelphia: F. A. Davis Co. (1922).

Edwards, W. The theory of decision making, *Psychological Bulletin* (1954), 51, 380–417.

Endleman, R. Familistic social change on the Israeli kibbutz. In L. L. Adler (ed.), Issues in cross-cultural research, *Annals of the New York Academy of Sciences* (1977), 285, 605–11.

Engels, F. *The origin of the family, private property and the state.* Chicago: Charles H. Kerr & Co. (1902).

Esselstyn, T. C. *Prostitution in the United States.* In J. N. Edwards (ed.), *Sex and society.* Chicago: Markham Publishing Co. (1972), 112–24.

Fang, B. Swinging: In retrospect, *Journal of Sex Research* (1976), 12, 3, 220–37.

Fast, J. *The incompatibility of men and women.* New York: Avon Books (1972).

Finger, F. W. Changes in sex practices and beliefs of male college students: Over 30 years, *Journal of Sex Research* (1975), 11, 4, 304–17.

Firestone, S. *The dialectic of sex: The case for feminist revolution.* London: Jonathan Cape (1971).

Fisher, S. *Understanding the female orgasm.* New York: Basic Books (1973).

Foss, G. L. The influence of androgens on sexuality in women, *Lancet* (1951), 260, 667–69.

Freud, S. *Totem and taboo.* New York: Random House (1918/1946).

——. Female sexuality, *International Journal of Psycho-Analysis* (1932), 13, 281–97.

Gagnon, J. H. *Human sexualities*. Glenview, Ill.: Scott, Foresman and Company (1977).

Gelman, D. Charting the gay life, *Newsweek* (March 27, 1978), 98–100.

Gokhale, B. B.; Master, R. S.; and Master, S. C. S. The visiting client (A pilot study on the client of the prostitute), *Indian Journal of Psychiatry* (1962), 4, 1, 39–45.

Goodman, J. D. The behavior of hypersexual delinquent girls, *American Journal of Psychiatry* (1976), 133, 662–68.

Gordon, M. and Shankweiler, P. J. Different equals less: Female sexuality in recent marriage manuals, *Journal of Marriage and the Family* (1971), 33, 3, 459–66.

Gorzynski, G. and Katz, J. L. The polycystic ovary syndrome: Psychosexual correlates, *Archives of Sexual Behavior* (1977), 6, 3, 215–22.

Greep, R. O. and Astwood, E. B. Endocrinology. In S. R. Geiger (ed.), *Handbook of Physiology*. Washington, D.C.: American Physiological Society (1975).

Greer, G. From the female eunuch. In M. E. Adelstein and J. G. Pival (eds.), *Women's liberation*. New York: St. Martin's Press (1972), pp. 27–36.

Gupta, A. S. and Lynn, D. B. A study of sexual behavior in females, *Journal of Sex Research* (1972), 8, 3, 207–18.

Hafez, E. S. E. and Schein, M. W. The behaviour of cattle. In E. S. E. Hafez (ed.), *The behaviour of domestic animals*. London: Bailliere, Tindall & Cox (1962), 247–96.

Hall, G. S. *Adolescence: Its psychology and its relations to physiology, anthropology, sociology, sex, crime, religion and education* (1905), 1.

Hamilton, W. D. The genetical theory of social behavior: I and II, *Journal of Theoretical Biology* (1964), 7, 1–52.

Harlow, H. F. Lust, latency and love: Simian secrets of successful sex, *Journal of Sex Research* (1975), 11, 2, 79–90.

Hart, G. Sexual behavior in a war environment, *Journal of Sex Research* (1975), 11, 3, 218–26.

Hartung, J. On natural selection and the inheritance of wealth, *Current Anthropology* (1976), 17, 4, 607–22.

Hedblon, J. H. Dimensions of lesbian sexual experience, *Archives of Sexual Behavior* (1973), 2, 4, 329–41.

Henshel, A. Swinging: A study of decision making in marriage.

In J. Huber (ed.), *Changing women in a changing society*. Chicago: The University of Chicago Press (1973), 123–29.

Herskovits, M. J. *Cultural anthropology*. New York: Alfred A. Knopf (1955).

Hessellund, H. On some sociosexual sex differences, *Journal of Sex Research* (1971), 7, 4, 263–73.

Hill, C. T.; Rubin, Z.; and Peplau, L. A. Breakups before marriage: The end of 103 affairs, *Journal of Social Issues* (1976), 32, 1, 147–68.

Hippler, A. E. Patterns of sexual behavior: The Athabascans of interior Alaska, *Ethos* (1974), 2, 1, 47–68.

Hite, Shere. *The Hite report*. New York: Dell Publishing Co. (1977).

Hoijer, H. and Beals, R. L. *An introduction to anthropology*. London: Macmillan Co. (1965).

Holroyd, J. C. and Brodsky, A. M. Psychologists' attitudes and practices regarding erotic and nonerotic physical contact with patients, *American Psychologist* (1977), 32, 10, 843–49.

Hopkins, M. K. The age of Roman girls at marriage, *Population Studies* (1965), 18, 3, 309–27.

Horney, K. The dread of woman, *International Journal of Psycho-Analysis* (1932), 33, 348–60.

Hunt, M. Up against the wall, male chauvinist pig. In M. E. Adelstein and J. G. Pival (eds.), *Women's liberation*. New York: St. Martin's Press (1972), 37–50.

———. *Sexual behavior in the 1970s*. Chicago: Playboy Press (1974).

Immelman, K. Ecological significance of imprinting and early experience, *Annual Review of Ecology and Systematics* (1975), 6, 15–37.

Isichei, P. A. C. Sex in traditional Asaba, *Cahiers d'Études Africaines* (1973), 13, 4, 682–99.

Kanekar, S. On being a psychologist in India, *American Psychologist* (1977), 32, 11, 974.

Kanin, E. J.; Davidson, K. R.; and Scheck, S. R. A research note on the male-female differentials in the experience of heterosexual love, *Journal of Sex Research* (1970), 6, 1, 64–72.

Kephart, W. M. *The family, society, and the individual*. Boston: Houghton Mifflin Co. (1966).

Kerr, C. *Sex for women*. New York: Grove Press (1978).

Kiefer, O. *Sexual life in ancient Rome*. New York: E. P. Dutton & Co. (1935).

Kinsey, A. C.; Pomeroy, W. B.; and Martin, C. E. *Sexual behavior in the human male.* Philadelphia: W. B. Saunders Company (1948).

Kinsey, A. C.; Pomeroy, W. B.; Martin, C. E.; and Gebhard, P. H. *Sexual behavior in the human female.* Philadelphia: W. B. Saunders Company (1953).

Klein, M. *Symposium on steroid hormones.* London: Ciba Research Foundation (1950).

Kling, S. G. *Sexual behavior and the law.* New York: Bernard Geis Associates (1965).

Kogan, N. and Wallach, M. A. Risk taking as a function of the situation: The person and the group. In *New directions in psychology: III.* New York: Holt, Rinehart & Winston (1967).

Komarovsky, M. *Dilemmas of masculinity: A study of college youth.* New York: W. W. Norton & Company (1976).

Kraemer, H. C.; Becker, H. B.; Brodie, H. K. H.; Doering, C. H.; Moos, R. H.; and Hamburg, D. A. Orgasmic frequency and plasma testosterone levels in normal human males, *Archives of Sexual Behavior* (1976), 5, 2, 125–32.

Kuhn, T. S. *The structure of scientific revolutions,* 2nd ed. Chicago: The University of Chicago Press (1970).

Larsen, K. S. An investigation of sexual behavior among Norwegian college students: A motivation study, *Journal of Marriage and the Family* (1971), 33, 1, 219–27.

Leshner, A. I. *An introduction to behavioral endocrinology.* New York: Oxford University Press (1978).

LeVine, R. A. Culture and personality. In B. J. Siegel, *Biennial Review of Anthropology.* Stanford, Calif.: Stanford University Press (1963), 107–45.

Lewinsohn, R. *A history of sexual customs,* tr. Alexander Mayce. New York: Harper & Brothers (1958).

Linton, R. *The study of man.* New York: Appleton-Century-Crofts (1936).

Lorenz, K. *Studies in animal and human behavior, Vol. I,* tr. Robert Martin. Cambridge, Mass.: Harvard University Press (1970).

Lowie, R. H. *An introduction to cultural anthropology.* New York: Rinehart (1940).

Maccoby, E. E. and Jacklin, C. N. *The psychology of sex differences.* Stanford, Calif.: Stanford University Press (1974).

Macrides, F.; Bartke, A.; and Dalterio, S. Strange females increase plasma testosterone levels in male mice, *Science* (1975), 189, 1104–6.

Malinowski, B. *The sexual life of savages in North-western Melanesia*, Vols. 1 and 2. New York: Horace Liveright (1929).

Masters, W. H. and Johnson, V. E. *Human sexual response*. Boston: Little, Brown & Company (1966).

———. *Human sexual inadequacy*. Boston: Little, Brown & Company (1970).

Mayr, E. Sexual selection and natural selection. In B. Campbell (ed.), *Sexual selection and the descent of man*. Chicago: Aldine Publishing Co. (1972), 87–104.

McClearn, G. E. and DeFries, J. C. *Introduction to behavioral genetics*. San Francisco: W. H. Freeman and Co. (1973).

Mead, M. *Male and female: a study of the sexes in a changing world*. New York: William Morrow & Co. (1949).

Meade, M. *Bitching*. London: Garnston Press Ltd. (1973).

Megargee, E. I. The psychology of violence: A critical review of theories of violence. In D. J. Mulvihill and M. M. Tumin (eds.), *Crimes of violence: A staff report to the National Commission on the Causes and Prevention of Violence*. NCCPV Report Series, Vol. 13. Washington, D.C.: U. S. Government Printing Office (1969).

Millet, K. *Sexual politics*. Garden City, N.Y.: Doubleday & Company, Inc. (1970).

Mitchell, J. Female sexuality, *Journal of Biosocial Science* (1973), 5, 1, 123–36.

Money, J. Components of eroticism in man: I. The hormones in relation to sexual morphology and sexual desire, *Journal of Nervous and Mental Diseases* (1961), 132, 239–48.

———. Use of an androgen-depleting hormone in the treatment of male sex offenders, *Journal of Sex Research* (1970), 6, 3, 165–72.

———. Sexology: behavioral, cultural, hormonal, neurological, etc., *Journal of Sex Research* (1973), 9, 1, 3–10.

———. Human behavior cytogenetics: Review of psychopathology in the syndromes—47, XXY; 47, XYY; and 45, X, *Journal of Sex Research* (1975), 11, 3, 181–200.

Money, J. and Clopper, R. R., Jr. Postpubertal psychosexual function in post-surgical male hypopituitarism, *Journal of Sex Research* (1975), 11, 1, 25–38.

Monod, J. *Chance and necessity*. New York: Alfred A. Knopf, (1971).

Morris, S. Darwin and the double standard, *Playboy* (August 1978), 109.

Mountcastle, V. B. *Medical physiology*. St. Louis, Mo.: C. V. Mosby Co. (1974).

Murdock, G. P. *Our primitive contemporaries*. New York: Macmillan Co. (1934).

Murphy, G. *Psychological thought from Pythagoras to Freud*. New York: Harcourt, Brace & World (1968).

Nyby, J.; Dizinno, G.; and Whitney, G. Sexual dimorphism in ultrasonic vocalizations of mice (*Mus musculus*): Gonadal hormone regulation, *Journal of Comparative and Physiological Psychology* (1977), 91, 1424–31.

Pietropinto, A. and Simenauer, J. *Beyond the male myth*. New York: New American Library (1978).

Popper, K., and Eccles, J. *The self and its brain: An argument for interactionism*. New York/London: Springer International, (1977).

Raboch, J.; Mellan, J.; and Starka, L. Adult cryptorchids: Sexual development and activity, *Archives of Sexual Behavior* (1977), 6, 5, 413–19.

Raboch, J. and Starka, L. Coital activity of men and the levels of plasmatic testosterone, *Journal of Sex Research* (1972), 8, 219–24.

Rainwater, L. Marital sexuality in four cultures of poverty, *Journal of Marriage and the Family* (1964), 26, 4, 457–66.

Rappeport, J. R. Antisocial behavior. In S. Arieti and E. B. Brody (eds.), *American handbook of psychiatry*, Vol. 3. New York: Basic Books (1974).

Reiche, R. and Dannecker, M. Male homosexuality in West Germany: A sociological investigation, *Journal of Sex Research* (1977), 13, 1, 35–53.

Reyburn, W. *The inferior sex*. Englewood Cliffs, N.J.: Prentice-Hall (1972).

Robinson, P. *The modernization of sex*. New York: Harper & Row (1977).

Rollin, B. Motherhood: Who needs it? In M. E. Adelstein and J. G. Pival (eds.), *Women's liberation*. New York: St. Martin's Press (1972), 59–69.

Rosoff, M. Don't just lie there—do something, *Women* (1974), 4, 1, 44–46.

Rotter, J. B. Some implications of a social learning theory for the practice of psychotherapy. In D. Levis (ed.), *Learning ap-*

proaches to therapeutic behavior change. Chicago: Aldine Publishing Co. (1970).

Rowe, C. J. *An outline of psychiatry.* Dubuque, Ia.: Wm. C. Brown Co. (1975).

Rubin, Z. *Liking and loving: An invitation to social psychology.* New York: Holt, Rinehart & Winston (1973).

Russell, B. A free man's worship. In P. Edwards (ed.), *Why I am not a Christian and other essays on religion and related subjects.* New York: Simon & Schuster (1956).

Sanger, W. *The history of prostitution.* New York: Arno Press (1859/1972).

Schäfer, S. Sociosexual behavior in male and female homosexuals: A study in sex differences, *Archives of Sexual Behavior* (1977), 6, 5, 355–64.

Schmidt, G. and Sigush, V. Patterns of sexual behavior in West German workers and students, *Journal of Sex Research* (1971), 7, 2, 89–106.

Schneider, S.; Boucher, D.; Hansen, M.; Noonan, R.; Risch, S.; and Vandermeer, J. Is our biology to blame? *The American Biology Teacher* (October 1977), 432–37.

Schneidman, B. and McGuire, L. Group therapy for nonorgasmic women: Two age levels. *Archives of Sexual Behavior* (1976), 5, 3, 239–47.

Science for the People. Sociobiology: Tool for social oppression (1976), 8, 2, 7–9.

Seward, G. H. Sex roles in cross-cultural perspective. In L. L. Adler (ed.), Issues in cross-cultural research, *Annals of the New York Academy of Sciences* (1977), 285, 612–17.

Shultz, G. D. *How many more victims? Society and the sex criminal.* Philadelphia: J. B. Lippincott Co. (1965).

Shuttleworth, F. K. A biosocial and developmental theory of male and female sexuality, *Marriage and Family Living* (1959), 21, 2, 163–70.

Sigusch, V.; Schmidt, G.; Reinfeld, A.; and Wiedemann-Sutor, I. Psychosexual stimulation: Sex differences, *Journal of Sex Research* (1970), 6, 1, 10–24.

Skinner, B. F. *Contingencies of reinforcement: A theoretical analysis.* New York: Appleton-Century-Crofts (1969).

Sonenschein, D. The ethnography of male homosexual relationships, *Journal of Sexual Research* (1968), 4, 2, 69–83.

Sopchak, A. L. and Sutherland, A. M. Psychological impact of cancer and its treatment. VII. Exogenous hormones and their relation to life-long adaptation in women with metastatic cancer of the breast. *Cancer* (1960), 13, 528–31.

Staples, R. Male-female sexual variations: Functions of biology or culture, *Journal of Sex Research* (1973), 9, 1, 11–20.

Stassinopoulos, A. *The female woman.* New York: Dell Publishing Co. (1975).

Steele, D. G. and Walker, C. E. Male and female differences in reaction to erotic stimuli as related to sexual adjustment, *Archives of Sexual Behavior* (1974), 3, 5, 459–70.

Stoller, R. J. *Sex and gender.* New York: Science House (1968).

Taber, R. D. and Dassmann, R. F. The dynamics of three natural populations of deer, *Odoicoileus hemionus columbianus, Ecology* (1957), 38, 233–46.

Tavris, C. and Offir, C. *The longest war: Sex differences in perspective.* New York: Harcourt Brace Jovanovich (1977).

Taylor, G. R. *Sex in history.* New York: Vanguard Press (1954).

Thibaut, J. W. and Kelly, H. H. *The social psychology of groups.* New York: John Wiley & Sons (1959).

Thomas, W. I. *Sex and society.* New York: Arno Press (1974).

Time. Why you do what you do. (August 1, 1977), 63.

Trivers, R. L. The evolution of reciprocal altruism, *Quarterly Review of Biology* (1971), 46, 4, 35–57.

Vinacke, W. E. Variables in experimental games: Toward a field theory, *Psychological Bulletin* (1969), 71, 4, 293–318.

Wagner, N. N.; Fujita, B. N.; and Pion, R. Sexual behavior in high school: Data on a small sample, *Journal of Sex Research* (1973), 9, 2, 150–55.

Wallin, P. and Clark, A. Cultural norms and husbands' and wives' reports of their marital partners' preferred frequency of coitus relative to their own, *Sociometry* (1958), 21, 3, 247–54.

Ward, D. A. and Kassebaum, G. G. *Women's prison: Sex and social structure.* Chicago: Aldine Publishing Co. (1965).

———. Lesbian liaisons. In J. H. Gagnon and W. Simon (eds.), *The sexual scene.* Chicago: Aldine Publishing Co. (1970), 125–36.

Watson, J. B. *Behaviorism.* New York: W. W. Norton & Company (1924/1970).

Wilson, E. O. *Sociobiology: the new synthesis.* Cambridge, Mass.: Harvard University Press (1975).

———. Foreword. In D. P. Barash, *Sociobiology and behavior.* New York: Elsevier (1977).

Women: A journal of liberation (1974), 4, 4, 3.

Woolston, H. B. *Prostitution in the United States.* Montclair, N.J.: Patterson Smith (1969).

Zeiss, A. M.; Rosin, G. M.; and Zeiss, R. A. Orgasm during intercourse: A treatment strategy for women, *Journal of Consulting and Clinical Psychology* (1977), 45, 891–95.

Index

Abele, L. G., 102, 257
About Men (Chesler), 110, 258
Abrahamson, P. R., 78, 79, 257
Accepting: oneself and others, 236–39 ff.; reality, 232–39 ff.
Acton, William, 92
Adaptation, selective. *See* Selective adaptation
Adolescence, 275 (*see also* Children); sexual socialization and, 114–19 (*see also* Socialization)
Adolescence: Its Psychology and Its Relations to Physiology, Anthropology, Sociology, Sex, Crime, Religion and Education (Hall), 48–49, 261
Adrenal cortex, 121
Adultery, double standard and, 179, 180–81, 182
Affection. *See* Love (affection)
Against Our Will: Men, Women, and Rape (Brownmiller), 101, 104–5, 227, 229–30, 258
Age discrimination (older men and younger women), 194–98, 204
Aggressiveness, sexual, 3, 9–13, 15, 54, 68–69, 86–87, 115–19, 165, 189, 213, 217, 228, 246, 247 (*see also* Violence); courtship and, 162–77; hormones and, 128, 129, 154; as a healthy characteristic, 3; myth of sexual identity and, 5–6; rape and, 97–99 ff., 105 (*see also* Rape)
Alcohol use, 243–44
Amazons, 153
Anderson, D. C., 129, 134–35, 257
Androgens, 121–24, 125–36, 217, 228
"Androgynous role" concept, 8–9
Angell, James, 17
Anger and dread, male-female relations and, 222–49 *passim*
Animal behavior, sexual, 16, 17, 19–21, 22–50, 122, 191, 213 (*see also* specific aspects, concepts, studies); and courtship, 162–64, 167–68, 169–70; hormones and, 178–79; and maternal behavior, 201–3; and pleasure-pain principle in motivation and, 53 ff., 72, 80–81, 83, 87,

88, 102–3; promiscuity and, 160–61, 179, 180–81, 209–10
Anthropology, 6–7, 105–6, 115, 223–24 (*see also* Culture; specific aspects, studies); and sexual identity myth, 6–7
Appetite, sexual, measurement of, 72 ff. *See also* Drive, sex
Applied-learning theory, 56–58
Arafat, I. S., 78, 83, 140, 257
Arousal, sexual, male-female differences and, 12, 25–36 ff., 51 ff., 212–13, 227; attractiveness and, 169 ff., 186 ff., 212–13; and courtship and control strategies, 162–77; motivation and, 51 ff., 65 ff.; and orgasmic responsiveness, 37 ff. (*see also* Orgasms); promiscuity and, 154 (*see also* Promiscuity); sex hormones and, 122–36
Asayama, S., 78, 182, 257
Athabascans, 102
Athletic (physical) prowess, 169–70, 171, 173, 196, 213, 226
Attractiveness, sexual, 186 ff., 203–4, 212–13; beauty, 186–88, 203–4, 212; courtship and, 173; physical, 169–70, 171, 173, 196, 213; visual stimuli and, 186–94, 203–4
Autostimulation. *See* Masturbation
Averages, 207. *See also* Exceptions, generalities and
Avery, A. W., 155, 257
Azrin, N. H., 95, 257

Barash, D. P., 7, 56, 87, 88, 102, 162, 164, 169, 179, 180, 195, 209, 213, 257
Barbach, Lonnie G., 12, 43, 44, 66, 81, 182, 239, 257
Barrett and Marshall, 29, 258
Bass-Hass, Rita, 77, 258
Beach, Frank A., 35, 83, 258
Beauty, 186–88 ff., 203–4. *See also* Attractiveness
Behavior, human (social), 15–21 (*see also* Sexual behavior; Sociobiology; specific aspects, concepts, kinds, studies); determinism and, 217–20;

exceptions, emotions, and ethics
and, 205–21; nature-nurture controversy and, 4–5, 55–65; pleasure-
pain principle and motivation and,
51 ff., 64–111; practice and change
in, 214–15; promiscuity and faithfulness and, 137–61, 208–10; sexual
identity myth and, 4–13; stereotyping and, 211–12, 239, 255
Behaviorism, 4–5, 14–15, 17–19, 55,
58 ff., 202; descriptive, 56–58; and
determinism, 218–20, 252; and instincts, 18–19, 55, 56–58, 219–20
(*see also* Instincts); and motivation
and sexual behavior, 55–65, 70 ff.;
and nature-nurture controversy,
55–65
Behaviorism (Watson), 14, 267
Beliefs (belief systems), 63–65, 72,
75, 135, 146, 249, 250–53; exceptions, emotions, and ethics and,
205–21 (*see also* Exceptions, generalities and)
Bell, Alan, 147
Bentham, Jeremy, 53, 95
Bernard, Jessie, 199
Beyond the Male Myth, 197–98, 265
Billings, Victoria, 83, 166, 171, 245,
258
Biology (biological evolution, biological factors), sexual behavior
and, 2–3, 7, 13, 16–21, 22–50, 51 ff.,
65–111, 112–19, 250–53 (*see also*
Evolution; Sexual behavior; specific
aspects, concepts, kinds, studies);
courtship and control strategies
and, 162–77, 225 ff.; and determinism and, 217–20; exceptions, emotions, and ethics and, 205–21; genetics and sociobiology and, 19–21
(*see also* Genetics; Sociobiology);
hormones and sex drive and, 120–
36; and identity myth (*see* Sexual
identity myth); and male-female
sex differences (*see* Male-female
sex differences); and motivation,
51 ff., 65–111; nature-nurture controversy and, 51–65; and promiscuity and faithfulness, 140–61, 179–85,
208–10
Birds, 167–68, 169–70, 179, 180–81,
209
Bitching (Meade), 9–10, 264
Blake, J., 199, 258
Blanchard, M., 8, 258
Boas, F., 150, 258
Bolton, R., 7, 258
Bonding, mother-child, 203

Brain, evolution and, 251
Breasts, 186–88, 189
Breeding. *See* Reproduction
Breland, Keller, 18–19, 201–3, 258
Breland, Marian, 18–19, 201–3, 258
Bremer, J., 122, 258
Brodsky, Annette, 108, 262
Brownmiller, Susan, 86, 90, 97, 99,
101, 102–3, 104–5, 158, 194, 223,
227, 228, 229–30, 258
Bruce, Lenny, 163
Bullard, M. K., 195, 258
Bullfrogs, courtship and, 162, 163–64
Bullough, V. L., 87, 182, 258
Burdine, Shipley, Papas, and Del-
atestryl, 126, 258
Burgess and Holmstrom, 97, 258
Burgess and Wallin, 175, 258
Buttocks, 186–88

Campbell, Donald, 215–16
Carr, Harvey, 17
Castration, 122, 128
Celibacy, 208
Change, genetics and, 214–15; determinism and, 217–20
Chaucer, Geoffrey, 186, 187
Chesler, Phyllis, 110, 258
Children (child-raising, offspring),
22–25 (*see also* Adolescence; Re-
production); abhorrence of rape
and, 99–100; courtship and control
strategies and, 168 ff. (*see also*
Courtship); genetics and changes
and, 214–15; and masturbation (*see*
Masturbation); maternal behavior
and, 198–203, 204, 238; promiscuity
and, 140–45, 180–81, 185, 209–10
(*see also* Promiscuity); sexual
arousal and coitus and, 27–35; and
sexual socialization, 113–19
Chimpanzees, 88, 102–3. *See also*
Monkeys
Clark, A., 36, 72, 267
Clavan, S., 8, 258
Clinical psychology, 5, 58, 255
Clitoridectomies, 182
Clopper, R. R., Jr., 123, 264
Cognitive expectancy-value theories,
53–54, 57
Combs and Kenkel, 171, 175–76, 259
Conditioning, 19, 201–3 (*see also*
Culture; Learning; Socialization);
and nature-nurture controversy,
56–58 ff., 112 ff.
Control, courtship and, 164–77, 213
(*see also* Courtship); of desire and
sex behavior, 243–44, 248–49; de-

terminism and, 217–20; and male-female relations, 224–27
"Coolidge effect, the," 160–61
Co-ordination (agility), physical, courtship and selection for, 169, 170, 171
Copulation (coitus, intercourse), 22–50; arousal and, 25–36 ff.; arousal on observing, 191–92; attractiveness and, 169 ff., 186–88, 212–13; biological evolution and survival and, 22–50; courtship and control strategies and, 162–77, 213; double standard and, 177–85, 203, 209; first, 75–76; hormones and sex drive and, 120–36; interpersonal relations and, 155–61; love and, 155–61; orgasmic responsiveness and, 37–50, 237, 238; pleasure as motivation in sex behavior and, 51 ff., 65 ff.; promiscuity and faithfulness and, 137 ff., 208–10 (*see also* Promiscuity); reproduction as aim of, 23–25 (*see also* Reproduction)
Cotton, W. L., 78, 83, 140, 147–48, 149, 257, 259
Courtship (courtship and control strategies), 23, 51, 162–77, 213 (*see also* Control, courtship and); older men and younger women and, 194–98, 204; sex hormones and, 128–29; survival characteristics and survival and, 168–77
Coyness, female, courtship and control and, 164–77
Crime, risk-taking for sex and, 93–109
Crook, J. H., 189, 259
Cryptorchids, hormone-therapy studies with, 123–24, 130
Cuckolded, 180, 185
Culture (cultural evidence, cultural factors), 7, 112–19, 136, 186 (*see also* Learning; Socialization; specific aspects, concepts, studies); double standard and, 182–83; and male-female relations, 223–24; masturbation and, 78–79, 83; and maternal behavior, 200–3; motivation and sex behavior and, 51–65; nature-nurture controversy and, 4–5, 55–65; 112–19; orgasmic ability and, 47–50; and polygamy, 150–53; and sexual freedom, 114–19; virginity and, 183, 184–85

Daly and Wilson, 35, 122, 151, 153, 259
Danielsson, B., 116, 117–18, 259

Darrow, Clarence, 219–20
Darwin (Charles) and Darwinism, 7, 16, 17, 18–19, 20–21, 87, 113, 136, 169
Dating: courtship and selection and, 171–72, 175–76; double standard and, 178–85
Davis, A. J., 99, 101–2, 104, 259
Dawkins, R., 9, 20–21, 141, 167–68, 169, 175, 185, 195–96, 259
Deception. *See* Lying
Denfield, D., 84–85, 89, 159, 259
Descriptive behaviorism, 56–58, 59
Desire, sexual, male-female differences and, 6 (*see also* Drive, sex; specific aspects, studies); controlling, 243–44, 248–49; and courtship and control strategies, 164–77, 225 ff.; genetic influence on, 61, 62–65, 112–19, 217 ff.; hormones and, 120–36; and motivation and sex behavior, 61, 62 ff., 65–111, 112–19, 208, 210, 227, 230, 241–44, 248; and promiscuity and faithfulness, 153–61
Determinism, 217–20, 252
Dewey, John, 17
Dewsbury and Rethlingshafer, 160, 259
Dilemmas of Masculinity: A Study of College Youth, 179, 263
Disgust (disappointment), female-male relations and, 227–28, 231, 248
Dizinno, G., 58, 129, 260, 265
Domination, rape and, 97–100, 101–3
Double standard, 146, 157, 178–85, 203, 209, 216–17
Drakeford and Hamm, 159, 260
Dreams, sexual, 47, 130
Dress (clothing), 173, 186, 189
Driscoll and Davis, 155, 260
Drive, sex, male-female differences and, 5–6, 18, 53, 54, 65–111 *passim,* 112–19, 221, 225, 227 (*see also* Desire, sexual; specific aspects, concepts, studies); and courtship and control strategies, 165–77; determinism and, 218–20; hormones and, 120–36, 154, 208, 228; measurement of, 72 ff.; promiscuity and, 153–61 (*see also* Promiscuity); reinforcers and, 56–58
Dworkin, Andrea, 8, 90–91, 194, 234, 260
Dworkin, G., 221, 260

Ecology, 15
Economic factors, 247 (*see also* Hedonic value; Wealth); promiscuity

and faithfulness and, 152–53, 184–85

Edwards, W., 53, 260

Eggs (ova), 60–61, 67–69, 94, 99, 104, 136, 140, 143–45, 189, 190; and courtship and control strategies, 162–77, 227

Ejaculation (*see also* Orgasms; Potency): dreams and, 130; sex hormones and, 122–23, 124

Ellis, Albert, 245, 260

Ellis, Havelock, 4, 169, 173, 186–87, 191, 260

Emotions. *See* Feelings; specific kinds

Endleman, Robert, 200–1, 260

Endocrine glands, 121–36

Engels, F., 182, 260

Enjoyment, sexual. *See* Hedonic value; Pleasure-pain principle

Environmental and species-specific pressures, 208–10

Environmental factors, 4–5, 10, 14–15, 208–10 (*see also* Culture); nature-nurture controversy and, 4–5 (*see also* Nature-nurture controversy; specific aspects, studies)

Enzymes, 62, 251

Erection, 51, 190; sex hormones and, 122–23

Estrogens, 121–22, 124 ff.

Ethics, sociobiology and, 215–21

Ethology, 15, 58

Evolution (evolutionary logic), sex behavior and, 2–3, 7, 13, 16–21, 22–50, 67 ff., 112–19, 251–53 (*see also* specific aspects, concepts, individuals, studies); adaptation and (*see* Selective adaptation); biology and (*see* Biology; specific aspects, concepts, studies); exceptions, emotions, and ethics and, 205–21; and genetics (*see* Genetics); hormones and sex drive and, 120–36; male-female sex differences and (*see* Male-female sex differences); motivation and, 57 ff., 65–111 *passim;* sociobiology and, 16–21, 22–50 (*see also* Sociobiology)

Exceptions, generalities and, 205–21; conflicting motivations and, 208; environmental and species-specific pressures and, 208–10; genetic and physiological anomalies and, 208; mistaken imputations and, 210–11; overlapping distributions and, 206–7; stereotyping and, 211–12

Existential-humanistic psychology, 58–59

Extramarital sex, 229 (*see also* Promiscuity); double standard and, 182–83

Fairness (unfairness), sex behavior and, 212–13

Faithfulness, promiscuity and, 137–61, 208–10, 235–36, 238 (*see also* Monogamy; Polygamy); courtship and control strategies and, 167–77; double standard and, 178–85

Family, the (*see also* Children; Marriage): maternal behavior and, 198–203, 204

Fang, B., 84, 159, 260

Fantasy (imagination), sexual, 190; hormones and, 122, 123, 129, 130

Fast, J., 194, 224, 260

Feelings (emotions), male-female differences in sex behavior and, 59–65, 210–11, 222–49 (*see also* Relationships, male-female); accepting, respecting, and protecting, 232–49; and anger, dread, hurts, and misunderstandings, 222–49; and courtship and control strategies, 164–77, 224 ff.; genes and, 59–65; and love (*see* Love); measuring, 69 ff.; and promiscuity and faithfulness, 139–61 *passim;* and sexual responsiveness, 155–61

Female-male sex differences. *See* Male-female sex differences; specific aspects, concepts, kinds, studies

Female orgasmic responsivity, 38 ff. *See also* Orgasms

Female sex hormones (estrogens), 121–22, 124 ff.

Female Woman, The, 8, 267

Feminists (radical feminists, women's movement), 7–9, 10, 65–66, 79, 80–81, 84–85, 90–91, 102, 114, 166, 194, 195, 235–36, 254–56. *See also* specific aspects, concepts, individuals, studies

Fertilization and gestation, 143–44; coitus data and probability of, 29

Fighting, 86–87. *See also* Aggressiveness; Violence

Firestone, Shulamith, 8–9, 260

Fisher, S., 44, 45–46, 260

Fittest, survival of, 20–21, 113, 180. *See also* Genetics; Selective adaptation; Survival

Food (hunger, thirst), analogy of sex drive and, 218, 225, 241–42, 243

Ford, C. S., 35

For Yourself: The Fulfillment of Female Sexuality, 66, 257
Foss, G. L., 125–26, 130
Franks, Bobby, 219
Free will, determinism and, 220
Freud, Sigmund, 5, 17, 53, 209–10, 223, 260–61; and primary process, 59
Friendship, 11–13, 241
Frigidity, 126, 155
Frogs, 162, 163–64
Fun. *See* Pleasure-pain principle
Functionalism, 17

Gagnon, John H., 130, 260
Galton, Francis, 17
Gelman, D., 147, 261
Generalities, exceptions and. *See* Exceptions, generalities and
Genetic and physiological anomalies, 208
Genetics (genes, gene pool, genetic survival), sex behavior and, 7, 10, 13, 15, 16, 18–19, 20–21, 22–50, 112–19, 140 ff., 189–90, 250–51 (*see also* Biology; Evolution; specific aspects, concepts, individuals, studies); adaptation and (*see* Selective adaptation); arousal and coitus and, 23–35 (*see also* Arousal, sexual; Copulation); and change, 214–15; and control and determinism, 217–20; courtship and, 162 ff. (*see also* Courtship); ethical implications and, 216–21; hormones and sex drive and, 136 (*see also* Drive, sex; Hormones, sex); and male-female sex differences (*see* Male-female sex differences); motivation and, 52 ff., 65–111 *passim;* orgasmic responsiveness and, 37–43; and promiscuity (*see* Promiscuity); survival of the fittest and, 20–21, 113, 180
Genitalia, arousal on observing of, 190–91
Gilchrist, S., 102, 257
Girl-watching, 188–94
God (Creator-design theory), 251, 253
Gokhale, Master, and Master, 91, 261
Gonads, 121. *See also* Testosterone
Goodall, Jane, 102–3
Goodman, Jerome, 125, 126–27, 130, 261
Gordon, M., 84, 89, 109, 259, 261
Gorzynski and Katz, 128, 130, 261
Greep and Astwood, 129, 261
Greer, Germaine, 170, 171, 224, 261

Group sex (mate-swapping, swinging), 84–85, 159
Guiterman, Arthur, 22
Gupta and Lynn, 76, 261

Hafez and Schein, 160–61, 261
Hall, G. Stanley, 48–49, 261
Hamilton, William D., 16, 261
Hamlet, 135, 161
Handicapped, the, sexual disadvantages of, 213
Harems, 153, 172, 179, 209–10
Harlow, Harry, 80, 261
Hart, G., 90, 163, 261
Hartung, J., 226–27, 261
Hedblon, J. H., 149, 261
Hedonic value, male-female differences in motivation and sex behavior and, 52–54, 59 ff., 66–111 *passim*, 136 (*see also* Pleasure-pain principle); and courtship and control strategies, 165–77; hormones and sex drive and, 120–36; maternal behavior and, 198–203, 204; older men and younger women and, 194–98, 204; visual stimuli and, 186–94, 204
Henshel, A., 84, 261–62
Herskovits, M. J., 151, 262
Hesselund, H., 5, 36, 75, 262
Hill, Rubin, and Peplau, 176–77, 262
Hippler, A. E., 102, 224, 262
Hips, 186–88, 190
Hirsutism, sex hormones and, 128
History of Prostitution, The (Sanger), 87–88, 89, 266
History of Sexual Customs, A (Lewinsohn), 152, 263
Hite, Shere, 35–36, 43–44, 80, 120, 155, 157, 159–60, 220, 262
Hobhouse, Leonard, 17
Hoijer and Beals, 151, 262
Holroyd, Jean C., 108, 262
Holz, W. C., 95, 257
Homosexuals: female (*see* Lesbians); and frequency of sex, 77, 111; and masturbation, 79; and promiscuity and faithfulness, 146–49; and prostitution, 89–90; and rape, 102, 104–5
Hopkins, M. K., 194, 262
Hormones, sex, male-female differences in sex behavior and, 62, 119, 120–36, 160–61; light-switch theory and, 129–31; and sex drive, 120–36, 154, 160–61
Horney, Karen, 223, 262
Hourglass figure, 186–88

Human nature (*see also* Behavior,
  human; specific aspects, concepts,
  kinds, studies): biology and (*see*
  Biology); exceptions, emotions, and
  ethics and, 205–21; instincts and,
  14–21 (*see also* Instincts); nature-
  nurture controversy and, 4–5, 55 ff.;
  sexual identity myth and, 4–13, 14–
  21 (*see also* Sexual identity myth);
  sociobiology and, 14–21 (*see also*
  Sociobiology)
Human Sexualities, 130, 261
Human Sexual Response, 6, 264. *See
  also* Masters and Johnson
Hummingbirds, 88
Hunt, Morton, 8, 75, 262
Hymenoptera, social behavior in, 16

Immelman, K., 58, 262
Imprinting, learning and, 58
Inheritance: of acquired characteristics, 213; of wealth, sexual power
  and, 226–27
Instincts, 5, 17, 51–65; and determinism, 219–20; and maternal behavior, 200–3; nature-nurture controversy and, 51–65 (*see also*
  Nature-nurture controversy);
  pleasure-pain principle and sex
  behavior and, 51–65; sociobiology
  and, 14–21, 51–61 (*see also* specific
  aspects, concepts)
Isichei, P. A. C., 183, 262
Israeli kibbutzim, maternal behavior
  in, 200–3

James, William, 17, 140
Johnson, Virginia E. *See* Masters and
  Johnson

Kanekar, S., 146, 262
Kanin, Davidson, and Scheck, 176, 262
Kardener, Fuller, and Mensh, 108–9
Kephart, W. M., 158–59, 176, 262
Kerr, Carmen, 43, 76, 157, 262
Kiefer, O., 87, 262
Kinsey, Pomeroy, Martin, and Geb-
  hard, 35–36, 44, 45, 46, 49, 78, 79,
  82, 88, 89–90, 93, 143, 147, 149, 150,
  163, 183–84, 185, 190–94, 229, 233–
  34, 237, 244, 247, 263
Kinsey Institute, 77, 147
Klein, M., 131, 263
Kling, S. G., 150, 263
Kogan and Wallach, 53, 263
Komarovsky, Mirra, 179, 263
Kraemer, Becker, Brodie, Doering,
  Moos, and Hamburg, 124, 263

Kuhn, Thomas S., 16, 64, 263

Lamarck, Jean, 214
Learning, 4–5, 112–19 (*see also* Conditioning; Culture; Socialization);
  and change, 214–15; effect on orgasmic ability, 47–50; homosexuality and, 146–47; and masturbation,
  79–85; motivation and sex behavior
  and, 51–65; nature-nurture controversy and, 4–5, 55–65, 112 ff.;
  sexual roles (*see* Roles [role-
  playing], sexual)
Leopold and Loeb trial, 219–20
Lesbians, 76–77, 111; and masturbation, 79; and promiscuity, 147, 148–
  49, 158; and prostitution, 89–90;
  and rape, 104–5
Leshner, A. I., 122, 124, 263
LeVine, R. A., 7, 263
Lewinsohn, R., 152, 263
Libido (*see also* Drive, sex): sex
  hormones and, 123–36 (*see also*
  Hormones, sex)
Life, beginning of, 250–53
Linton, R., 151, 152, 263
Listening, acceptance of others and,
  240–41
Loeb, Jacques, 17
Longest War, The, 223, 267
Lorenz, K., 58, 263
Love (affection), 5, 140, 155–61; and
  courtship and conflict strategies,
  175–77; and promiscuity and faith-
  fulness, 140, 150, 154, 155–61; ro-
  mance and (*see* Romance); and
  sex, 155–56, 158–61
Lowie, R. H., 151, 263
Lucretius, 53
Lying (deception), sexual behavior
  and: as a courtship strategy, 174–
  75, 177; and privacy and secrecy,
  234, 236

McClearn and DeFries, 19, 264
McDougall, William, 17
Macho image, 228
Male-female sex differences, sexual
  behavior and, 1 ff., 14–21, 22–50,
  51–65, 112–19 (*see also* Sexual behavior; specific aspects, concepts,
  kinds, studies); anger, dread, hurts
  and misunderstandings and, 222–
  49; arousal and, 25–36 (*see also*
  Arousal, sexual); biology and genetics and, 21, 22–50 (*see also* Biology; Genetics); and copulation
  (*see* Copulation); courtship and

control strategies and, 162–77, 224 ff. (*see also* Courtship); determinism and, 217–20; and double standard, 178–85 (*see also* Double standard); exceptions, emotions, and ethics and, 205–21; and feelings (*see* Feelings); homosexuals and (*see* Homosexuals); hormones and sex drive and, 120–36; and interpersonal relations (*see* Relationships, male-female); and maternal behavior, 198–203, 204; and myth of sexual identity, 4–31; nature-nurture controversy and, 4–5, 55–65; older men and younger women, 199–204; pleasure-pain principle and motivation and, 51 ff., 65–111; and pornography, 193–94; and promiscuity and faithfulness, 137–61, 208 ff.; and reproduction and orgasmic responsiveness, 37–50 (*see also* Orgasms; Reproduction, sexual); and risk-taking, 85–87, 93–109; stereotypes and, 211–12; and visual stimuli, 186–94, 204 (*see also* Visual stimuli)

Malinowski, B., 106–7, 113–15, 140, 264

Marriage, 137–61 *passim* (*see also* Children; Family, the); courtship and control strategies and, 162–77; double standard and, 179–85; maternal behavior and, 198–203; older men and younger women and, 194–98, 204; promiscuity and faithfulness and, 137–61 *passim*, 230, 235–39 (*see also* Monogamy; Polygamy)

Maslow, Abraham, 58–59

Masters and Johnson, 5–6, 38, 156, 157, 264

Masturbation, 45, 48–49, 77–83, 110–11, 182; and frequency as a measurement of sexual satisfaction, 77–83

Materialistic monism, 253

Maternal behavior, 198–203

May, Rollo, 58–59

Mayr, E., 20, 264

Mead, George Herbert, 17

Mead, Margaret, 23, 24, 83, 115–17, 194, 199, 264

Meade, Marion, 9–10, 75, 82, 88–89, 155, 188, 194, 247, 264

Medroxyprogesterone acetate, 122–23

Megargee, Edwin I., 54, 264

Menstrual disturbances, sex hormones and, 128

Mice, sex hormones and, 128–29

Millet, Kate, 179, 264

"Misbehavior of Organisms, The" (Breland and Breland), 201–3, 258

Mitchell, Juliet, "Female Sexuality" by, 6–7, 254, 264

Money, J., 121, 122–23, 124, 125, 129, 264

Monkeys, 23–24, 80–81, 191, 209. *See also* Chimpanzees

Monod, J., 251, 264

Monogamy, 5, 140, 142–45, 147, 179, 180, 201–10, 217, 236 (*see also* Faithfulness); polygamy and, 150–53 (*see also* Polygamy; Promiscuity)

Morality (immorality), sociobiology and, 215–21

Morgan, Lloyd, 17, 135

Morris, S., 163

Motherhood, maternal behavior and, 198–203. *See also* Children

Motivation, male-female differences in sex behavior and, 51 ff., 65–111, 208, 210–11 (*see also* Hedonic value; Pleasure-pain principle; specific aspects, concepts, kinds, studies); conflicting, 208

Mowrer, Hobart, 53

Mtessa, King (Uganda), 151

Murdock, G. P., 152, 265

Mutations (accidents), genetic material and, 214–15, 251

Natural selection theory, 251–53. *See also* Selective adaptation

Nature-nurture controversy, 4–5, 51–65, 112 ff., 220, 254. *See also* Conditioning; Culture; Learning; Socialization; specific concepts, individuals, studies

Need, sexual, 18, 73 ff., 136, 230. *See also* Drive, sex

Neofeminism, 7–9. *See also* Feminism

Nudity, as a visual stimulus, 193–94

Nurture-nature controversy. *See* Nature-nurture controversy

Nyby, Dizinno, and Whitney, 58, 129, 265

Nymphomania, 165

Offspring. *See* Children

Older men and younger women, 194–98, 204

Onanism, 48. *See also* Masturbation

"One-night stand," 147

On the origin of species . . . (Darwin), 16, 259

Operant and respondent conditioning, 57, 201–2

Orgasms (orgasmic ability and responsiveness), male-female differences and, 37–43, 65–66, 67–69, 83, 157, 163, 237, 238; multiple, 66, 83, 84; and sex hormones, 122, 124, 129, 131, 136
Ova. *See* Eggs (ova)
Ovid, 69–70

Pain-pleasure principle. *See* Pleasure-pain principle
Papas, A. T., 126, 258
Passion, crimes of, 97
Peeping (window peeping), 192–93
Personality, 7; and courtship and control strategies, 174–75
Petting, premarital, 146–47
Philandering. *See* Promiscuity
Physical (athletic) prowess, 169–70, 171, 173, 196, 213, 226
Physicians (professionals), risk-taking for sex by, 108–9
Physiological and genetic anomalies, 208
Physiology, 5, 15. *See also* Biology
Pietropinto and Simenauer, 44, 183, 197–98, 265
Pigs, 201–3
Playboy Foundation study, 44, 75
Pleasure-pain principle, male-female differences in motivation and sex behavior and, 52–54, 59 ff., 65–111, 116, 136 (*see also* Hedonic value); and courtship and control strategies, 167–77; first coitus and, 75–76; hormones and sex drive and, 120–36; lesbians and, 76–77; and masturbation, 83, 110–11; maternal behavior and, 198–203, 204; measuring, 69 ff.; older men and younger women and, 194–98, 204; promiscuity and faithfulness and, 138, 141 ff., 155–57; prostitution and, 87–93; and rape, 93–109; and risk-taking, 85–87, 93–109; sociobiology and, 67 ff.; and swinging (group sex), 84–85; and visual stimuli, 186–94, 204
Political power, sex and, 226–27
Polycystic ovary syndrome (POS), 127–28, 208
Polygamy (polygyny, polyandry), 140, 150–53, 208–10
Popper and Eccles, 251–52, 265
Pornography, 159, 193–94
Posteriors, 186–88
Potency, sex hormones and, 122, 124
Power and status, 171–72, 224–27.

See also Control; specific kinds
Predictions, stereotypes and, 211–12
Pregnancies, 142–45 (*see also* Children; Eggs; Reproduction); older men and younger women and, 196–98; sex drive and, 110–11, 188
Premarital sex, 140, 146–47, 155–56; double standard and, 179–85; virginity and, 183–85
Prestige. *See* Power and status
Primary process, 59
Primates, 23–24. *See also* Animal behavior; specific kinds, studies
Prisons: lesbian relations in, 105, 158; rape in, 99, 101–2, 104–5, 107–8
Professionals, risk-taking for sex by, 108–9
Promiscuity, faithfulness and, 137–61, 208–10, 235–36, 238 (*see also* Monogamy; Polygamy); courtship and control strategies and, 167–77; double standard and, 178–85
Prostitution, 87–93, 149–50, 163, 228–29; promiscuity and, 149–50, 159
Prostitution (Acton), 92, 257
Prostitution in the United States (Woolston), 150, 268
Psychiatrists, risk-taking for sex by, 108–9
Psychoanalytic psychology, 58, 59
Psychology, 4–6, 7, 91–92, 95, 140, 232 (*see also* specific aspects, concepts, individuals, studies); behavioristic, 4–5, 14–15, 17–19 (*see also* Behaviorism); clinical, 5, 18, 255; and instinct theory, 17–18, 55 ff.; and motivation and sex behavior, 51–65; and nature-nurture controversy, 55–65; psychoanalytic, 58, 59; role in sexual identity myth of, 4–6, 7; sociobiology and, 17
Psychopaths, 174–75
Punishment, rape and risk-taking and, 94–97

Rabkin, Richard, 199
Raboch, Mellan, and Starka, 123–24, 130, 131, 132–33, 265
Rainwater, L., 76, 156–57, 265
Rape, 68, 94–109, 170, 227, 229–30; abhorrence of, 99–100; by females, 104, 105–7; gang, 102, 103; intellectual, 239; as a male phenomenon, 103–4; of men, 98–99, 101–2, 104–5; prevalence and history of, 101–3; in prisons, 99, 101–2, 104–5, 107–8; punishment and, 94–97; risk-taking and, 68, 94–109; sexual pleasure

and, 100, 107; violence and domination in, 97–99, 100, 101–3, 169–70
Reality, accepting, 232–39 ff.
Reiche and Dannecker, 148, 265
Reinforcement principles, sex behavior and, 56–58, 141–42, 201, 202, 218
Relationships, male-female (interpersonal relations), 9–13, 162–77, 222–49; acceptance of reality in, 232–39 ff.; anger, dread, hurts, and misunderstandings in, 1 ff., 222–49; consideration of others in, 246–49; courtship and control strategies and, 162–77, 224 ff.; double standard and, 178–85, 209; exceptions, emotions, and ethics and, 205–21 ff.; feelings and (*see* Feelings; specific aspects, kinds); female sexual responsiveness and, 155–61; homosexual (*see* Homosexuals); older men and younger women and, 194–98, 204; and promiscuity and faithfulness, 137–61 *passim*, 208–10; sex differences and (*see* Male-female sex differences); sex and love and, 158–61 (*see also* Love)
Religious beliefs, 252–53
Reproduction, sexual (*see also* Children; Copulation; Eggs; Genetics; Sperms; specific aspects, concepts, studies); arousal and, 25–36 ff.; biology and, 21, 22–50 (*see also* Biology); courtship and (*see* Courtship); double standard and, 180–85; desire and drive and (*see* Desire, sexual; Drive, sex); orgasmic responsiveness and, 37–50; and pleasure-pain principle and motivation in sex behavior, 51–65 (*see also* Hedonic value; Pleasure-pain principle; Sexual behavior; specific aspects); promiscuity and, 140 ff.
Reyburn, W., 170, 265
Reynolds, Burt, 193
Ridley, C. A., 155, 257
Risks (risk-taking), male-female differences in sex behavior and, 68, 85–87, 93–109
Robinson, P., 4, 5, 46, 156, 247, 265
Rogers, Carl, 58–59
Roles (role-playing), sexual, 6–7, 8–9, 10, 13, 117, 157, 233, 234, 254 (*see also* Culture; Instincts; Learning; Socialization; specific aspects, studies); and courtship and control strategies, 165–77; *macho* image and, 228

Rollin, B., 199, 265
Romance, 199, 237 (*see also* Love); courtship and dating and, 175–77; pornography and, 159
Rosoff, Margaret, 237, 265
Rotter, J. B., 53, 265–66
Rubin, Zick, 176, 266
Russell, Bertrand, 252–53, 266

Samoans, 115–19
Sanger, William, 87–88, 89, 266
Satisfaction. *See* Hedonic value; Pleasure-pain principle
Schafer, S., 79, 149, 266
Schmidt and Sigusch, 78, 79, 266
Schneider, Boucher, Hansen, Noonan, Risch, and Vandermeer, 218–19, 266
Schneidman and McGuire, 45, 266
Science for the People group, 217–18, 219
Seduction (seductive behavior), female, 172–73, 224, 231, 233
Selective adaptation (natural adaptation), human sexuality and, 2–3, 7, 251–53 (*see also* Evolution; Genetics); arousal and, 25–36; attractiveness and, 187–88; courtship and control strategies and, 162–77, 213; hormones and sex drive and, 136; maternal behavior and, 203, 204; older men and younger women and, 194–98, 204; orgasmic responsiveness and, 38–50; and pleasure-pain principle and motivation, 67–69, 80, 81, 88; promiscuity and faithfulness and, 143 ff., 180–85, 209; reproduction and survival and, 24, 25 (*see also* Reproduction; Survival); visual stimuli and, 188–94
Selfish Gene, The, 20, 259
Selfish genes, 20, 185, 259
Seward, G. H., 144, 266
Sex, Evolution and Behavior (Daly and Wilson), 35, 259
Sex and Society, 152, 267
Sex-hormone-binding globulin, 134–35
Sex in History, 86–87, 267
Sexual behavior (*see also* Behavior, human; specific aspects, concepts, developments, kinds, studies): adaptation and (*see* Selective adaptation); arousal and, 25–36; biological evolution and (*see* Biology; Evolution); change in, 214–15; and copulation and reproduction (*see* Copulation; Reproduction); excep-

tions, emotions, and ethics and, 205–21; and feelings (*see* Feelings); hormones and sex drive and, 120–36; male-female differences in (*see* Male-female sex differences); nature-nurture controversy and (*see* Nature-nurture controversy); pleasure-pain principle and motivation in, 51 ff., 65–111; sociobiology and (*see* Sociobiology)

Sexual Behavior and the Law (Kling), 150, 263

Sexual freedom (sexual liberation, sexual revolution), 1–3, 9–13, 44, 78, 84, 239; double standard and (*see* Double standard); in other cultures, 114–19; of the sixties, 44, 78

Sexual identity myth, 4–13 (*see also* Male-female sex differences, specific aspects, concepts, studies); biology and genetics and, 5, 7, 19–21, 22–50 (*see also* Biology; Genetics); cultural evidence and, 112–19 (*see also* Culture; specific studies); instincts and (*see* Instincts); nature-nurture controversy and, 4–5 (*see also* Nature-nurture controversy); radical feminists and, 7–9 (*see also* Feminism); role of psychology in, 4–6; role of sociology and anthropology in, 6–7; sociobiology and, 14–21, 22–50 (*see also* Sociobiology; specific aspects)

Shankweiler, P. J., 109, 140, 261

Shipley, T. E., 125, 258

Shultz, Gladys D., 100, 266

Shuttleworth, F. K., 43, 46, 47, 79–80, 266

Signals, sexual, visual stimuli and, 189–94. *See also* Visual stimuli

Sigusch, Schmidt, Reinfeld, and Wiedemann-Sutor, 159, 194, 266

Skinner, B. F., 18, 53, 56, 57, 95, 219, 266

Social Darwinism, 7

Socialization, sex behavior and, 8–9, 15, 112–19, 146–47, 254 (*see also* Conditioning; Culture; Learning; specific aspects, concepts, studies); and homosexuality, 146–47; nature-nurture controversy and (*see* Nature-nurture controversy); and prostitution, 93; and sex roles, 8–9, 254 (*see also* Roles [role-playing], sexual)

Social sciences, 77, 91–93, 112 ff., 120 (*see also* specific aspects, concepts, individuals, kinds, studies); ethical implications and, 215–21; exceptions, emotions, and ethics and, 205–21; and prostitution, 91–93; and rape, 95, 97–99; sociobiology and, 15, 16, 17 ff. (*see also* Sociobiology); and stereotypes, 211–12

Sociobiology, 14–21, 167–68, 178–204, 232, 250 (*see also* specific aspects, concepts, individuals, studies); and biological evolution, 19–21 (*see also* Biology; Evolution); and exceptions, emotions, and ethical implications, 205–21; and instincts and sexual identity myth, 14–21 (*see also* Sexual identity myth); and nature-nurture controversy, 51–65, 112 ff.; origin of, 16; and use of term "strategies," 141; what it is, defined, 15, 19–21

Sociobiology: The New Synthesis (Wilson), 16, 267. *See also* Wilson, Edward O.

Sociology (sociologists), 6–7, 140, 166, 218 (*see also* Social sciences; specific concepts, individuals, studies); role in sexual identity myth of, 6–7

Sociopathic personalities, 174–75

Socrates, 53

Solomon, King, 151, 173

Sonenschein, D., 147, 266

Sopchak and Sutherland, 125, 126, 132, 266–67

Soul, the, 253

Spencer, Herbert, 20

Sperms, 60–61, 67–69, 94, 99, 104, 140, 141, 143, 185. *See also* Eggs

Staples, R., 140, 267

Stassinopoulos, Arianna, 8, 267

Status and power, 171–72, 226–27. *See also* Control; specific kinds

Steele and Walker, 194, 267

Stereotypes (stereotyping), 211–12, 239, 255

Stimulus generalization concept, 47

Strategies: in courtship and control, 162–77, 196; use of term in sociobiology, 141

Sublimation, sex drive and, 110

Survival, biological evolution and sex behavior and, 20–21, 22–50 113–19 (*see also* Biology; Evolution; Genetics; Sexual behavior; specific aspects, concepts, studies); aggressiveness and, 217 (*see also* Aggressiveness); fittest and, 20–21, 113, 180 (*see also* Selective adaptation); hormones and sex drive and, 136

(*see also* Drive, sex; Hormones, sex)
Swinging (group sex, mate-swapping), 84–85, 159

Taber and Dassmann, 23, 267
Tavris and Offir, 223, 267
Taylor, G. R., 86–87, 267
Testosterone, 121, 122–24, 125–36, 154, 208
Therapists, risk-taking for sex by, 108–9
Thibaut and Kelly, 53, 267
Thomas, W. I., 145, 151, 152, 267
Thorndike, Edward, 17, 53
Time magazine, 16, 17, 87, 88, 267
Todas, the, 151
Tolman, Edward S., 53
Traits, survival, 24–25; attractiveness and (*see* Attractiveness); courtship and, 168–77; genetics and change and, 214–15; instincts and (*see* Instincts)
Trivers, Robert L., 9, 16, 175, 267
Trobrianders, 106–7, 113–16, 119

Value (gain), pleasure-pain principle as motivation in sex behavior and, 52–54, 59 ff., 66–111 *passim*, 208. *See also* Hedonic value; Pleasure-pain principle
Varicocele, coital frequencies and, 132–33
Variety, sexual, promiscuity and, 145–61, 189, 208, 229
Viet Nam War, prostitution in, 90, 228–29
Vinacke, W. E., 53, 267

Violence (*see also* Aggressiveness; Fighting): female responsiveness to, 170, 171 (*see also* Physical [athletic] prowess); rape and, 97–100, 101–3
Virginity, double standard and, 183–85
Visual stimuli (visual signals), 159, 163, 186–94, 203–4, 244–45 (*see also* Attractiveness; specific kinds); pornography as, 193–94
Voyeurism, 192–93

Wagner, Fujita, and Pion, 185, 267
Wallin, P., 36, 72, 175, 258, 267
Ward and Kassebaum, 105, 158, 267
Wars, rape and, 101, 102, 107
Watson, John B., 14–15, 18, 19, 60, 267
Wealth (money), 226; courtship and, 171, 172
Whitney, G., 58, 129, 260, 265
Wilson, Edward O., 15, 16, 20, 267
Wilson, Margo, 35, 259
Woman Hating (Dworkin), 90–91, 260
Women: A Journal of Liberation, 8, 195, 197, 249, 267
Women's Realm, 170
Women's Lib, 8. *See also* Feminism; Sexual freedom
Women's movement. *See* Feminism
Woolston, H. B., 150, 268

Yausa, 106–7
Younger women and older men, 194–98, 204

Zeiss, Rosin, and Zeiss, 45, 268